SAY IT LOUD!

MY MEMORIES OF
JAMES BROWN,
SOUL BROTHER NO.1

DON RHODES
Foreword by Brenda Lee

The Lyons Press
Guilford, Connecticut
An imprint of The Globe Pequot Press

Library of Congress Cataloging-in-Publication Data

Rhodes, Don.
 Say it loud! : my memories of James Brown, soul brother number one / Don Rhodes ; foreword by Brenda Lee.
     p. cm.
 Includes bibliographical references and index.
 ISBN 978-1-59921-362-0 (alk. paper)
 1. Brown, James, 1933-2006. 2. Soul musicians—United States—Biography.
I. Title.
 ML420.B818R56 2008
 782.421644092--dc22
 [B]

                                                                2008024562

Printed in the United States of America

10 9 8 7 6 5 4 3 2 1

This book is dedicated to Joseph and Susie Brown, Minnie Walker, Velma Warren Brown, Allyn Lee, Emma and Leon Austin, Charles Bobbit, Ella Overton, Robert "Flash" Gordon, Laura Garvin, Henry Howard, William Glenn, Charles A. Reid Jr., Danny Ray, and Bobby Byrd—and all the others who kept the faith and loved James Brown as much as I did.

Anything he did, he did it whole heartedly. He did it from the heart. . . No matter what anybody says or anybody thinks, he was a good person, and he believed in giving. He did. He really did. He believed in giving, and he would give it his best. And, however these things [legal matters] turn out it's nobody to blame but themselves. They can't blame him, because he gave it all. . . . I can say that I truly loved him and want nothing to be a mockery of him, because he certainly doesn't deserve it. I look at it like this: If a man leaves and takes care of his family, then he's all right, because a lot of men leave and forget about their family.

There are people who want to believe the bad things about him and they don't want to look at the good, but in my heart I know he was a good person. That's all that matters—no matter how many books are written because I've read a lot of stuff that I knew wasn't true about him and heard a lot of stuff that I knew wasn't true about him. The way I loved him in life is the way I love him in death, and that's just the way it is.

—Velma Warren Brown
First Wife of James Brown
Toccoa, Georgia, February 8, 2008

CONTENTS

FOREWORD

I would love to say that James Brown, the 5-foot-6-inch, pompadoured "Mr. Dynamite," and I, the 4-foot-9-inch, bouffanted "Little Miss Dynamite," had the opportunity to perform together, but that, unfortunately, would never be.

Nevertheless, we were connected in many other distinctive ways.

We both had our first, career-making, debut hits in 1956—James with the cry ballad "Please, Please, Please" and me with the rockabilly tune "Jambalaya." He and I both performed many times individually on the storied stage of Bell Auditorium in Augusta, Georgia, and were both greatly influenced by the blues, big band, gospel, and country music that pulsated on Augusta's radio stations.

We both lived and worked in Georgia and South Carolina, with me singing on WRDW television station in North Augusta, South Carolina—James' home state—and James later buying WRDW radio station in my "adopted" hometown of Augusta.

James loved country music and performed once on the Grand Ole Opry stage, and I love soul music, even first meeting my husband, Ronnie Shacklett, at a Jackie Wilson concert in Nashville.

We are both inductees into the Georgia Music Hall of Fame and the Rock and Roll Hall of Fame.

And last but not least, both James and I came up poor doing what we could as children to help earn money for our families; with me picking cotton and with James picking up pieces of coal from railroad tracks so his family could have some heat in the winter. But we both ended up selling more than 100 million records each and touring internationally with fans in many countries.

It's a great honor to share so much in common with James Brown, but perhaps one of my biggest thrills was seeing him perform live in Nashville. His raw emotion was palatable, and his incredible energy and trademark dance moves drove the crowd completely wild, me included.

I absolutely loved his signature, one-three beat and funky horn arrangements. And, of course, the screaming fans couldn't get enough when he dropped, exhausted, to the floor in his famous lavender cape only to rush back to the microphone to give us more. He was truly a phenomenal performer.

So, here's to you, James. You are unequivocally one of the major musical influences of my time, and I feel privileged to have been along side you in the world of entertainment.

—BRENDA LEE
Nashville, Tennessee

PREFACE

On an average work or weekend day, I wake up at 5 a.m. regardless of the alarm on my clock radio. My three dogs always need out whether it's a holiday or not. But on Christmas Day, 2006, I slept until about 6 a.m.

The previous Friday I had been watching the early TV news when I saw that James Brown would be at the Imperial Theatre in Augusta, Georgia, just before noon for his annual Christmas toy giveaway to needy children.

As it had sometimes happened during my forty years of friendship with James Brown, I was being given the cold shoulder by the Brown camp. I wasn't sure why; most likely I had written something that his fourth wife, Tomi Rae, didn't like. JB never got mad at me. It always was someone else who was "looking after his best interests."

Whenever that happened, I always kept in mind this was the same James Brown who autographed a scrapbook that I had put together about him in 1988 "To Don, My young bro who never fails to amaze me. Living in America, James Brown, I'm Real." The "I'm Real" referred to his then new album; typically always promoting his latest projects.

Watching the news that Friday morning I thought maybe the Christmas season of 2006 would be a good time to find out if I was again welcome in the inner Brown fold. But as the weather that day grew increasingly cold and wet, I chickened out; deciding to stay in my warm home across the Savannah River in North Augusta, South Carolina, less than three miles from the Imperial Theatre.

It was a decision I will forever deeply regret.

That evening on the local TV newscast, I saw the coverage of JB's toy giveaway at the Imperial. There were the usually excited kids with their mothers waiting hours in line, and there was JB wearing a brown western hat with round silver medallions on the band. He loved western hats and was photographed often in public wearing that particular one. But I noticed JB wasn't really giving out a lot of toys but letting others do it.

He was attempting to look cheery and sound upbeat, but I was struck by how very frail he appeared. Frail was not a word usually associated with JB. He had been a tough kid who became a tough adult, and he exuded that physicality on stage over five decades of professional performing. He was a live wire of celebrity electricity that no one could touch. He didn't earn the title of The Hardest Working Man in Show Business by sitting on his butt.

Still, I dismissed his look of frailty.

On the night of Saturday, December 23, my life partner, Eddie Smith, and I joined our friends, Bill and Linda Macky, for an evening at the Mission nightclub in downtown Augusta to see a thrown-together band called "Tobacco Roadkill" consisting of close friends and expert local musicians. They were drummer Jamie Jones and guitarists Patrick Blanchard Jr. and James Brown's own lead guitarist Keith Jenkins—a tall, handsome redhead who usually played just to JB's right.

At midnight, it became Christmas Eve and my 61st birthday. And when the band concluded at about 1 a.m., I spent some time talking with Jenkins and praising his incredible guitar solo on "Ramblin' Man." If he knew then how sick his boss was that very day he never let on; he was to join JB and the band the week after Christmas for more shows, including two New Year's Eve shows at B. B. King Blues Club & Grill in New York City.

For me, the rest of that day passed rather quietly.

Then came Christmas Day morning when I arose at about 6 a.m. and turned on the TV and learned James Brown had died about four hours earlier at a hospital in Atlanta, two and a half hours west of Augusta.

Once I got over the initial shock, I went to the Web site of the *Augusta Chronicle,* www.augustachronicle.com, and saw there was nothing about JB dying. But why would there be? This was a little past 6 a.m. on Christmas Day when most Web site people and *Chronicle* reporters were off for the holiday. Most reporters and editors arrived about mid-morning or closer to noon on a normal weekday to put out the next day's edition.

The only thing I saw on the Web site about JB was a link to the story about his toy giveaway at the Imperial three days earlier. I grabbed the telephone book and looked up the home number of Dennis Sodomka, executive editor of the *Chronicle* and my former boss when I was the entertainment editor in the *Chronicle* newsroom. The phone rang a few times and a very groggy sounding Sodomka came on the line. I blurted out, "Dennis, this is Don. I hate to bother you this early but Channel 6 is reporting that James Brown has died in Atlanta, and there is nothing on the *Chronicle* Web site. Y'all need to get on this." And I added, "This is going to be HUGE!!"

Before saying goodbye, I told Sodomka that I would be heading for my office to write something for the next day's paper. Even though I had transferred twelve years earlier from the *Chronicle* newsroom to the corporate communications office of the *Chronicle*'s Augusta-based parent company, Morris Communications, I still have kept close ties with the newsroom including writing my weekly country music column, "Ramblin' Rhodes," for the *Chronicle*'s Applause entertainment section and occasional guest editorials for the *Chronicle*'s editorial pages.

I took a quick shower and got dressed in good clothes because Eddie and I were planning to see the first showing in Augusta of the movie *Dream Girls* at 2 p.m. at Regal Cinemas Augusta Exchange 20. I also grabbed my large scrapbook about JB, which he had autographed for me years before.

On the way to the newsroom, I stopped at the Waffle House on Georgia Avenue in downtown North Augusta to get some breakfast. There were several customers along with the jovial Christmas Day crew.

While waiting on my order, I mentioned to a young black short order cook standing nearby, "Did you hear about James Brown dying?" He said back, "Yeah, I did hear something about that on the news."

"Hear about what?" said a white waitress. He told her the news about the same time four black female customers came in with two wearing Santa Claus hats. The white waitress handed them menus and said, "Did you hear that James Brown died this morning?"

The news was passing fast.

After eating and paying the bill, I crossed the 13th Street bridge into Augusta and passed Reynolds Street (where I normally would turn left heading for the News Building) and instead went up two blocks to take a left onto Broad Street so I could drive by the new statue of James Brown.

In all of the huge state of Georgia, there are only three statues to entertainers: One is of the late great soul singer Otis Redding in Macon; another is of the incomparable Ray Charles in Albany; and the third is of James Brown in the middle of the 700 block of Broad Street a short distance from James Brown Boulevard.

I was standing next to JB at Augusta Common on November 15, 2003, when he was shown a clay model of the statue. It depicted JB standing erect with a full head of hair, wearing a suit and floor-length cape and holding an old-style, stand-up microphone. JB took a hard look at the model in a clear plastic case that day, broke into his wide familiar grin and exclaimed joyfully, "Looks like Thomas Jefferson! Looks like Thomas Jefferson!"

And he was totally right. It looked very much like the statue of Jefferson at his memorial in Washington, D.C.

On that Christmas Day morning of 2006, it looked wet and cold from the previous weekend's rain. Someone had placed a lone Poinsettia plant at its base, and wind had toppled it on its side.

Two blocks later, I parked and went upstairs to my second

floor office, turned on the computer, and wrote a long tribute, concluding:

> *One of the greatest honors I've had as a journalist was when then [Augusta] Mayor Bob Young asked me to write the wording for the metal marker near Mr. Brown's statue.*
>
> *And this is what I wrote: "Singer, songwriter, musician and one-of-a-kind performer James Brown has thrilled millions around the world with his hit recordings and electrifying performances. The 1983 Georgia Music Hall of Fame inductee, 1986 Rock and Roll Hall of Fame inductee and 2003 Kennedy Center honoree has called Augusta "home" since moving here when he was five. It was in Augusta's Lenox Theater that he first received recognition for his talent by winning an amateur contest. His songs have enriched the world, and his personality and generosity have enriched this city."*
>
> *What I should have wrote, however, is what he told me in 1986 when I asked what he regarded as the keys for success.*
>
> *He replied, "Just work hard, give the people their money's worth and be sincere in what you do. It's worked for me."*

By the time I had finished writing the tribute, *Chronicle* metro editor Bill Kirby had arrived in the newsroom. I e-mailed the column to him from my office two buildings away and then took a print-out version to Kirby, a longtime friend, former coworker, and popular local columnist.

"I know it's long, so cut it down like you want," I told Kirby.

Back at my house, Eddie and I got ready to head out to the Augusta Exchange to see the movie. But on impulse before leaving, I checked into the *Chronicle*'s Web site and was pleased to find there were now two local items posted about James Brown: a basic news story compiled by Bill Kirby and Donnie Fetter and also my tribute article.

Instead of editing it down, Kirby had left it pretty much in its entirety. The article was posted on the *Chronicle*'s Web site on Christmas Day at 11:03 a.m., making it one of the first online tributes posted anywhere after Brown's death.

The movie *Dream Girls* is based on the 1986 book *Dreamgirl: My Life as a Supreme* by Mary Wilson of The Supremes vocal group, whom Brown knew well even though he was said to have held a grudge about Tamla-Motown Records failing to ever sign him. There is a character in the movie called James "Thunder" Early portrayed by actor Eddie Murphy, obviously based on Murphy's love of James Brown.

When Murphy sings his final number in the movie, "Jimmy's Rap," there is no question that the interpretation is totally based on Brown, including JB's trademark soul rhythm section and his famous growls and wails.

The audience in that theater burst into applause after Murphy finished his number; which seemed to me an expression of tribute to both Murphy and Brown. I knew there very likely were many in that Augusta audience who had either encountered JB around Augusta or who were just there because of the loss of a guy who gave so much back to the area.

And I knew in that moment in that darkened theater on the afternoon of that Christmas Day, Soul Brother Number One James Brown may have died earlier that very same day in Atlanta, but his massive amount of recordings and video images and written accounts would ensure that his memory and fame would endure forever.

Don Rhodes
Augusta, Georgia
Hometown of James Brown

ACKNOWLEDGMENTS

First of all, thanks to my life partner and closest friend, Ervin Edward "Eddie" Smith Jr., for being there with me to share so many fun moments with James Brown. Eddie loved JB coming up to him at his last wedding reception and saying, "I know who you be. You be Don's partner."

And to the great four-legged friends and confidants in my life: Fluffy, Little Bit, Wolfie, Foxie, Reba, Jasper, Rusty, Will, and Jayme Brown, who brought me up when two-legged folks brought me down.

And, in no particular order, my gratefulness also goes out to:

My father, Ollen Columbus Rhodes, and his wife, Jean Swann Rhodes; my sisters Linda Groover, Jan Harris, and Ann Holland; my brothers, Larry Rhodes, Mike Spence, and Doug Spence and their families and my late mother, Ella Sampert Rhodes, who gave me my love of reading and music.

The amazing and wonderful music legend Brenda Lee for letting me share so many great times with her and her ultra cool husband, Ronnie Shacklett, over the past 30-something years and writing the foreword for this book and to their daughter, Julie Clay, for her help.

My frequent lunch buddies Duncan Wheale, Pat Claiborne, Jeff Barnes, Todd Beasley, Free Pennington, and Johnny Edwards who enthusiastically encouraged my research, who listened to my latest James Brown trivia discovery without acting too bored and who, in fact, asked some pretty good questions that prompted further research.

JB's first wife, Velma Warren Brown, and her son, Terry, and grandson, Forlando Brown, who generously spent a wonderful, sunny afternoon in Toccoa, Georgia, showing my father and sister, Linda, around at the places where the legend of James Brown and the Famous Flames began. Anyone who knows Velma personally would say that James was luckier to have found Velma than she to find him.

At Morris Communications Company, my immediate corporate services coworkers Kay Pruitt, Mark Albertin, Cathy Martindale, and Pete May for making it a joy to go to work (most days at least) and to the Augusta Futurity/National Barrel Horse Association friends on my floor: Sherry Fulmer, Tranis Harper, Rick Hardy, Renee Jenkins, Cookey Caruso, and Len Carter.

Also at Morris Communications Company to Billy Morris and his wonderful wife, Sissie; sons, Will and Tyler; and daughter, Susie, for their longtime support of my creative efforts both in and out of the office, which hopefully reflect honor back on their great, international, multimedia company based on Broad Street in Augusta, Georgia.

Don Bailey, president of the *Augusta Chronicle,* and Executive Editor Dennis Sodomka for allowing me extensive usage of the *Chronicle's* photo and news files, including the incredible augustaarchives.com electronic search tool that allows James Brown fans to read the articles in the *Chronicle* just as Brown himself did.

Also at the *Chronicle,* special thanks to Sean Moores, Tami Roose, Rhonda Hollimon, and Michael Snyder for their generous assistance with the photos for this book; and to David Playford and John Barnes of the *Augusta Herald* for allowing me to pursue the James Brown legend in the first place with series and other feature articles.

Also thanks to the many reporters worldwide, but especially in Augusta, who covered JB's good days and bad days—with many like me being in awe of the "hardest working man in show business." Especially thanks to Greg Gelpi of the *Augusta Chronicle* for sharing his personal memories of covering JB's last turkeys and toys giveaways in the weeks before JB's death and Johnny Edwards of the *Chronicle* for his personal memories covering JB's funeral at the Apollo in New York City.

Charlie Reid Jr. for sharing the awesome and even funny details of JB's three funerals in New York, South Carolina, and Georgia and of his working with JB on the Third World nightclub and to Lowell Dorn for sharing with me the details of recording *The Payback* album.

Former Augusta mayor Bob Young, who also has loved JB since the '60s and saw him in Vietnam like I did, for giving me the great honor of writing the words on the metal plaque next to the statue of JB. It was fun sitting next to Bob and his wife, Gwen Fulcher, at JB's wedding to Tomi Rae and JB's funeral in Augusta and being with them at JB's Christmas party.

Larry Harris for being Joe "Pop" Brown's neighbor and sharing stories about JB's early life in Augusta and Warren Jennings for sharing his wonderful collection of Louis Jordan CDs to give me a better understanding of why JB loved Jordan so much.

William Glenn, Leon and Emma Austin, Robert "Flash" Gordon, Allyn Lee, Bill Berry, Danny Ray, Little Richard, Flo Carter, Ramblin' Tommy Scott, Bobby and Vicki Byrd, Henry Howard, Gloria Daniel, and others who were there in his early days and who kindly shared with me their stories about the guy they loved and respected for most of his life.

Members of JB's bands and staffers of his offices and homes who generously helped me through the years get close to the real JB, especially Charles Bobbit, Roosevelt Johnson, Elif (Pesmen) Crawford, Ella Overton, Fred Daviss, Al Garner, and Keith Jenkins.

The many Augusta mayors who tried to honor James Brown at one time or another including Deke Copenhaver, Charles A. DeVaney, Edward M. McIntyre, Lewis A. "Pop" Newman, George A. Sancken Jr., and Larry Sconyers.

The many researchers and James Brown enthusiasts who generously shared their wealth of knowledge, historical materials, and opinions, especially Lisa Love and Joe Johnson at the Georgia Music Hall of Fame in Macon; radio talk show host

Austin Rhodes; musicians and friends Pat Blanchard Sr., "Buzz" Clifford, Sandy Martin, Russ Mobley, R. J. Smith, Mike Theiss, Pat Blanchard Jr., and Derrick Monk; lawyer and Brown estate trustee Albert H. "Buddy" Dallas; Soul Bar owner Coco Rubio, Nancy Glaser, and Guy Robbins at the Augusta Museum of History; and John J. O'Shea and Carol Waggoner-Angleton at Augusta State University.

My great friends at Globe Pequot Press/Lyons Press in Guilford, Connecticut, including Scott Watrous, Kathryn Mennone, Christine Etlinger, Shelley Wolf, Bob Sembiante (who also deeply loves music and is an excellent singer), Mary Norris, Ellen Urban, Rose Marye Boudreaux, and Jane Sheppard (who designed this book's outstanding cover), and, most especially, to my new close friend Erin Turner, who edited this book from her office and home in Montana. Thanks, Erin, for making my dream come true of having not one but two national books following our early 2008 joint collaboration: *Ty Cobb: Safe At Home.*

Finally, thanks to James Brown himself who not only was one of the most interesting journalistic subjects I've ever come across in my 40-plus years of published writing but was kind to me when he really didn't have to be. I miss you, JB. There never will be another like you.

ONE

Death Comes to the Godfather

My faith in God is the only thing that brings me through. Faith is the only actual thing that keeps me going.

—James Brown
May 14, 1988
Augusta (Georgia) *Chronicle*

The Reverend Al Sharpton, ordained minister and political activist, was awakened from a sound sleep at his home on Christmas Day 2006 about 3 a.m. by a startling phone call from Charles Bobbit, James Brown's long-time road manager and trusted aide.

Sharpton would later tell CNN cable TV host Larry King that Bobbit broke the horrible news by simply saying, "Your man is gone."

"What do you mean?" Sharpton responded, knowing from an earlier call from Bobbit that 73-year-old Brown was in Crawford Long Hospital in midtown Atlanta being treated for pneumonia.

"Your dad died an hour ago," Bobbit added, referring to the "father-son" relationship Sharpton had forged over the years with his mentor, close friend, and father figure.

Although Brown was 73 and had battled diabetes and prostate cancer in recent years, his death still came as a shock to almost everyone. This, after all, was the same man who, in the last year of his life, performed in China for the first time and also presented his usually high energy show in Australia, Korea, England, and other countries as well as throughout the United States; keeping up a tough schedule far younger entertainers couldn't match.

Nobody—not Sharpton, not Brown's children, not even his close friend Bobbit who was with him his final moments—thought for a second that the early hours of Christmas morning would be James Brown's last hours alive on Earth.

As the news spread rapidly from that hospital in Atlanta to places around the world, memories of James Brown flooded those who had known him personally and those who only knew of him through his music and moments in the media.

"Little Richard" Penniman had been there from the start. At his first meeting with James Brown, Bobby Byrd and the other Famous Flames in Bill's Rendezvous nightclub in Toccoa, Georgia, Penniman had been so impressed that he suggested they move to Penniman's hometown of Macon, Georgia, where they might find work. They took his advice, and the Flames recorded "Please, Please, Please" at Macon radio station WIBB on November 1, 1955.

"I heard about (his death) Monday night," Penniman said. "I couldn't believe that. It was too early. God bless him. . . . He was a great songwriter and hard-working entertainer, even before he had any fame. . . . His impact on R&B and soul was unbelievable. There was nothing like it. He was a great dancer. He did a move everyone used to call the 'Suzie Q.'

"After he started to do it on stage, we started calling it the 'James Brown.' Rap music came from him. . . . All the licks and hooks came from him. His impact on blacks and whites, red, brown and yellow, it was felt everywhere."

In Toccoa, Georgia, JB's first wife, Velma, was awakened by her son, Terry, who had been told about his father's death by Terry's son, Forlando, a student at West Georgia College.

Terry said, "Mama, daddy is dead." I couldn't believe it, the first Mrs. James Brown would tell me in Toccoa a few months after JB's death. This may sound crazy, but you know I still feel his presence . . . When he passed, that was a shock

2

to me because I had been with him the Friday the week before
at the house in Beech Island. . . . He was in good spirits, but I
could tell in his face that he was tired and his feet were swollen.
I thought about that a lot later, but it was far from my mind
when I saw him. I never thought he would die. He had told me
what his plans were about going to the dentist in Atlanta, so
that was so far from my mind.

She said that JB was at peace with his God with he died. "I think God gave him the talent, and he went out there to use it. He believed in God, and he knew that God would get him where he needed to be."

One of the first persons to get a call from Bobbit was Elif Crawford (formerly Pesmen), who was JB's personal office assistant for the last eight years of his life. She got the call about 1:45 a.m. and immediately started calls notifying JB's daughter, Venisha, and the band members.

Like other of JB's staffers, she would find it hard to grasp in coming days how his death was going to affect his family, friends, and business associates. "It's very hard. All week, I cried one minute and I was OK the next," she would say. And almost immediately what came to her mind was JB's generosity with his Thanksgiving free turkey giveaways and Christmas toy giveaways in Augusta.

"I know those meant a lot to him," she told this author. "He planned his tour schedules around those events, and he would instruct us in the office and his booking agents to make sure we didn't conflict with those events. How many celebrities do you know would give up their concert income every year for something like that?"

Derrick Monk, who produced Brown's critically lauded 1998 CD *I'm Back* and played organ at Brown's last wedding, to Tomi Rae Hynie, would tell reporters that he was in bed when he heard of JB's death. He sat up in bed in shock and then cried. He later would say the tears were not just for JB and his family but also in the realization that he would never again work with the Godfather. Monk would add, "The man made me feel that I was a musician, and that I did mean something as a musician, and suddenly that man was gone. I also felt like a bird getting kicked out of the tree, saying 'OK, you've got to fly now and use all the stuff I gave you, Monk.'"

Another Augusta-area person who had crossed JB's path several times was Jennie Montgomery, the long time popular co-anchor of the evening newscast on Augusta's oldest TV station, WJBF, Channel 6. It would be Montgomery who would inform many of Brown's friends in Augusta of his death, as she had happened to pull morning-anchor duty that Christmas Day morning.

"I was indeed the first news anchor to break the news in Augusta since WJBF was the only station with a live newscast Christmas morning," she would tell me later. "I got a phone call at my home about 2:45 a.m. I was just getting up to jump in the shower and get to work by 4 a.m. The call was from the morning show producer, Rachel Weinstein. I was stunned by what she said, and I flat high-tailed it into the newsroom.

"By the time my morning show producer was making the calls to confirm it, The Associated Press wires were flashing the alerts. CNN broke in with it, too."

Allyn Lee had known James Brown since they were children living in '40s black Augusta. He grew up to become one of the most popular disc jockeys in Augusta and in Montgomery, Alabama, in the '60s. He even booked Brown into shows in Augusta's Bell Auditorium when he was working at WTHB radio station.

Whenever Brown was performing in Montgomery, he often would visit in Lee's home, and, likewise, Lee was a frequent visitor to Brown's late '60s, early '70s home on Walton Way Extension in Augusta in the middle of rich white residents living on "The Hill" section.

"We swam in his pool at the Walton Way house," Lee would tell me. "I cooked for him when he came to my house both in Montgomery and where I live now. His favorite food was T-bone steaks, and he loved champagne. I always kept a bottle of it around for him."

Lee and his wife, Lu, had watched the TV newscasts on Friday, December 22, and remarked to each that their long time friend was not looking good at his annual toy giveaway earlier in the day.

"We woke up at Christmas morning at 4 o'clock to visit that day with my two daughters in Atlanta. We saw Jennie Montgomery's early newscast and were shocked and saddened like everyone else."

One of the best early published tributes to JB was by Clarissa Walker writing a guest editorial for the *Augusta Chronicle*. Walker, who works as the international student administrator at Dean College in Franklin, Massachusetts, was a staff writer for the *Chronicle* in 1999 and 2000.

"I grew up in east Augusta, but, after graduating from Davidson Fine Arts School in 1990, I traveled and lived abroad. Working as a newspaper reporter in Agana, Guam, I met my Chuukese next-door neighbor during my first days living in the village of Mangilao. Upon learning of my hometown, his eyes brightened as if something had clicked, and he belted out in a thick Micronesian accent 'Ow! I feel good! Na-na-na na-na-na-na!' Those were all of the lyrics he knew, but I told him, 'Yeah. That's the right place.'

"In a beautiful dance club called the Rhapsody in downtown Rio de Janeiro, I felt ownership and hometown pride when a frenzied, dancing crowd of Carioca—as those indigenous to Rio call themselves—encircled a Portuguese singer when he sang the first line of the Godfather's anthem. What's most amazing is that most of that crowd, including the singer, didn't speak or understand English. Yet signature James Brown—polished horn riffs and

5

the feeling of release in his guttural vocals—had captured them. I left full-time journalism in 2001 and began a career in international education.

"Intermittently, I worked in Chengdu, China, and was able to conduct research for my master's thesis in Geneva, Switzerland. I remember the beginnings of these experiences as awkward and isolating. In these situations, you fumble. Those around you—blocked by language, cultural, stereotype barriers—fumble around looking for a common thread. Often, for me, JB was the first nugget of familiarity shared."

TWO

The Early Years

I hope to someday turn this building (old Silas X. Floyd elementary school) into the James Brown School of Music. I love this area and the people in it. The school looks good. But you look around and can see the houses are dilapidated. It's visible in this community, this town and in America that we have regressed. . . . If I can put hope into the eyes of just one child, it's worth it.

James Brown
June 25, 1991
Augusta Chronicle

Who's Who in America has given James Brown's date and place of birth as June 17, 1928, in Pulaski, Tennessee, but James Brown himself always claimed he was born on May 3, 1933, in a small wooden shack that no longer exists on private property off U.S. Highway 278 in rural Barnwell County, South Carolina, near the small town of Snelling.

Family legend has it that Brown came into the world as a stillborn, but his aunt, Minnie Walker, supposedly blew life back into him and gave the world the voice that millions would hear. His father was said to have walked nine miles into Barnwell to record his birth, but no official record of that has turned up at this writing.

JB's father, Joseph Brown, had been born as Joseph Gardner on March 29, 1911, in Barnwell County. His adopted last name of Brown came about when his mother left South Carolina for New York with a white man and left her son behind with a woman named Mattie Brown. The boy eventually took her last name with Joseph Gardner becoming Joseph Brown.

JB's mother, Susie Behling, was born on August 8, 1916, in Colleton County, South Carolina in the southeastern part of the state known as the Low Country which touches on the Atlantic Ocean. Her parents were Monnie and Rebecca Bryant Behling. Susie was educated in both Colleton and Bamberg counties.

It is not as important how Joseph Brown and Susie Behling met as it is the fact that when their only child was about four or five, Joseph Brown decided to move his family 40 miles west from rural Barnwell County, South Carolina, to the growing big Georgia city of Augusta.

As often told by James Brown in later years, the family moved into a house of prostitution at 944 Twiggs Street owned and operated by Joe Brown's aunt, usually identified as "Handsome Honey Washington." (Her real name was Hansone.) One of her sons, William Glenn, would become James Brown's friend from childhood and longtime office manager.

About 1946, Joe Brown again would move his family—this time into a house that would be shared with another aunt, Minnie Walker, the same woman who had breathed life into the newborn James Brown.

An often told, but apparently erroneous, story is that James Brown's mother, Susie, left the family in South Carolina before they moved to Augusta and ran off to New York City just as Joe Brown's mother (JB's grandmother) had done. JB apparently would tell a biographer that he didn't see his mother again until some 20 years later when he was appearing at the Apollo Theater and there was a knock on his dressing room door and there stood his mother.

While that is a compelling and sensitive story, it apparently is not true according to official records and insider accounts. The 1947–1948 and 1949 Augusta directories list Susie as living with Joe Brown. And two of JB's longtime friends—who asked to remain anonymous—also contend that Susie, indeed, did move with the family from Barnwell County to Augusta and did not willingly abandon her family.

"The account that I got was Aunt Honey's house had two or three stories to it, and the Browns were staying on the second floor, and Pop threw Susie out of the second floor window. And so it wasn't very long before she ran for her life out of Augusta.

"It was James' second wife, Deidre, who decided to try and find Susie in New York City and somehow did," the friend related. "Susie supposedly told Dee Dee that she had to flee for her life because Pop Brown had promised to kill her if she tried to take his son away from him. She also told Dee Dee, 'All of these years I wanted my son to know how proud I have been of him.' And that's why she showed up at the Apollo, but James thought she was just coming because he was famous and would not see her."

After Deidre Brown reunited her husband with his mother, Susie would remain in James Brown's life. He would move her in her final years from New York to Augusta so she would be near him and his father.

"He tried to put them back together so they could be a real family," JB's friend said. "That was something he always wanted, and I think that's where the families of his early friends played such an instrumental role in his childhood; that he could see what a real family life and home life could be like.

"But that was one thing out of all of his fame and fortune and everything else that he never was able to accomplish and enjoy. I think that because of that early relation so early with his mother and the feeling he had been abandoned and not wanted by a woman is why he had such a hard time really, really relating to women."

No matter where James Brown lived in Augusta or whom he lived with, it was those formative years growing up in Augusta that made him friends who would last until his death—friends

9

who would be there in the lowest moments of his adult years. It would be Augusta also where he would be infused with musical influences that would create the recordings that would sell millions of copies worldwide.

By all accounts, James Brown was a survivor; doing what he could to make money for food, clothes, and shelter for his family. He was everywhere all over the downtown Augusta area in his pre-teen and teen years and became well known to Augustans before he became well known to the world.

Country-gospel singer Flo Carter, who was a friend to JB for several decades, recalls that her mother, Ada Collins, had young James Brown running errands for her and hotel guests when she was the executive housekeeper at the massive Bon Air Hotel in its heyday. He would set up shoeshine stands on various corners in downtown Augusta where soldiers from Camp Gordon would pass, and he would dance for the coins they would throw his way.

Allyn Lee, a popular radio disc jockey and show promoter turned car salesman, recalls knowing James Brown when they were youngsters in Augusta:

"There were sections of Augusta where you couldn't go past certain streets because of the tough guys in those areas," he said. "And if you did pass through, you had to crawl. But James Brown always walked tall. I don't care where we were (Brown and Lee together), he could handle it. He was never afraid."

Leon Austin, later to front his own band Leon Austin & The Buicks and owner of Leon's DeSoto Club, first met JB when they were in the third grade at Silas X. Floyd Elementary School.

JB would go to Austin's home on Wrightsboro Road, where the Austin family had a piano, and Leon would help improve JB's playing. JB in later years always gave Leon credit for developing his talent in playing keyboards. JB in those childhood years also was learning to play different instruments including a harmonica that his father brought home.

In 1944, James Brown won his first talent contest singing a mournful ballad called "So Long" at the popular Lenox Theater in Augusta.

James Brown began getting a wider reputation as a singer and entertainer thanks in large part to an elementary school teacher who believed in him.

Laura Garvin, who taught seventh graders at Silas X. Floyd Elementary School and lived not far from the Brown family at 950 Hopkins Street between Ninth and 10th streets, was one of the first educated professionals to encourage JB's talents as also was the Floyd school's principal and future Augusta city councilman, Yewston N. Myers.

"Neither of us called him James or Brown," Garvin told reporter Keith Claussen of the *Augusta Chronicle* in 1969. "It was always James Brown. It just seemed to go like that.

"We used to have little performances in the class," she further recalled of JB's school years in the late 1940s. "I could tell when James Brown was in the mood for a show, and he would do it whenever I asked. He enjoyed performing for the children.

"Now the school has one big fund raising project a year, but back then we did lot of little things. We would charge 10 cents to see James Brown, and the children would just pile in. So, we had to rule out classroom shows. Sometimes we would move the show into the library. There was a piano there, and James Brown would play it or dance or sing. That was the real beginning."

Both Garvin and Myers described JB as being an excellent student who came across calm, cool, and collected. But they knew of his tough family life and that he had to miss school sometimes for his family or for himself.

"He would stay out of school two and three days a week, but when he came to class, he would still do more than the other children," Garvin recalled. "Nothing could make you dislike him. When he came back to class, I would call him up to my desk and he would lean against the radiator. I would ask him why he had been absent, but he never told me. He'd just smile that big smile, and you couldn't say anything else to him."

She said that even when she was positive that he had not opened a book, he still would shoot his hand up when she asked questions in the classroom and always had the right answers.

"He had so much potential," she said of noticing his above average talents. "He could sing so well. He was very musically inclined, very cooperative. He was a well-rounded student, good in all his subjects; almost brilliant. James Brown says that if he had listened to me and Mr. Myers he would have gone on to high school. He regrets it now, but has done well without it. He has several honorary degrees from colleges and universities."

Today, Silas X. Floyd Elementary School is closed. The dreams that James Brown and his fourth wife, Tomi Rae, had of transforming it into a neighborhood performing arts center are on indefinite hold. But, past students of Silas X. Floyd have vivid memories of their former classmate and of the world-famous entertainer delighting schoolchildren with his impromptu visits.

Besides music, JB's love of sports also was offering him a way out of his poverty and a way to get his name known to a lot of people.

"I used to hang from trees outside Jennings Park (actually Jennings Stadium at Allen Park located on Walton Way) and watch the ballgame," Brown told sports writer Mitch Mitchell in an article published in the *Augusta Chronicle* on May 3, 1969.

JB went on to say that he played a lot of baseball himself and was offered a contract with the Chicago White Sox but couldn't accept it, for a very good reason. He added, "I couldn't sign a contract with the White Sox because I was on parole and couldn't leave town."

JB further noted, "I played football, too, and had a chance to go to school, but a poverty stricken family will make a man do a lotta things. I try to tell kids to stay in school, to get their lessons, because being a pro athlete isn't enough. My advice is to study as hard as you can because it's better to be a smart mediocre star than being a dumb one."

One of the money-making things young JB tried was boxing. Local fight promoter Sam Gantt said Brown was also a good boxer for his weight and added, "If he'd stayed fighting, he would have been a masterpiece. He had it in him; courage, desire, and he'd do whatever you said do. When he got hit, he'd never get mad. He'd stay calm. He was a pretty good puncher, too."

The *Chronicle* reported on January 29, 1946, of a boxing match in the Municipal Auditorium (later renamed Bell Auditorium), where Brown would later perform his fast footwork while singing his hits: "James Brown, a nice jabbing welter [welter weight], scrapped Kid Owens to a four-round draw in the opener. Brown displayed a fine left, which, after proper tutelage, could be developed into a very damaging weapon."

The next month on February 12, the *Chronicle* wrote about another fight in the Municipal Auditorium saying, "David Walker, 139, will run up against James Brown, 140, a left-jabbing specialist who has shown lots of class in previous scraps, meeting in a four rounder. Both boys are Negroes."

Brown conceded many times in his life that the tough nature and poverty of his growing up years forced him to take drastic measures which may not have been always been right but which were absolutely necessary for him and his family to survive in the days before, during, and after World War II. There were thousands of soldiers with money at Camp Gordon, and a boom time after the war, and James Brown wanted like a lot of others to take advantage of the money that was around to be spent.

But that way of life of hustling or stealing to get by ended abruptly in the spring of 1949 when he was caught breaking and entering cars on the upper end of Broad Street. The Richmond County Grand Jury on May 31, 1949, returned a true bill against him (meaning there was enough evidence for a trial) for "four cases of breaking and entering and larceny from an automobile."

Solicitor George Hains on June 4 announced the complete criminal docket for the Richmond County Superior Court including Brown's case set for Monday, June 13. When James Brown came before him and submitted his guilty plea, Judge Anderson sentenced Brown to two to four years of prison in each of the four cases: eight to sixteen years.

And, yet, while Brown must have felt that his whole world had come crashing down on top of him and that his life was basically over, it was only beginning.

For if he not been caught that day breaking into cars and stealing items, he would not have been served time at a prison near Toccoa, Georgia, and would not have met Bobby Byrd. And, if he had not met Bobby Byrd, he would not have started singing with Byrd and would not have formed the Famous Flames.

And if he had not formed the Famous Flames and they had not met Little Richard who steered them toward music opportunities in Macon, Georgia, the world may never have known James Brown, the singer and entertainer.

So, that's why the author of this book always has contended that one of the luckiest breaks of James Brown's very lucky life was being caught by the city police on Broad Street in Augusta, Georgia, that spring day in 1949.

THREE

Taking Flight with Byrd's Help

I sang a lot of James Brown songs. He can't do any wrong by me I used to sing things like "Cold Sweat" and "I Feel Good." I once heard him sing "If I Ruled the World" on Johnny Carson's [late night TV] show, and I'm still looking for a copy of that recording if there ever was one made.

—Rock star Patty Smyth
May 21, 1987
Augusta Chronicle

One can only speculate on what would have happened to James Brown had he not met Bobby Byrd—singer, songwriter, music arranger, and all-around nice guy.

Possibly after serving his time in prison, James Brown may have moved back to Augusta and tried to jump-start a music career. Or he may have given up on that and entered some other line of work. His options, being young and black and a former jailbird in the late 1950s, would have been severely limited in segregated Augusta.

But fate would have it another way.

After his sentencing on June 13, 1949, JB was first sent to the Georgia Juvenile Training Institute in Rome, Georgia. But in November 1951, all the institute's inmates and staff were transferred to Camp Toccoa, a former paratrooper training camp on Currahee Mountain, the southernmost peak in the Blue Ridge mountain range.

The work camp facility outside Toccoa, Georgia, known officially as the Georgia Boys Industrial Institute, was a minimum-

15

security prison. The guards did not carry guns, and the only barrier to the outside world was a small barbed-wire fence that the inmates knew they could not cross without severe repercussions.

By the fall of 1951, young gospel singer Bobby Byrd was becoming known in the northeast Georgia area through his a cappella group, the Gospel Starlighters, reportedly also known as the Avons when they sang with instruments.

Byrd, born in Toccoa on August 15, 1934, was about a year younger than James Brown, and, like JB, he loved sports. He graduated as valedictorian of his class at Whitman Street High School in 1953 and was very active in Mount Zion Baptist Church on Whitman Street.

His gospel group took its musical religious messages to the inmates of the Georgia Boys Industrial Institute, where Byrd said he was told, "We've got a man in here called 'Music Box' who can really sing and play."

"Music Box," James Brown of course, had attracted the attention of a Toccoa car dealer, not for his music but more for his muscles and his obvious willingness to do hard work.

S. C. Lawson, owner of Lawson's Motor Company, was working on a project to create a lake near the unincorporated town of Hollywood in Habersham County, Georgia, using broken-up concrete from the Camp Toccoa paratrooper base, with labor supplied by young men from the Georgia Boys Industrial Institute.

Young and muscular from his days of boxing and playing other sports in Augusta, James Brown was one of the inmates helping to load the broken concrete onto trucks bound for the lake. Lawson saw Brown working and was impressed by his hard work and enthusiasm.

The story goes that Lawson was told by a guard that Brown could be released if he had a job guaranteed for two years, and Lawson agreed to be his sponsor. On June 14, 1952, James Brown was released from prison; it had been exactly three years and one day after being sentenced in Richmond County Superior Court.

According to JB's first wife, Velma Warren Brown Ridley, when James got out of prison he moved into a house in Toccoa owned by Lena Wilson, near the corner of Sage and Sautee Streets. There were few places in Toccoa in the segregated South for young blacks to stay other than as boarders in the homes of local black citizens.

"He used to go down to a barber shop on Broad Street owned by Nathaniel Davis to have his hair shaped," Velma told me. "You know how he was about his hair. Nathaniel's wife, Dora, had started this gospel group and James started singing with it. Johnnie Mae Wheeler and her sister, Yvonne, also were singing in that group. After he started with the group, he left Miss Lena's house and moved into the basement of the Davis house on Emily Street near Hughes."

Velma believes that is when Bobby Byrd actually met James. The Byrd family home at 114 Weston Sautee Street, was just around the corner from where JB was living at 508 Sage.

Eventually, Brown started singing with Byrd's gospel group, which also consisted of Sylvester Keels, Doyle Ogelsby, Nashplende Knox, Fred Pulliam, and Nafloyd Scott. They sang secular as well as gospel songs and rehearsed at Byrd's house on Sautee Street, at Scott's house at 629 South Broad Street, and Keels's house at 506 Spring Street.

Among their favorite gospel groups was the Swanee Quintet of Augusta, which Brown knew from his days of shining shoes on Augusta streets, and also the Five Blind Boys of Alabama. But they also loved other popular soul, blues, and borderline rock music. Byrd was fond of Big Joe Turner and Billy Eckstine songs, Pulliam tried to copy Lowell Fulsom, Keels sang hits by Clyde McPhatter, and Brown especially enjoyed the music of Roy Brown and Wynonie Harris, who had appeared in person on April 26, 1949, at the Harlem Theatre in Augusta—three months before JB was sentenced to prison.

Brown, Byrd, and Scott also loved the smooth sounds of the Spaniels, the Orioles, the Clovers, the 5 Royales and, of course, the great Louis Jordan. And on the rocking side they also loved Hank Ballard and the Midnighters, and they traveled to Greenville, South Carolina, to see them in person. Ballard later would say that he became so impressed with the young vocal group from Toccoa that he convinced Syd Nathan to sign the group to the King Records label.

By November of 1952, the Gospel Starlighters (aka Avons) had become so hot around Toccoa that they changed their name to the Flames. Some members later said they adopted the name from another group called the Hollywood Flames. The group added drums and piano played by Brown, Byrd, and Keels, and added Nafloyd's brother, Baroy, on bass guitar. Brown, Keels, and Byrd alternated on drums and piano depending on who was singing lead vocal.

Meanwhile, James Brown had been working a series of jobs. He left Lawson Motor Company and went to work for Howell Lawson's brother, J. C., who had a Chrysler dealership called Currahee Motor Company. He later worked for Plastic Laminators and as a janitor at the white Toccoa High School (now Toccoa Elementary School).

The Flames became identified with two popular places in Toccoa: the Ritz Theater on West Doyle Street and Bill's Rendezvous Club on Hughes Street. The Flames performed during the intermission between movies at the Ritz, where at that time, the whites sat downstairs and the blacks sat in the balconies. People would throw money onto the stage in appreciation, and JB would dance over near the money, bending over backwards, picking it up, and keeping on dancing.

Berry Trimier became the Flames' manager and began booking them for white parties at nearby college campuses, such as Clemson in South Carolina, and the University of Georgia in Athens, and at black nightclubs, including Little John's Grill in

Clemson, South Carolina; the Cotton Patch and the Hole in the Wall nightclubs in Canon, Georgia, and Bill's Rendezvous Club in Toccoa.

Members of the Flames recall playing early in the night at Bill's Rendezvous Club, owned by Bill and Delores Keith, and then heading a few blocks over and across the railroad tracks to perform for thirty minutes during the intermission at the Ritz Theater, and then heading back to Bill's to finish the night.

More and more it became important for James Brown to take as many gigs as he could, for on June 27, 1953, he married Velma Warren. They had met at Mount Zion Baptist Church in Toccoa, which Bobby Byrd also attended. Velma and Bobby also attended school together on Whitman Street. She was the daughter of a carpenter from Birmingham, Alabama.

"We dated for some months. Six at the most," Velma said. "He would come to the house [274 Craig Street] and get me, because that's the way my parents were. He had to leave by nine o'clock. My daddy would walk through the house and clear up his throat and that meant, 'Go!' "

When asked where JB proposed to her, she said,

I'll be honest. Everywhere. He wanted to get married at first, but I didn't know if I wanted to or not. Then the tables changed. Everything goes around comes around. Believe me when I tell you that it does, because I had been to Charleston and had come back here. He thought I was going back to Charleston again, but I wasn't going back to Charleston. I really cared for him. That's truthful. I really did. And by that time I loved him.

I could see where he wanted something. He was very ambitious. He was. He was very ambitious. He wasn't going back to poverty, and he knew with me he wasn't going back to poverty. That wasn't going to happen. If you were at there in front, as far as I was concerned, you're going to stay in the front. And he could sing, and that's what he wanted to do, and I wasn't going to cripple him in singing cause that was his baby.

According to most accounts JB and Velma were married in the church he attended, Trinity CME (Colored Methodist Episcopal) at 329 West Franklin Street, but Velma said they actually were married directly across the street from the church in a house at 326 Franklin that served as the parsonage for the Trinity preacher.

"This is where we said 'I dos,' right here in this house," Velma said as we stood in front of the deteriorated structure. "We married about 7 o'clock on a Saturday night. He set it up like the way he wanted it to be. He went and bought the license. And we married that Saturday night right here in the living room. My sister was the witness, and the preacher was F. N. Rushing. That's been so long ago. We didn't have any parents there. There were about five of us."

There was no honeymoon for the new couple. "We were working people," Velma said. "You couldn't have no honeymoon then. There wasn't no money for a honeymoon. He stopped working at Lawson's Motors. He had bought a green, '35 Ford—I never will forget that—and started working a thread mill and started helping down there."

JB, apparently planning out the marriage, already, had rented a house in the Summer Hill section of Toccoa on a short street that was built over a hillside drop off near what was then Toccoa High School and already had put furniture in it.

Velma recalls vividly the early days of the Flames performing at Bill's Rendezvous Club. "He'd play the piano on one side, and after he played his little thing, then he'd go to the mike and sing. They had the drums and all of that with Nate Floyd and his brother Baby Roy playing the guitar. James played the drums. Bobby [Byrd] was singing. I think sometimes he [James] played the piano."

Early in those days, Velma, as JB's new wife, played a role in keeping away overly adoring female fans. "Well, how do I say this?" Velma said. "I figure he thought, 'You are here, and they won't bother me.' He was like that, you know, because he knew the way I was, and I knew the way he was. So, we were protective of one another. I didn't have problems out of women while I was with him. You know playing in a small town like this. You can imagine how it was. So, I was there to keep down a lot of stuff, and he tried to keep stuff down as much as he could. He was just like that."

After their marriage and their sons Larry, Teddy, and Terry came along, JB and Velma still kept attending their respective churches. "He would take us to my church at Mount Zion, and then go to his church at Trinity. Then he'd come back and pick us up. I raised our kids in church and went to Sunday School with them. I didn't just send them."

In those early days, JB started taking Velma and the kids to Augusta to visit family. She recalls them staying with his aunt, Minnie Walker.

As the Flames began growing in popularity in the northeast Georgia and northwest South Carolina region, they began calling themselves "the Famous Flames," and were dressing much better onstage thanks to Andrews-Hamby men's clothing store in Toccoa. Owners Jim Andrews and Fred Hamby dressed them in suits with peg-leg pants and long coats in unusual colors.

A pivotal moment for the Flames was the night they met Macon-born entertainer "Little Richard" Penniman at Bill's Rendezvous Club.

"I first met James in Toccoa, Georgia, when I was doing a show in that town," Little Richard said to me on Saturday night, September 21, 1996, during the celebrity gala for the grand opening of the Georgia Music Hall of Fame in Macon. "James and his group, the Famous Flames, asked if they could sing at intermission of my show. They called themselves 'Famous' even then. I'll never forget that.

"I could hear them [from] backstage and what they were doing to the audience. James sang 'Please, Please, Please.' I thought they weren't going to give me my microphone back! I said to myself, 'I'd better go out and look and see what was happening.' They were fantastic!"

Little Richard and his bandleader, Lucas "Fats" Gonder, were so knocked out by the Famous Flames that they encouraged them to go to Macon and audition for Little Richard's manager, Clint Brantley, who owned a nightclub called the Two Spot.

And so in late 1955, the Famous Flames left northeast Georgia for what they hoped would lead them to fame and wealth. Velma Brown remembers JB telling her about the encounter with Little Richard and his advice to move to Macon.

"He talked about it, but they didn't go right immediately then. They went later," she said. "By then, we had our sons, Teddy and Terry. He couldn't just jump up and leave. He had to make a decision to see how I was going along with it. But you know he was going along with it his way because he loved music."

When the Flames started going back and forth between Macon and Toccoa, Velma stayed home with the kids and JB and the Flames would stay with friends in their homes in Macon. There were few motels that would accept blacks at the time.

The separation led to marital problems between Velma and James, with Velma eventually coming to know about affairs that James was having with other women.

"We were talking about it and trying, but you see it had gotten all messed up and mixed up then," she said. "You know some things you can't go back to. Some things you can't go back to. Sometimes you're better off as friends. We stayed friends."

Knowing about James Brown's legendary temper and his later history of domestic violence, I asked Velma specifically if he ever struck her. She said, "No, because I didn't take that stuff. One thing about it, when it starts, you have to stop it. If you don't ever stop it, it continues. So, before it started, I let him know that I'd been raised one way, and you can't re-raise me. If your temper is bad, take it out on somebody else. That's what I never did ever understand—the person they say he became. I didn't know him that way. So, it's no point in me saying anything about that stuff. 'Cause I didn't know him that way."

JB and Velma separated in 1964 but did not formally divorce until five years later. He made sure that Velma and his sons and later grandchildren were taken care of by building Velma a $150,000 brick home on Prather Bridge Road. JB stayed close and in touch with Velma the rest of his life.

"I didn't have to worry about our sons getting out of hand, because when they did get out of hand, I could send them to him. And that made it good, because they knew good and well how he was [strict]. . . . He would call me from all over, even China, and he would let me know who he was with, and sometimes I would drive to where he was to visit with him. We were good friends, and we stayed that way."

JB would later bring his second wife, Deidre, and third wife, Adrienne, to Toccoa when he visited Velma and the kids, and he would go there for important times in Velma's life.

"Everything major that happened in my family, James was here," she said. "If there was a funeral or something, he would come. When my mother passed, he didn't come, but he sent Dee Dee and his daddy. But when my sister died, he came."

She said that JB even would slip into town secretly and stay at Velma's house when he just needed to get away from everything. "During all those marriages and all of that stuff, he would say that he felt at peace when he came up here," Velma said. "And we would just sit down and talk and talk and talk and talk. He always said that the house belonged to us. We were just good friends. That's all."

FOUR

Macon and the World Beyond

The first I thought of using them [his capes] was
in doing a show in Chattanooga with B. B. King,
Bobby Bland and two or three other acts. I went off
stage and I was singing "Please, Please, Please,"
and they threw a towel around me. I threw it off and
came back, and they threw another towel around
me and I threw it off and came back. I thought of
Gorgeous George [the pro wrestler] when he wore
them to his wrestling matches. So I got the capes.

—James Brown
December 4, 1984
Augusta Chronicle

By late 1955, the basic makeup of the Flames was Bobby
Byrd, Johnny Terry, Sylvester Keels, Nashplende Knox,
Nafloyd Scott, and James Brown. And one Saturday, the Flames
approached Little Richard's manager, Clint Brantley, at his
nightclub, Two Spot, for an audition. Brantley had been drinking
heavily the night before and wasn't in the mood to hear them,
but he consented and asked them to do a spiritual to pick up his
spirits.

The Flames decided to do "Looking for My Mother," which
had the line "When I get to heaven, / I'm going to look for my
mother." The Flames had worked up a performance routine where
they would walk around the stage, each one mournfully looking
for his mother, when they sang the heart-wrenching ballad.

Brantley later recalled that audition and routine saying, "They
looked up under the tables, all behind the stove and all behind the

24

refrigerator, and they never did find her!" Brantley said he told the Flames afterward, "Boys, y'all can sing!"

He signed the group to a management deal and arranged for them to record a demo session at downtown Macon radio station WIBB-AM, then located in the basement of the old Professional Building (now called the Robert E. Lee Building) at 830 Mulberry Street. The group picked the soulful and rhythmic "Please, Please, Please" JB and the Flames supposedly had been inspired to write from an Orioles song, "Baby Please Don't Go." Some members of the Flames said they also had heard "Baby Please Don't Go" performed by a popular Augusta group called Bill Johnson and the Four Steps of Rhythm.

Charles "Big Saul" Green, a popular WIBB disc jockey, was at the reel-to-reel tape control board (which JB later bought and donated to the Georgia Music Hall of Fame) for that historic session on November 1, 1955. The microphones hung from the ceiling and JB was too short to get close to them. So Green got a soft drink crate for him to stand on for the recording session. Bobby Byrd was playing piano for the session, and Nafloyd Scott was on guitar.

As the Flames' manager, Brantley sent a copy of the recording to Hamp Swain, an influential disc jockey at another Macon radio station, WBML-AM. Swain had first aired Little Richard's recordings and later would help another home-grown Macon vocalist named Otis Redding get his big break. The radio station phone lines lit up immediately with callers wanting to hear the recording again and wanting to know more about the singers. Swain knew from the tremendous reaction that the Flames were going to be getting hotter.

But it was James Brown himself who took the next major step in making "Please, Please, Please" and the Flames a huge success. He took a copy of the recording to Gwen Kesler at Southland Record Distributing Company in Atlanta, which distributed King Records—founded in 1943 by Sydney Nathan in Cincinnati,

Ohio—and its subsidiary labels, such as Federal, also started by Nathan in 1950. The headquarters and recording studio of King Records was in a former ice-storage building.

Three versions exist on what happened next, with each of them sounding logical and credible about what actually happened.

One version is that Kesler played the recording for King Records representative Ralph Bass, a native of the Bronx, New York, who ended up producing many hits of rhythm and blues recordings in his long career. He worked for many great R&B labels, including King, Savoy, Federal, and Chess.

The other version is that Bass was driving through Atlanta when he heard the Flames' recording of "Please, Please, Please" and was so impressed that he headed straight for Macon to sign the group with King Records.

Another credible version is told by rhythm and blues pioneer Henry Stone, of whom James Brown later spoke highly of on Larry King's talk show on the CNN cable TV network. Stone contended he was in Miami, Florida, when he got a phone call from Syd Nathan, founder and president of King Record, who had heard about the recording made in Macon. Nathan had been told that the Flames were becoming extremely popular in the Macon area.

Stone said he immediately headed for Macon to get the group signed by his own DeLuxe label, which was distributed by King Records.

"At the same time Nathan had called me, he had also contacted Federal Records A&R [artist and repertoire] man, Ralph Bass," Stone recalled. "Bass, who was in Birmingham, Alabama, at the time, also hightailed it to Macon. . . . Bass, who was closer to Macon, beat me there by one day. He picked up the master demo and sent it on to King Records in Cincinnati."

Interestingly enough, Bobby Byrd remembers that—even before moving to Macon and signing with King Records—the Famous Flames had been a guest on Piano Red's program on WAOK-AM in Atlanta. Piano Red, who later became popular with crowds in the Underground Atlanta entertainment district, had arranged for them to record with a label called NRC. He said the Flames recorded "Sentimental Reasons" for NRC in a studio in Greenville, South Carolina, not far from Toccoa.

The Famous Flames journeyed to the King/Federal studios and on February 4, 1956, recorded four singles: "Please, Please, Please," "I Feel That Old Feeling Coming On," "I Don't Know," and "Why Do You Do Me?"

The Federal Records version of "Please, Please, Please" recorded with the label's session musicians was not an easy session. King founder Nathan was said to have walked out of the building in disgust after an argument with King music director Gene Redd over the odd chord changes in the Flames' arrangements. Redd, however, realized what groundbreaking sounds he was hearing and proceeded with the session.

Later, JB told the *Augusta Chronicle* about the unique sound, "I couldn't go to Mozart, Schubert, Beethoven, Bach or Tchaikovsky, because you have to be educated. So I changed the music from two and four beats to one and three, so you were on the downbeat instead of the upbeat."

The single "Please, Please, Please" was released on the Federal label on March 3, 1956, and by April 11 had peaked at number six on the nation's rhythm and blues sales charts. One of the legendary radio station giants who helped make "Please, Please, Please" a national hit was a white disc jockey in Nashville, Tennessee, named John Richbourg who broadcast rhythm and blues and early black rock records over powerful WLAC-AM under his broadcast name "John R."

When I was a student at the University of Georgia in Athens in the mid-1960s, my friends and I would drive out into the nearby countryside at night and sit on the car and listen to John R's radio show being beamed into north middle Georgia. We thought John R was a black disc jockey, as so many others did, because of the sound of his voice and the music he played.

Another disc jockey closer to Brown's hometown of Augusta who was playing "Please, Please, Please" and Brown's other early releases was Mal "Your Pal" Cook with his 10 a.m. to 1 p.m. show on WAUG-AM.

He sang with an Army glee club on radio and TV throughout California during his military service and worked as an announcer for WLIB in New York. Back home in Augusta, he became one of the city's most popular radio announcers and was able to help launch the career of hometown guy James Brown.

With the quick success of "Please, Please, Please," it seemed as if the Flames could do no wrong, but it was more than two years before they had another major hit single when JB's stirring organ ballad "Try Me" was released on the Federal label October 1, 1958. It became the Flames' first number one record.

Over the years to come, "Please, Please, Please" became Brown's signature song as much as "I Got You," which most fans know from its refrain line, "I feel good." "Please, Please, Please" would drive fans into a frenzy with Brown dropping to his knees and being covered by a cape, which was thrown over Brown's back for most of his career by Danny Ray, longtime master of ceremonies at Brown's stage shows.

As Brown was being helped up and off the stage and, in later years while his later female backup vocalists chanted, "Please, please, please, don't go, I love you so," Brown would fling off the cape and come back to the stand-up microphone and let out more shouting, mournful sounds only to go through the same process two more times with different capes thrown over his shoulders by Danny Ray.

The first major wedge to divide the Famous Flames came when Bobby Byrd discovered that their manager, Brantley, was paying JB more then the other five Flames in spite of the group's agreeing from the start that everything would be divided equally. Supposedly, Brantley tried to quiet Byrd by paying him more also for being the group's primary songwriter and music arranger, but the rest of the Flames found out and that put a damper on everything.

The second major wedge came when Ben Bart of Universal Attractions in New York City became the group's manager and was in charge of their performance bookings, with JB leaving the original Flames' manager, Brantley, behind in Macon to work with other acts. It was Bart who supposedly changed the group's billing to "James Brown and the Famous Flames."

As might be expected, that went over about as well as when years later Motown founder Berry Gordy changed the name of his popular female trio from the Supremes to "Diana Ross and the Supremes." The rest of the Flames were not happy with the billing, just as Flo Ballard and Mary Wilson weren't exactly tickled to death with Ross getting the extra star treatment.

So, the original Flames went their separate ways in the late 1950s, and Byrd headed back to Toccoa. He worked as a darkroom assistant at Troup's Photo Service and, along with Keels, remained active on the Toccoa music scene. Scott also continued with his music after moving to Pensacola, Florida, but Knox apparently mostly dropped out of music after moving to Miami. JB's old prison buddy, Johnny Terry, turned his sights to music in New York City.

In spite of any hard feelings over being pushed aside, Bobby Byrd was an important musical part of James Brown's life over the following decades and continued to play an important role in JB's success.

He rehearsed Brown's bands to stage-worthy perfection and worked out of the King Records office in Cincinnati "doctoring" songs for Brown and other artists so the songs would sound more like hits.

He cowrote many of Brown's smash hit singles, even though he did not receive credit on some of them. The ones he did receive label credit include "Lost Someone" (1961), "Licking Stick" (1968), "(Get Up I Feel Like Being a) Sex Machine" (1970), and "Get Up, Get into It, Get Involved" (1970).

29

And he and his wife, former Brown backup vocalist Vicki Anderson, were in attendance at Brown's fourth and last wedding at JB's South Carolina home and at his final funeral service in Augusta, Georgia. And, even after they both died, the names of Bobby Byrd and James Brown would be forever linked in the hearts and ears of rhythm and blues fans.

FIVE

Live at the Apollo

They [King Records company executives] didn't
think I could do it [record a live album]. They thought
I was crazy. I spent my own money. It cost, $5,700.
Today, it would cost $400,000. It probably has sold
25 million copies, I guess. I've never been paid yet,
but I guess one of these days I'll get paid.

—James Brown
December 4, 1984
Augusta Chronicle

Before Elvis Presley and James Brown came along with their sounds that combined spirituals, jazz, country, and blues, there were other recordings trying that mix, including Louis Jordan's 1945 million-seller "Caldonia"; Arthur "Big Boy" Crudup's 1947 recording "That's All Right (Mama)"; Wynonie Harris's 1947 King Records single "Good Rockin' Tonight"; Willie Mae "Big Mama" Thornton's 1952 recording "(You Ain't Nothing But a) Hound Dog"; Bill Haley's 1954 megahit "Rock Around the Clock,"; Big Joe Turner's 1954 release "Shake, Rattle and Roll", Chuck Berry's 1955 hit "Maybellene"; and Ray Charles's hit of the same year, "I've Got A Woman."

But it seems like all hell broke loose with rock and roll and on the nation's stages when Elvis Presley started releasing his RCA singles in early 1956, and James Brown began recording for King Records that same year. Only four days after Ralph Bass had signed James Brown to King Records, RCA Records in Nashville released Presley's first RCA single, "Heartbreak Hotel" on January 27, 1956.

Two major cultural changes had just happened in Augusta, Georgia, which changed the face of local music. WJBF television station went on the air on November 25, 1953, and WRDW television, built next door in North Augusta, South Carolina, went on the air on February 14, 1954. Augusta area teenagers, like other U.S. teenagers, were not only hearing rock music on the radio but they were seeing their rock and soul music heroes and heroines performing before their very eyes on black-and-white electronic screens. It was a cultural revolution for the still segregated South.

Just a few years later, an incredible concert billed as the "Fantabulous Rock & Roll Show" came to Bell Auditorium on October 15, 1957, featuring the first Augusta appearance of Ray Charles and His Orchestra along with Mickey and Sylvia, the Moonglows, the Del Vikings, Larry Williams and His Orchestra, Big Joe Turner, the Velours, Bo Diddley and His Trio, Roy Brown, Tiny Topsy, Vicky Nelson, Nappy Brown, and Annie Laurie. Advance tickets were $1.50; tickets sold at the door were $2.

The advertisements for the show noted "White Spectators in Music Hall," which meant whites would be allowed to sit in the Music Hall section on the south side of the auditorium, which shared a common stage with the main auditorium section. It was shameful that Augusta then was enforcing segregated seating at rock shows, but at least white Augustans were getting a chance to see some of the best acts in black rock and soul music.

White and black music fans throughout most of the nation, including the Southern states, were all ready for a breakthrough rock and soul album. Their wait ended on October 24, 1962, when James Brown and his revue recorded their spine-tingling *Live at the Apollo* album.

By 1960, Brown had moved to New York and was tearing up the stage with his pulsating sounds and energetic performances. He wanted to try a live album, but Syd Nathan of King Records had no vision when it came to what James Brown knew in his heart and soul what his fans really wanted. Nathan contended that no one would buy reissued songs or would want a live recording of a show that was being performed virtually every night on the road.

Brown, however, knew how audiences were reacting to his stage shows and to his hits on the soul music radio stations including "Please, Please, Please" (1956), "Try Me" (1958), and "Night Train" (1962). He believed in having a live album so much that Brown—then twenty-nine years old—paid to rent the Apollo Theater in Harlem at 253 West 125th Street, promoted the shows, and paid for the recording sessions. Brown made his first Apollo appearance in 1959, supporting another King Records artist, Little Willie John.

The night of October 24, 1962, was freezing in Harlem, but fifteen hundred people stood in two lines to get into the show. Brown's staff handed out free cups of coffee to people waiting outside. Lucky fans who bought tickets were not told the event was being recorded until they got into the theater.

Lucas "Fats" Gonder, who also played organ in JB's orchestra introduced James Brown that night, and besides Gonder on organ—occasionally letting Bobby Byrd take over the instrument, such as on "Lost Someone"—the other musicians were: Louis Hamblin, music director and principal trumpet; Teddy Washington and Mack Johnson, trumpets; St. Clair Pinckney, principal tenor saxophone and soloist on "Think"; Al "Brisco" Clark, tenor and baritone saxophones; Clifford "Ace King" MacMillan, tenor saxophone; Dickie Wells, trombone; Les Buie, guitar and acting road manager; Hubert Perry, bass guitar; Clayton Fillyau, principal drums; and Sam Latham, also drums.

The Famous Flames backing JB that historic night were Bobby Byrd, Bobby Bennett, and Eugene "Baby Lloyd" Stallworth.

After the introduction by Gonder, JB opened the show with "I'll Go Crazy" and followed it with "Try Me," "Think," "I Don't Mind," and "Lost Someone." Then came a medley consisting of "Please, Please, Please," "You've Got Power," "I Found Someone,"

"Why Do You Do Me Like You Do," "I Want You So Bad," "I Love You Yes I Do," "Strange Things Happen," "Bewildered," and then a reprise of "Please, Please, Please." Finally came the closing number: "Night Train."

The original 78 rpm live album was titled *The Apollo Theatre Presents, in Person, The James Brown Show,* and it became a benchmark in recording history, usually listed by rock music authorities as one of the best live albums ever. It remained on Billboard magazine's music charts for an unprecedented sixty-six weeks, peaking at number two.

Nathan was so sure it was going to be a disaster that only five thousand copies were pressed initially. But, just like in boxing with his one-two powerful punches, Brown had landed his own one-two punches with the success of his Apollo album that established him as one of the greatest entertainers of all time.

The Apollo album let white, black, and other ethnic fans *hear* how exciting Brown could sound onstage in a live performance. But the Teenage Awards Music International (T.A.M.I.) show filmed October 28–29, 1964, in the Santa Monica, California, auditorium would let moviegoers both *see* and *hear* how exciting his performances could be.

He was up against some tough competition with other acts on the show: being the Supremes, the Beach Boys, the Rolling Stones, Lesley Gore, Billy J. Kramer and the Dakotas, Marvin Gaye, Chuck Berry, and Smokey Robinson and the Miracles.

But he and the Famous Flames and his band literally stole the show with the resulting film, *The T.A.M.I. Show,* which became a teen sensation in worldwide movie theaters. It permanently cemented his fast-growing reputation as "the Hardest-Working Man in Show Business."

SIX

Getting Ready to Come Home

I met the Beatles in England when I was doing the *Ready, Steady, Go* television show with the Animals, and they were there. They weren't on the show. They just came to see me. I think of the song "Something (in the Way She Moves)" and its writer, George Harrison, because he said out of 121 covers of "Something," James Brown did the best one.

—James Brown
December 4, 1984
Augusta Chronicle

The times they were achanging in the 1960s, as Bob Dylan would eloquently proclaim in his similarly titled single, especially as the politically minded Doves and Hawks fought over the rights and wrongs of the escalating conflict in Vietnam, and as idealistic young and old Americans tried to comprehend the early 1960s assassination of U.S. President John F. Kennedy and the late 1960s assassinations of his brother, U.S. Senator Robert Kennedy, and of the civil rights leader, the Reverend Martin Luther King Jr.

And nowhere were the times achanging more than in the old South where barriers of segregation were finally being broken down, partly because of white music and film celebrities who marched arm-in-arm with black protest leaders.

Throughout the sixties, popular music itself would change from the simple acoustic folk melodies of New England coffeehouses to the frenzied electric rock tunes of San Francisco's hippie culture, and from the soft and smooth sounds of synchronized

Motown artists to the sexy, rough growls of James Brown's self-penned anthems.

JB was trying hard to keep up with those changes in music and culture as evidenced by his monster hit single "Papa's Got a Brand New Bag" recorded on February 1, 1965, which describes an older guy trying to stay up with the latest dances and times.

American rock and soul music artists were finding it increasingly difficult to get their songs on the rock music charts in the mid-1960s because of the invasion of the British music acts that were led by the Beatles' first tour of America in 1964.

That almost was exactly the same pushed-aside feeling that traditional American country music artists had experienced in the late 1950s with the explosion of rockabilly artists such as Elvis Presley, Jerry Lee Lewis, Conway Twitty, and Carl Perkins.

It's a good bet that Brown was concerned about the increasing popularity of British artists, especially since it came just as he was beginning to get more airplay on rock music stations—which was vital for the promotion of the big money concerts and huge record sales.

And surely he must have taken note when British acts began invading his own home state in 1965 just as "Papa's Got a Brand New Bag" was released that year in March.

A sharp entertainment promoter named Ralph Bridges, owner of Atlanta-based Alkahest Artists & Attractions, recognized the enormity of the new British acts and their popularity with American teenagers. His son, Scott Bridges, later would carry on his father's work.

About that time, I was writing for the University of Georgia's student newspaper, *The Red and Black*, and had first made contact with Bridges when he booked folk music trio Peter, Paul, & Mary at the old Atlanta Municipal Auditorium on January 24, 1965. Bridges not only allowed me full backstage access but also encouraged me to return for future shows. His angle, of course, was seeking some free publicity to let University of Georgia students in nearby Athens know about his shows.

Atlanta teenagers went totally nuts when promoter Bridges booked the Beatles at the relatively-new Atlanta-Fulton County Stadium on August 18, 1965, as a stop on their second U.S. tour. I remember that visit well as Bridges granted me access to the Beatles' press conference held at the stadium. When the conference was over and The Beatles went through the locker room doors, the other reporters left but I hung around. That's how I got to meet John Lennon. I remember he had large jingle bells on an ankle strap. He was polite and signed a piece of blue-lined paper from my reporter's notebook but apparently was a bit miffed at running into an autograph hound. I heard him say to his companion as they were walking away, "Might have known I would have run into one of those bahs-tards."

I often thought in later years what an honor it was being called a "bahs-tard" by the bigger-than-life singer-songwriter.

Just a week after the Beatles left Atlanta, Bridges brought Dick Clark's Spring Caravan of Stars tour to Atlanta's Municipal Auditorium, featuring British heartthrobs Peter & Gordon ("World without Love," "I Go to Pieces," and "Nobody I Know"), an upcoming powerhouse singer from Wales named Tom Jones, and also American acts the Turtles (who tried to sound British), Billy Joe Royal, Ronnie Dove, the Shirelles, Mel Carter, Brian Hyland, and some others.

James Brown and other American soul and rock artists quickly learned that they had nothing to fear from the new British artists, who eagerly sang their praises in telling interviewers that they had based their own music on the fifties and sixties recordings of American rock and soul artists.

Unlike his friend, Elvis Presley, who never toured or performed overseas except for his U.S. Army service while he was stationed in Germany, James Brown was a frequent global traveler, adored by fans throughout the world. He began popping up on England's

TV shows such as *Ready, Steady, Go,* as well as on American TV shows such as *Shindig* and *American Bandstand.*

"He was a whirlwind of energy and precision, and he was always very generous and supportive to me in the early days of the Stones," said British lead vocalist Mick Jagger of the Rolling Stones upon Brown's death. "His passing is a huge loss to music."

Jagger, whose dance steps were influenced by Brown, had said earlier of the American legend, "His show didn't just have to do with the artist but had to do with the audience, the way he and they interacted. Their reaction was always interesting, like being in a church."

As James Brown grew more and more successful in the late fifties and early sixties, he undoubtedly wanted his hometown friends and family to share in his success, and he must have taken some personal satisfaction in being able to go back home a musical hero.

Those early trips back to Augusta included a show and dance at the Paramount Country Club helping Mal "Your Pal" Cook celebrate his eighth anniversary of broadcasting over WAUG-AM. Cook, returned the favor, by booking Brown into Bell Auditorium for a show on May 10, 1964, that featured "Mr. Dynamite, James Brown," the Famous Flames, the James Brown Orchestra, Otis Redding, Dionne Warwick, Solomon Burke, Garnet Mims, the Tams, the Orlons, Dean and Jean, Anna King (a vocalist with the Brown revue), Timmy Shaw, and others. Tickets were $3 in advance or $3.50 at the door.

Allyn Lee, the popular Augusta disc jockey and JB's childhood friend, also would bring Brown back to Augusta for shows when Lee was a popular disc jockey on WTHB-AM.

On August 17, 1966, Brown was back in the Bell in Augusta with his eighteen-piece orchestra and Bobby Byrd, James Crawford, and the Swanee Quintet. Two months after that show, Brown was a guest on Ed Sullivan's hugely popular, color-broadcast network variety TV show. The *Chronicle* on Sunday, October 30, 1966, noted in its TV listings: "8 p.m. (12)—Ed Sullivan (Color). Nancy

Sinatra, popular singing star, and James Brown, Augusta singer, are among the guest artists."

Apparently, Augustans couldn't get enough of James Brown in those days, because he was back before the year was out performing in Bell Auditorium on December 8, 1966, and with him were the Famous Flames, the Jewels, Bobby Byrd ("Oh What a Night"); Byrd's future wife, Vicki Anderson ("Never Let Me Go"); James Crawford ("Honest I Do"), and what was billed as the "Go-Go Dancing Girls." It was the sixties, after all.

Just a few days before that pre-Christmas show in Augusta, Brown had made national news when a thirty-minute, "near violent" brawl erupted at a Brown show in Kansas City, Missouri, on Thursday night, November 24, 1966, that injured thirteen people, five of whom were police officers.

More than eight thousand people were in the building for the "rock 'n' roll" dance and show, with an estimated two thousand either fighting or trying to block police efforts.

According to the Associated Press story in Brown's hometown newspaper, the *Augusta Chronicle*, the brawl resulted from a dance contest that had taken place to the music of Brown's eighteen piece orchestra. The contest had come down to two couples competing for the prize of $150. Contest judges called it a draw, which didn't sit well with the audience.

"Police said most of the audience appeared to favor a couple which had put on the most daring dance, described by one officer as a 'simulated sex act' in which both participants were down on the floor on their hands and knees," the report stated.

"Fist fights broke out. Whisky bottles began flying. Lt. Maynard Brazeal called off the rest of the show. His announcement from the stage was greeted by a flying whisky bottle that hit him on the chin. More empty bottles were thrown from the balcony."

The offshoot of the brawl, the story noted, was that city officials were "taking a hard look" at the type of entertainment that would be permitted in the auditorium in the future.

Three months later, in February of 1967, Brown's next single release was "Kansas City" with the lines, "I'm going to Kansas City. Kansas City, here I come. / Going to Kansas City. Kansas City, here I come. / They got some crazy little bopsters here. I'm gonna get me one."

In the fall of 1966, I crossed paths with Brown for the first time, backstage at the University of Georgia's coliseum. Some of the songs he performed that night included "Prisoner of Love," "I Got You (I Feel Good)," "Ain't That a Groove," and a ten-minute version of "It's a Man's, Man's, Man's World," which had been released in April.

The "Man's World" number was especially memorable because it was staged with the members of his female backup group, the Jewels, and dancers on various levels of large platforms with very cool mood lighting. When Brown closed with "Please, Please, Please," six capes were thrown over him before he finally left the stage.

I remember that two of his sons were standing in the wings that night, and he hugged them when he came offstage. They apparently had come down from nearby Toccoa where they lived with their mother. By that time, Brown and his wife, Velma, had been separated for two years.

By the time of Brown's appearance at the University of Georgia, the campus had been seeing its share of racist speakers such as Mississippi governor Ross Barnett, as well as civil rights advocates such as Roy Wilkins, executive director of the NAACP, whose speeches I had covered for the campus newspaper, the *Red and Black*.

Like many other prominent black entertainers in the 1960s, Brown was doing his part to stir up some good old white boys and good old white girls in the South to do the right thing and give blacks their equal rights for a decent education in a decent school, a good meal in a good restaurant, a nice house in a nice neighborhood, and a well-paying job at a progressive company.

Brown joined Sammy Davis Jr., Marlon Brando, Anthony Franciosa, Burt Lancaster, and athlete Rafer Johnson on June 25, 1966, for a rally at Tougaloo College on the outskirts of Jackson, Mississippi, to boost the morale of marchers who were protesting the shooting of civil rights leader James Meredith.

James Brown saw that the way out of poverty and degradation for most blacks was a good education, even though he himself had dropped out in the seventh grade. He translated those thoughts into his 1966 hit single "Don't Be a Dropout," which had the often repeated line, "Without an education, you might as well be dead." Later that same year in December, Brown established a $1,000 scholarship at his old elementary school, Silas X. Floyd, for deserving students. He presented the grant to his former principal, Yewston N. Myers.

His efforts to promote education were recognized in his own hometown when Augusta mayor George A. Sancken Jr. in late August of 1967 presented Brown with an official key to the city of Augusta for his achievements in the entertainment field and for his contributions to a national program called Don't Be a Dropout: Stay in School. The *Augusta Chronicle* noted that the singer had just given two concerts in Bell Auditorium under the sponsorship of WAUG radio station.

Augusta was never far from his thoughts, which was apparent in his single release of "There Was a Time" in December of 1967 that had these words:

Ha, in my home town / Where I used to stay
The name of the place, ha / Is Augusta, G.A.

The year 1967 was an extremely productive and successful one for Brown recordingwise, with some of his legendary singles released that year: "Bring It Up" in January, "Kansas City" in February, "Think" in March, "Let Yourself Go" in April, "Cold Sweat" in July, "Get It Together" in October, and "I Can't Stand Myself" and "There Was a Time" both in December. The year ended on a high note for James Brown with the release of two of his greatest-ever recordings; it also ended on a low with the death of his good friend and musical competitor from Macon, Otis Redding, who was only twenty-six when his twin-engine Beechcraft airplane plunged into icy Lake Monona at 3:30 p.m. on December 10, 1967, just a few miles from the airport at his destination of Madison, Wisconsin.

Redding had produced a major hit single by another Georgia-born artist, Arthur Conley, called "Sweet Soul Music," which paid tribute to James Brown by calling him "the king of them all, y'all." But it was another King that the world was thinking about on April 4, 1968, when Baptist preacher and civil rights leader Martin Luther King Jr., Southern born and reared, was shot to death on the balcony of a motel in Memphis, Tennessee.

Many black Augustans—possibly even James Brown's relatives—had come to personally know the Reverend Dr. King and his father. The Reverend Martin Luther King Sr., in fact, had conducted a week-long revival at Tabernacle Baptist Church in Augusta in February 1934 about a year before James Brown was born. The Reverend Dr. Martin Luther King Jr. had been in Augusta a couple of times. His last visit was on March 24, 1968, at Beulah Grove Baptist Church just a couple of weeks before his death. About a month before Dr. King's assassination in Memphis, James Brown was back in Bell Auditorium on February 11 with the show billed as an "all star cast of 40 stars of radio, TV, stage & screen."

The advertisement proclaimed "in person, the world's No. 1 entertainer" and promised he would be singing "Cold Sweat," "Get It Together," "Bring It Up," "Can't Stand It," and "There Was a Time."

The next month he cemented his relationship with Augusta by buying the WRDW-AM radio station—the same station that he had shined shoes in front of when it was located downtown. By the time Brown bought it, the station had moved into a trailer (mobile home) on Eisenhower Drive, named after frequent Augusta visitor and former U.S. President Dwight D. Eisenhower.

42

"An agreement to transfer Radio Station WRDW to JB Broadcasting of Augusta Limited, an enterprise of James Brown, the Negro radio, television and recording artist, has been signed," the *Augusta Chronicle* announced on March 5, 1968, adding that the sale price was "said to involve $377,500." That surely made white businessmen and others in Augusta acutely aware of Brown's buying power. He may have left Augusta poor and in the custody of the police, but he was working his way back into the city by letting his money talk for him.

Brown, who knew firsthand the power of radio, had acquired WGYW the previous year in Knoxville, Tennessee, and had managed to get the Federal Communications Commission (FCC) to change the radio station's call letters to WJBE for James Brown Enterprises.

The day after King was shot to death, Brown was scheduled to perform in Boston Garden auditorium. There had been talk of canceling the show because of the great amount of unrest in the city and fear of a riot by angry residents of Boston's black community of eighty thousand. But cooler heads prevailed when city officials came to the conclusion it would be better to have black citizens in Boston Garden watching Brown and his revue than roaming the streets seeking trouble.

Someone came up with the idea that even more black citizens could be kept occupied if the show was televised live over the local public broadcasting television station. The only problem was that Brown had taped a network show the previous Friday in New York City with a contract clause saying he could not appear on TV until that show aired.

City leaders pleaded with Brown, and he finally agreed to do the live TV appearance provided the city government would guarantee his $60,000 show expenses which would cover his costs if he was sued by the New York City network. He was afraid no one would show up, and the promoter wouldn't pay him and his entourage. Mayor Kevin White agreed to the deal, Boston media later reported.

Even though Boston Garden held fourteen thousand people, only two thousand showed up for the concert. But Brown put on his usual strong show that was being broadcast live. He talked during the show to those both in the Garden and in the TV audience about the importance of staying calm and protesting peacefully as the Reverend King would have wanted.

Immediately after the concert ended, the local TV station that was broadcasting it replayed the tape. Peter Wolf, lead vocalist with the J. Geils Band, told the *Boston Globe*, "I remember going through the South End and every window seemed to be watching James Brown."

There is no doubt about the major effect of Brown's influence, and Boston leaders forever gave Brown all the credit for averting a possible and probable disaster in their city. The interesting footnote to that Boston performance is that—even though Brown at first didn't want to do the live TV show—it now can be found on DVD, on the Internet, and segments have aired repeatedly over the years including on YouTube.com and in the TV tributes after his death.

Back in Brown's hometown of Augusta, his family and friends and fans were not only told of the good that Brown was doing to calm citizens angry over King's assassination, but the *Chronicle*'s editorial page published the remarks Brown made on television the next day, which had been read into the *Congressional Record* by New York state's Republican Senator Jacob Javits.

Those very personal and eloquent words that revealed how Brown felt about his own years growing up in Augusta were:

> *I want to start by saying that I can't come up with a written speech because I am not a speech maker. I am not a writer. But I can tell you what's happening. Now, I know how everybody feels because I feel the same way.*
>
> *Number one, I feel sad because we have a black man that died for the movement and the progress for the betterment of the nation and of the black race.*

I want to say—we were in Boston last night—[and] we were having a problem there. . . . We put on a program that lasted three hours and fifteen minutes, taped it, televised it. We were supposed to do a show at the Garden there.

Normally, we have 15 to 16,000 people. But we asked the people to stay home. They were just watching the show [on TV]. We had a real bad problem there. When I finished talking to the people and we finished doing the show—the amazing thing—35 minutes after we got on the air, everybody cleared the streets.

They didn't clear the streets because I asked them to. They cleared it because they know that they were doing wrong. But they wanted someone to identify with them—that's me, I'm down there.

I guess you know how I started as a shoeshine boy in Augusta, Georgia. I didn't get a chance to finish the seventh grade, but I made it. I made it because He believed in me— because I had honesty and dignity and sincerity and I wanted to be somebody.

The other day I was talking to the kids—stay in school and don't be a dropout, because if I hadn't lucked out and through the good will of their people, I wouldn't be here.

Education is the answer. Know what you are talking about. Be Qualified. Be ready. Then you will have a chance. Be ready, know what you are doing.

You know in Augusta, Georgia, I used to shine shoes on the steps of the radio station, WRDW. I think we started at three cents, then went to five or eight. I never did get to a dime. But today, I own that radio station.

Now, I say to you, I'm your brother. I know what it's at. I've been there. I am not using my imagination. I am talking from experience. I have picked cotton. I did everything. I was nine years old before I got my first pair of underwear from a store. All my clothes were made from sacks and things like that. You know what I'm talking about.

This is our language. We know where it's at. But I know that I had to make it. I had to have the determination to go on and my determination was to be somebody, and that's what I am because you made me that. Now, I say to you—I heard the gentleman talking tonight about how many policemen they got on the force.

We don't need that. This is America. This is our country. We don't need that. We are not going to tear the country up because we love the country. You aren't going to burn your house down. You aren't going to cut up the streets, throw your shoes in the trashcan. . . . This is your home, your life.

I just left Africa. I always wanted to go to Africa because I wanted to know where my soul came from. I wanted to know where it really started.

They say I have so much in common—my music, I even have the drums, the syncopation, the movement, the sound. So I went to Africa and I found people working for $200 a year, $40 a month. Then I thought of something else. But, do you know, with all the minor things that have happened out there, America is the greatest country in the world.

Everybody has had their problems. My home is Augusta, Georgia, and you know I had my problems. I know what they are. But the main thing is that you've got determination, enough believing confidence in yourself to go all the way.

Don't leave the kid homeless tomorrow with no place to go back to. He can't go to school. He can't get a formal education.

We wanted a hero, so we got one. We didn't get it just like we wanted, but we got one. But we got something to live for. We've got an image to maintain. We got a man of the world. We got a man of the world. We got a dream we want to fulfill.

We can do more with that dream now than he ever did because we know what he left. He believed in it enough to die

for it: we should have the respect and dignity for our fellow
man, our country, ourselves to hold that image and maintain it
and keep the respect of it.

Among the performers in Brown's revue for the famous
Boston Garden concert was his featured vocalist Marva Whitney
who did her part in calming viewers by singing "Tell Mama." She
was also there onstage beside Brown in June of that same year for
one of the noblest adventures of his life—performing for white
and black soldiers in Vietnam—and she was there at the very end
to sing at Brown's funeral in Augusta.

Brown's performances in Vietnam touched my heart and soul,
because I was there that extremely hot day in the huge outdoor
amphitheater at Long Binh Post when Brown and the few revue
members he was allowed to bring with him took the stage.

He never forgot it after I told him about being there, and he
almost always would introduce me to his friends and business
associates saying, "You know, he saw me in Vietnam."

Earlier in 1968, he released the singles "You've Got To
Change Your Mind" in February, "I Got The Feelin'" in March,
and "Licking Stick" and "America Is My Home" in May.

The emotions that Brown had experienced earlier in the year—
getting over Redding's death, King's assassination, the intense
concert in Boston Garden, and the overwhelmingly gratifying trip
to entertain soldiers in Vietnam—resulted in one of the greatest
songs of his career.

It was a song that was more than just words and music. And
like his television remarks he made about his Boston show, this
particular song would have a profound social effect on a racially
divided nation.

That song was "Say It Loud—I'm Black and I'm Proud."

SEVEN

Saying It Loud and Being Proud

> When I went to his room, on two napkins on the table was a song, "Say It Loud—I'm Black and I'm Proud." He said, "Mr. Bobbit, I want you to get the band together. Send them down to the Valley, and get a studio. We are going to record this record tonight. Get me 30 children. I want you to get me 30 children to sing on this song."
>
> —Charles Bobbit

Brown tried his whole life to do the Christian thing and be color blind. He never came across as a black militant, and he made white friends and business associates feel as welcome in his presence as his black friends and business associates. Just as the Reverend Martin Luther King Jr. and the Reverend Billy Graham, he truly believed that everyone of all races should try to get along.

He totally believed in that children's song that many racists sang in white churches in the 1950s and 1960s without being sincere about it: "Red and yellow, / black and white, / they are precious in his sight. / Jesus loves the little children of the world." Right up to his death, he never let any nasty experiences with racism stop him from loving his fans of all races and from being very proud of his own race.

Charles Bobbit, his longtime personal manager and the last person to talk with Brown just before he died, told this story at JB's funeral in the James Brown Arena in Augusta:

All of you walk around saying [and], singing—"Say It Loud—I'm Black and I'm Proud." Let me tell you how that was done. The young lady, Ms. Marva Whitney who sang for you a short while ago, myself and Mr. Brown, were in Los Angeles, California. We just finished a date.

[It was] raining, storming like nothing. Mr. Brown, he always had a lot to say. So, we were sitting in there talking, looking at television, and there was black crime going on. He said, "How come black people can't love each other? How come they can't get together? How come they can't respect each another?"

I was tired and I agreed, "mm-hmm," which was true. He said, "Oh, my, my, my, OK, you can go to your room." . . . I went to my room. I thought, "Oh, man, I can turn on the television," and watched for 20 minutes exactly [until] he called me [saying], "Mr. Bobby, come here."

When I went to his room, on two napkins on the table was a song, "Say It Loud—I'm Black and I'm Proud." He said, "Mr. Bobbit, I want you to get the band together. Send them down to the [San Fernando] Valley, and get a studio. We are going to record this record tonight. Get me 30 children. I want you to get me 30 children to sing on this song."

It's storming, and it's almost in the middle of the night. I said, "Mr. Brown, where am I going to get 30 children from?" He said, "You're the manager. You can do it."

I went to a church and watched. I found this lady, and I got an old school bus and we rode around Watts and got 30 children, brought them down to the studio, recorded "Say It Loud—I'm Black and I'm Proud." I gave them $10 [each] and a James Brown album. That's how the song that you love so well was played.

Brown's trombone player, Fred Wesley, also told part of that story to Scott Freeman who wrote about it in "James Brown: Soul Brother No. 1 (1933–2006): The story of a Georgian who rose from poverty to become a cultural icon, as told by the people who knew him best" for the January 10, 2007, issue of *Creative Loafing* magazine.

Wesley, who had just joined the band earlier that year in 1968 and eventually became Brown's music director, said his first recording session was for "Say It Loud—I'm Black and I'm Proud."

He told Freeman, "We were in California and had the day off, and we were laying around the hotel. Somebody came in and said, 'We're going into the studio.' James Brown walked in [the studio] with a bunch of kids, and he said, 'Say it loud!' And the kids said, 'I'm black and I'm proud!' We went back on the road a couple of weeks later. We were in Houston. And James Brown came out onstage and said, 'Say it loud!' And everybody in the auditorium, about ten thousand people, yelled back, 'I'm black and I'm proud!' It happened that quick."

Brown's single was released in August of 1968 and went to number one on the soul music charts and number ten on the pop music charts. Millions of copies have been sold over the years.

On September 21, 1968, it was announced that James Brown had been contacted by the principal and two teachers of Silas X. Floyd school—all alumni of Augusta's predominantly black Paine College—and that he had agreed to give a benefit performance the following January or February to help raise emergency money for Paine College following a disastrous fire in August that had burned the Haygood Hall administration building.

Dr. I. E. "Ike" Washington, principal of A. R. Johnson Junior High and later an Augusta city councilman, was serving as chairman of the benefit performance. The story in the *Augusta Chronicle* announcing Brown's concert added, "Working with him will be Miss Laura Garvin, one of Brown's former teachers and an influential factor in the singer's acceptance of the alumni request."

The Brown concert was set for 8 p.m., February 4, 1969, in Bell Auditorium with a parade in Brown's honor on Broad Street in downtown Augusta beginning at 4 p.m. that same afternoon.

The month before the concert, a story in the *Chronicle* on January 10, 1969, announced that the hometown guy who had recorded twenty-four records that had sold more than a million copies each was going into the food franchise business with the formation of a corporation called Gold Platter Inc.

His new business partners were former Augustan Herbert L. Parks, formerly president of the First of Georgia Insurance Group, who would be president of the Gold Platter Corporation, and current Augusta resident Jack E. Fink, a textile executive, who would be secretary-treasurer.

The corporation would be headquartered in Macon and would initially sponsor a chain of eating establishments called "James Brown's Gold Platter" restaurants. You know—gold records, gold platters. Get it?

According to the announcement, the menu would consist of chicken, fish, and soul food such as collard greens, black-eyed peas, and hush puppies. Two restaurants, company owned, would open in Macon on June 1, the corporation promised, and would be used as a base for training franchisers and evaluating the menu.

One aspect of the company, James Brown said from his by now office branch in Los Angeles office, is that black citizens would be encouraged to buy franchises, which would cost a minimum of $25,000 each. Brown said in his statement he hoped the corporation would become "a vehicle and an example for the interchange and the interfusion of black and white capital by the profit incentive."

Brown later would tell interviewers that the restaurants did "pretty well" but he decided to get back on the road and give them up. He contended that he made a lot of money from them.

On the afternoon of February 4, 1969, Brown's private red, white, and blue Lear jet—said to have cost $715,000—touched down just after 3 p.m. at Bush Field airport, the same airport he would fly in and out of thousands of times in years to come.

When it taxied to a stop near the terminal, Brown stepped out onto a red carpet. He smiled and bowed to the crowd waiting not far away. The January afternoon was chilly, but the day was sunny without clouds. The *Augusta Chronicle* noted Brown was wearing a seal coat said to have cost $800. His wife, Deidre, also stepped from the plane wearing "an opulent silver fox coat."

Several young black women were content to just touch his coat, while other spectators handed him $10 bills to autograph. Some reached out to him with copies of the latest edition of the internationally-distributed *Look* magazine that had gone on sale at Augusta newsstands that very morning for fifty cents per copy.

The issue, dated February 18, 1969, had three things on the cover to attract readers: a headline proclaiming "P.O.W.—My Four Years in a VC Prison, a photo on the bottom right of U.S. Senator Edmund Muskie with the caption "A close-up of the loser as a big winner" (he had been the vice presidential candidate on the losing 1968 Democratic ticket), and a photo on the bottom left of James Brown with the intriguing caption "Is he the most important black man in America?"

The article on the inside pages by *Look* assistant editor Thomas Barry was titled "The Importance of Being Mr. James Brown." It told Brown's rags-to-riches story—getting his first store-bought underwear at age nine, picking cotton, dancing for nickels and dimes from local soldiers, entering reform school at sixteen, and being paroled at nineteen.

According to the article, just the previous December, James Brown at age thirty-five had become the first black man in the thirty-year history of *Cash Box* magazine to be cited as best male vocalist on a single pop record (sales to the entire record buying public).

"To millions of kids on ghetto street corners, he is living proof that a black man can make it big and still come back to listen to their troubles," Barry wrote.

He noted that Brown performed 250 to 300 days a year charging no more than $5 for adults and ninety-nine cents for children. His tour gross from concerts had risen from $450,000 in 1963 to $2.5 million in 1968, 10 percent of which went to charities and youth groups. The additional income from investments, record sales, and song publishing boosted his total 1968 gross income to $4.5 million, the article claimed.

Additionally, Barry reported, in 1968 alone Brown had traveled more than one hundred thousand miles and had entertained more than 3 million people and had sold 4.4 million copies of his single records. He employed eighty-five people and owned two radio stations. This was particularly significant, as only five 5 of the nation's 528 "soul music" stations were owned by blacks.

His net worth included three hundred pairs of shoes, about five hundred to one thousand suits, a gray Lincoln Mark III automobile, a silver and black Rolls Royce, a yellow Excalibur sports car, a Victorian castle in Queens, New York, said to cost $120,000, and, oh yes, that Lear jet that cost roughly $715,000—all in 1968 dollars!

Instead of Deidre being identified as Brown's wife, as the Augusta newspapers had done, *Look* identified her as his "close companion over the past year," and noted that he was separated from his wife who lived in Toccoa in a twenty-room mansion he had built for her and their children.

Brown told Barry that in spite all of his hopes he still got very discouraged that things were not moving as quickly as he wanted for the betterment of black people.

"This country's gonna blow in two years unless the white man wakes up," he said. "The black man's got to be set free. He's got to be treated as a man. I don't say hire a cat cause he's black; just hire him if he's right. This country is like a crap game. I'll lose my money to any man long as the game is fair. But if I find the dice are crooked, I'll turn the table over. What we need are programs that are so out of sight they'll leave the militants with their mouths open. A militant is just a cat that's never been allowed to be a man."

Brown was supposed to have arrived in Augusta that morning for activities planned in his honor, including a morning press conference and a ceremony in the new Gilbert-Lambuth Chapel on the campus of Paine College. The ceremony went on without him with Millard A. Beckum, executive vice president of the Augusta Chamber of Commerce and former Augusta mayor, reading a proclamation from mayor George A. Sancken Jr. designating Tuesday as "James Brown and Paine College Day."

Brown told fans welcoming him at the airport about 3:30 p.m. that he needed to be leaving and said, "I've got a parade I have to be in at four." He nevertheless signed some more autographs before getting in a yellow Ford sedan and being driven from the airport.

Still, Brown had an important stop he wanted to make before heading downtown, and that was to the Youth Development Center on Georgia Highway 56 (Old Savannah Road), where young people were imprisoned just as he had been almost twenty years earlier.

The senior patrol of Boy Scout Troop 37 from the center stood at attention lining the sidewalk leading to the gymnasium where Brown was to speak to an assembly of the young inmates. A record player was blaring "I break out in a cold sweat" when Brown entered the gymnasium. The music stopped and Brown went up to a microphone.

It was then and there that Brown let those young inmates at the Youth Development Center know something that Brown had not told the rest of the world.

"I've had enough of New York," he said. "I'm coming home. Then I'll be able to spend a lot more time with you." The young inmates screamed their approval, according to *Chronicle* writer

Tom Turner who covered Brown's airport arrival and Youth Development Center appearance.

Brown made it to his Broad Street parade with two minutes to spare, arriving downtown at 3:58 p.m. The photos taken that day and the headline the next morning in the *Augusta Chronicle* told the story: "Thousands cheer soul singer Brown." His car literally was surrounded by people trying to get a glimpse of him, trying to put their hands through his car's window to touch him, trying to let him know how much he was loved and appreciated in his hometown.

Thousands of black faces beamed at their hometown hero, while four stories above Broad Street the stone white face of Confederate Private Berry Benson watched down from atop the Confederate Monument in the 700 block of Broad Street.

Brown was being honored on the very street where slaves from Africa were sold in the 1700s and early 1800s like any other merchandise. Brown, with his deep South Carolina roots, was most likely a descendant of those slaves brought into the Southern ports.

That night in Bell Auditorium, a packed crowd watched and saw him perform, with the proceeds going to benefit the students, faculty, and administration of Paine College.

Eleven days after James Brown Day in Augusta, the FCC announced its approval to transfer the operating license of WRDW-AM radio station from Radio Augusta Inc. to JB Broadcasting of Augusta Ltd., owned 90 percent by James Brown and 10 percent by New York City resident Gregory Moses.

The Associated Press article in the *Chronicle* announcing the FCC approval noted that Brown and Moses also co-owned WJBE-AM radio station in Knoxville, Tennessee.

Additionally the article noted that the FCC also had dismissed opposition from The Hunter Group Inc., operator of WAUG-AM and WAUG-FM in Augusta, who had contended that "WAUG, operating as a Negro-oriented station would be adversely affected because Brown, a recording artist, might control the distribution of his music."

The FCC, according to the article, also noted that WJBE in Knoxville had been operating without any complaints from its competitors. The FCC said JB Broadcasting had given assurances that no restrictive or unfair practices would be allowed in any way in regard to Brown's music.

Oddly, it was just the opposite, according to former Brown employees at WRDW, who contend that Brown himself enforced a discriminatory playing policy. The employees said that Brown was so pissed off in the sixties at not being offered a recording contract by Motown Records that he ordered that no Motown Records could be played on his radio stations.

And just like that, James Brown found himself owning the very radio station in his hometown where he once shined shoes, even though the station was at a different location in his childhood.

WRDW-AM became Augusta's first permanent radio station when it went on the air on June 25, 1930. The *Chronicle* reported the next day, "The initial test program over station WRDW, Augusta's radio broadcasting plant, from 1:05 until four o'clock yesterday morning delighted radio owners in the city and community. J. Bernard Carpenter, musician at the Imperial theatre, was the first to broadcast over the local station.

"Warren C. Davenport, co-partner in the ownership of the station with Clark Jack, said that the local broadcasting caused no interference with other stations (outside Augusta)," the *Chronicle* added. "Augusta fans switched from station WRDW to others by turning the dial only three or four notches in either direction."

The station originally was owned by Musicove Inc., which also sold radios, records, and sheet music from its building at 309 Eighth Street.

Augusta had flirted with the miracle of radio waves eight years before WRDW went on the air when the *Chronicle* tried an experimental station that lasted from early June to late September

1922. The station broadcast the first religious program in Augusta when the Reverend Joseph R. Sevier, pastor of First Presbyterian Church, delivered a sermon on Sunday, August 6, 1922, from the *Chronicle*'s broadcasting studio at Seventh and Broad Streets.

The Reverend Sevier likened prayers to radio signals and commented, "Prayer is communicating and almighty. It's sending to and receiving messages from God. Many are like the radio—senders only or receivers. But God wants you to be so connected with him that at all times you can send and receive."

Among the talented artists who broadcast live over WRDW in 1941 were mandolin player "Smilin' Bill" and guitarist "Ramblin' Scotty," who performed as the Kentucky Partners. Smilin' Bill was Curly Seckler, fresh from the band of Bill Monroe's brother, Charlie. He would go on to become a Foggy Mountain Boy in Lester Flatt and Earl Scruggs's band, and later with Flatt's Nashville Grass band.

Ramblin' Scotty was Tommy Scott, who was in movies and headlined his own Old Time Medicine Show, which toured internationally. At this writing he is ninety years old and lives in Toccoa, Georgia, not too many miles from JB's first wife, Velma.

On April 30, 1969, James Brown was in Augusta for the grand opening under his ownership of WRDW at 1480 Eisenhower Drive. The thirty-six-year-old entertainer had arrived at 3 p.m. in his private jet, attended a late lunch at the Town House restaurant, and then headed for the official opening of his station. Visitors were greeted with music from a local band and then led on tours of the facility.

Brown left town within a few hours after his arrival, with the *Chronicle* noting that he was due to perform in New Haven, Connecticut, two nights later followed by a trip to California for the filming of the Steve Allen, Joey Bishop, and Allen Ludden TV shows.

The *Chronicle* also reported that his future plans included a visit to Africa in August and a European tour in October.

For the rest of the year of 1969 he kept busy with show business and other business ventures. In July he angrily turned down a proclamation from the city of Los Angeles designating James Brown Day in the city because mayor Sam Yorty wouldn't be there to present it, but would send a deputy mayor instead.

"I believe in the dignity of man," Brown was said to have remarked. "If I can take the time to be there, I would assume he could, too," the *Chronicle* reported in an Associated Press distributed story.

His Gold Platter restaurant company took off big that same month of July 1969 when all two hundred thousand shares of Gold Platter Services Inc. were sold out when the stock issue reached the market through Johnson, Lane, Smith & Co. at $6 per share.

The *Chronicle* article announcing the stock issue said Brown owned 8.2 percent of the stock and would share in royalties, and that eleven franchises had been sold.

Meantime, not all was happy in Brown's life, as Superior Court Judge Gordon D. Schaber in Sacramento, California, in late July of 1969 ordered blood tests from Brown as a result of a paternity suit filed by Mary Florence Brown (no relation), twenty, former president of his Sacramento, California, fan club. She claimed that she and Brown had sex in Burlingame, California, in January of 1968, and that Brown was the father of her ten-month-old son, Michael Deon Brown. She wanted $5,000 a month in child support.

Brown was ordered to pay $500 per month in child support and $33,000 in attorneys' fees and costs and, according to the *Augusta Chronicle*, later was sued for not paying $3,536.52 of those fees and costs. The alleged son himself in 2007 was found by myself through some Web searches as being incarcerated at Rio Cosumnes Correctional Center in Elk Grove, California, on drug paraphernalia and parole violation charges and writing a blog on the Internet called "Being the son of the Godfather of Soul."

Although cracks were starting to show in Brown's personal life, they apparently had no effect on his stardom-driven professional life, which touched Augusta in a unique way when Brown decided to do another live album on October 1, 1969, in Bell Auditorium.

"Augusta's own James Brown will appear in a 'raw soul' concert with his 18-piece band, Wednesday, October 1, at 8 p.m. at Bell Auditorium," the *Chronicle* reported in cutlines beneath a photo of JB standing in front of his private jet plane.

"King Records will be in town to record this performance for later release as an album to be entitled *James Brown At Home*. In the above autographed photo (courtesy James Brown Enterprises, New York) Brown sports an $800 seal coat as he stands before this $750,000 red, white and blue Lear jet. Tickets for Wednesday's performance are available at Red Star Restaurant, Record Heaven and the Bell Auditorium box office."

There is no doubt that with his flashy lifestyle, the purchase of WRDW-AM radio station, and the announcement of his recording a live album in Bell Auditorium, James Brown was out to impress the home folks in Augusta.

And that certainly ended up being the case a few months later in 1970 when the governor of Georgia met with James Brown at his radio station to personally seek his help in diffusing a dangerous racial situation in Augusta that was on the verge of erupting almost like Boston had two years earlier.

EIGHT

Keeping the Hometown Calm

Unless you do something for yourselves, it won't get
done. How are we going to have equal opportunity
if we don't have equal minds?

—James Brown
January 3, 1971
from a live broadcast on WRDW-AM

In September 1970 two black fellow inmates at Richmond
County jail in Augusta—seventeen-year-old Sammy Lee Parks
and his sixteen-year-old juvenile accomplice—received only
ten-year sentences in Richmond County Superior Court for the
beating death of sixteen-year-old fellow black inmate Charles
Oatman after they were convicted of voluntary manslaughter
rather than murder.

Each of the defendants' attorneys had argued that it would be
difficult to determine who actually struck the blows that caused
Oatman's death.

Testimony in the case revealed that Oatman had been confined
in the eight-foot-by twelve-foot cell with Parks, three sixteen-year-
old juveniles, and an adult man who was paralyzed from the waist
down—a total of six people in the small cell that contained four
double-bunks, a flush toilet, and a television set.

The inmates, according to court testimony, had been playing
a card game called Pitty Pat in which the winner of the game
"won" the right to hit the loser in the palm of his hand with two
thick leather belts doubled over and bound with adhesive tape.
The belts were described as being two feet long, three inches wide,
and an inch thick, and were used regularly on Oatman. According

60

to the two state witnesses (who were inmates), the only time on Saturday, May 9, that Oatman was not being beaten was during meals when he was forced to put on his shirt so guards would not see his injuries.

One of the state's witnesses said he saw Parks and the other defendant repeatedly abuse Oatman up until the time he died after being beaten with a shoe, belt, and stick. The witness testified that the defendants tied Oatman's hands to the top bunk in the cell and "socked, stomped, and beat him in the stomach and chest" in spite of Oatman's begging them to leave him alone.

As told in court, the witnesses said they tried to let deputies know what was going on but were threatened by Parks and his partner that they (other inmates) would get the same cruel treatment if they said anything. The witness said he was told to say Oatman had fallen accidentally from the high bunk to the floor.

According to the autopsy performed on Oatman, the exact cause of his death was a hemorrhage under his skull from a severe blow to the left side of his head just behind the ear. Oatman had been listed as dead on arrival at University Hospital at 8:08 p.m. on May 9. He had been discovered unconscious in his cell.

The beating death was reported in the Augusta newspapers and was also described by Augusta city councilman Grady Abrams on his radio program.

On Sunday, May 10, Abrams told listeners that he had seen Oatman's body the night before at Mays Funeral Home (owned by another city council member, Carrie Mays) and that his body was covered with fork marks, that he had cigarette burns and also three lashes on his back, and that the back of his skull was busted open.

Abrams blamed prison guards for not intervening sooner during Oatman's long period of torture.

"I just couldn't imagine those kinds of injuries happening in the jail cell with three or four other inmates and the jail personnel not knowing about it," Abrams told the *Augusta Chronicle* in 2000 in recounting the incident.

Other black Augustans who agreed with Abrams gathered at May Park across from the jail on Fourth Street to get some answers. They then moved from there to historic Tabernacle Baptist Church, the scene of many 1960s civil rights rallies where their anger continued to grow.

The next day, on Monday, the protestors began gathering at the Augusta-Richmond County Municipal Building in the 500 block of Greene Street where, in the middle of Greene Street beneath an obelisk monument, are the remains of two signers of the Declaration of Independence (Lyman Hall and George Walton).

"Police had guns aimed at the crowd the whole time at the rally," recalled Mallory Millender, a professor at Paine College who was at the demonstration on Greene Street. "There were police standing on the second floor of the Municipal Building with guns pointing down at the backs of speakers."

Growing angrier at not getting any satisfactory answers or a proper government response, some of the protesters ripped down the state of Georgia flag from the pole in front of the building and set it on fire. Then they headed out from the Municipal Building toward Walton Way on the south and Druid Park Avenue on the west near Paine College and began setting grocery stores, apartment buildings, and other property ablaze.

Several dozen black and white citizens were injured and six black citizens were killed.

Georgia governor Lester Maddox, an ardent segregationist in the 1960s who turned away black citizens who wanted to eat at his Atlanta restaurant, the Pickrick, sent one thousand National Guardsmen and one hundred and fifty state troopers to quell the violence.

James Brown had been in Augusta when the riot broke out.

"You had tanks in the middle of the street and armored

trucks," Brown later said. "Me and my daddy and a couple more people were going through the community trying to stop them, talking to the looters and calm the people and not take sides. . . . [The riot] was Augusta's warning ticket."

Brown had to leave town for a concert in Flint, Michigan, but on Wednesday the thirty-seven-year-old entertainer flew back to Augusta in his private jet to appeal for calm in the city and county. Governor Maddox had requested his presence and agreed to meet with Brown late Wednesday, May 12, at Brown's WRDW radio station.

The governor had told Brown on the phone that he would not be as effective a communicator with the black citizens as Brown would be, and he urged Brown to take to the WRDW airwaves and make black citizens realize it was their city that was burning as well as that of the white citizens.

"The governor asked that I do all I could to relate because we don't need to lose any more lives," Brown later told reporters. "I'm acting in the interest of our country, of all our people."

The radio announcer who introduced "the governor of the state of Georgia and the Godfather of Soul, James Brown" to give their plea for peace was Marion "Mal Your Pal" Cook, who had brought the James Brown Revue with the Famous Flames to the Paramount Country Club in the sixties.

Cook himself later recalled that the governor, his aide, and James Brown gathered around a WRDW microphone placed on Cook's desk with Brown doing most the talking. Cook noted that the rioters did listen to Brown.

Brown had to resume his concert tour but promised to be on call to return anytime that he felt the city or its people needed him.

Thirty years after the riot, councilman and radio personality Abrams, who later was a labor relations manager for Bechtel Savannah River Inc. at the nuclear energy Savannah River Site, told reporter Clarissa J. Walker of the *Augusta Chronicle* that the incident forced white politicians to pay more attention to voices in the black community.

"Prior to that, they didn't pay much attention to any spokesman that we had speaking on behalf of the black community," Abrams said. "They took everything with a grain of salt."

Just a few days after JB met with Maddox, the entertainer's participation in another business endeavor called "Black and Brown Trading Stamps" was mentioned in the *Chronicle*. The program, which already had been in use in California grocery stores for about a year, involved grocery store customers being given a certain number of Black and Brown Trading Stamps (with JB's photo on them) based on their total purchase. The customers could paste the stamps in a booklet which, when full, could be redeemed at the participating grocery store for $3 cash.

JB had entered into the business venture with Art Powell, a former Oakland Raiders and New York Titans (later Jets) pro football star. Powell himself was known to take a stand for what was right, such as joining teammates Fred Williamson, Bo Roberson, and Clem Daniels in refusing to play an exhibition game at Ladd Stadium in Mobile, Alabama, in protest of its segregated seating.

Elmer Rush, sales manager for the company, told reporters that Augusta was the second city in the southeast with stores carrying the stamps; Atlanta was the first. He said the trading stamp program was aimed at helping develop minority communities by encouraging customers to shop at the grocery stores carrying the stamps.

As he became more and more involved with Augusta, JB put down more roots by purchasing an extremely large and expensive house in a wealthy section of the city.

A headline in the *Augusta Herald* on October 23, 1970, read, "James Brown Plans to Live in Augusta." The accompanying story said Brown had purchased a four-acre $115,000 estate on Walton Way Extension that included three large bedrooms, a swimming pool, and horse stables, and that his wife, Deidre, confirmed the Browns planned to give up their New York state residence to move to Augusta.

The story also noted that Brown bought twenty-five acres in his native South Carolina, near the Atomic Energy Commission's Savannah River Plant (the "bomb plant" as local residents call it but now known as the Savannah River Site) for $16,000—an incredible bargain.

"Mrs. Brown said they have not definitely decided how the property will be utilized but reportedly he is considering it for a recreation area. In addition to the large acreage, it contains a lake."

The truth is that reporters didn't know that Brown already had taken up residence in Augusta that was fairly permanent. He had bought a house at 2506 Parkway Drive just a few blocks from Daniel Village Airport (propeller planes and short runways) that he then gave to his father and stepmother, Olivia, for their residence. He moved his wife and Afghan dogs to a house a few blocks away on Hillsinger Drive, which he later gave to his wife's parents when he moved to the Walton Way house.

Larry Harris, a business licenses official with the Richmond County government, recalls that his family's house was on Clairmont Drive and backed up to the house of Joe and Olivia Brown. He played basketball with Brown's sons, Larry and Terry, from Brown's first marriage to Velma and would see JB in the neighborhood often. Harris remembers Brown driving through the neighborhood and telling the teens they should not be drinking wine or it would get them in trouble.

The news of JB's buying the four-acre estate on Walton Way Extension in the heart of what is still one of Augusta's richest, majority white neighborhoods undoubtedly shook up the white political and social structure of the area even more than JB's buying WRDW radio station. He wasn't content to just own a formerly white business in Augusta. He also was moving into the white hood!

During this period, rich white folks in the area were concentrated in three main areas: the historic Summerville Hill section of Victorian homes built in the 1800s, where Ty Cobb lived in the 1920s; the Walton Way Extension neighborhood of massive, ranch-style and two-story estates; and the suburban West Lake area off Stevens Creek Road with more modern, two-story, huge brick homes. The subdivision was developed by former Georgia governor Carl E. Sanders, the only native Augustan to serve as governor of Georgia in the twentieth century.

It's possible the local "Welcome Wagon" did call on the Browns at their new Walton Way Extension home to officially welcome them to the neighborhood, but most area residents regarded it as a sign that times definitely were changing, and Brown fully intended to bring about some more of those changes.

One of the favorite memories of most area residents was the black Santa Claus and black Wise Men that the Browns would put out each Christmas season on their front lawn just beyond the steel fence bordering Walton Way Extension. I remember driving past one afternoon and watching one of the Brown's Afghans knock over a Wise Man with its nose.

In March 1972, the *Augusta Herald* ran a notice that "the wife of soul singer James Brown" was offering a $300 award for the return of her newly-acquired Afghan valued at $1,000. She just had brought the dog from New York to Augusta, but it disappeared about 5:30 p.m. the same day.

"Fuzzy is described as weighing about 50 pounds, has long blond fur and a black face," the article noted. "Mrs. Brown said Fuzzy is 'very frightened' and can probably be caught only by enticing her with food. Fuzzy prefers cookies." Whether Fuzzy and the Browns were reunited is unknown.

For some strange reason in March 1971, just a few months after he bought the Walton Way Extension home, Brown appeared on *The Tonight Show Starring Johnny Carson* on a night when Joey Bishop was the guest host and told Bishop he was moving to Europe!

Whether he was kidding or not, Bishop asked the singer to stay in the United States, which was followed by applause from the studio audience. Brown said his 1970 hit single "(Get Up I Feel Like Being a) Sex Machine" had sold two million copies in Europe compared to one million copies in the United States.

Brown had just returned to the States from three concerts in England (two in London and one in Birmingham) and had opened a two-week engagement at New York City's upscale Copacabana nightclub the night before his appearance with Bishop. He introduced his new wife, Deidre, and his father, Joe Brown, during the TV broadcast and sang "Sunny" and "Let It Be Me" (two very middle-of-the-road ballads) before saying good-bye to the audience with the peace sign.

Why JB would announce out-of-the-blue that he was moving to Europe is unclear. Maybe it was just a joking, off-the-cuff remark from the euphoria created by his adoring fans at the three England concerts. Maybe the Welcome Wagon in Augusta had not been welcoming enough.

Still, he never followed through with his moving plans. It wouldn't be the last time he would say that he planned to move from Augusta, especially after the terrible days ahead with his run-ins with Augusta area law enforcement agencies. The truth is, except for leaving his house on Walton Way Extension in the mid-1970s and moving across the Savannah River to his South Carolina estate fifteen miles away near Beech Island, Brown would live the rest of his life in the Augusta area.

He continued to use his fame and his radio station, WRDW, as his personal voice in the Augusta community.

"Unless you do something for yourselves, it won't get done," he told black Augustans and area listeners in a broadcast on January 3, 1971. "How are we going to have equal opportunity if we don't have equal minds?" he added attributing business failures and interracial violence to insufficient education of blacks.

He also urged "merely surviving" families to consider birth control measures, the *Augusta Chronicle* reported in a story about Brown's broadcast, and he described the poverty cycle that resulted from children born to families that are financially unable to take care of their children. He surely must have been speaking from his heart and soul in thinking of his own childhood.

In addition to his James Brown Enterprises and JB Broadcasting Ltd. companies, Brown had created "Man's World Enterprises Inc.," which was described in an advertisement in the 1972 City of Augusta business directory as "a James Brown affiliate" and the "exclusive booking agency" of the James Brown Show, and the management and promotion agency for singers and musicians.

Man's World Enterprises settled into a building at 1122 Greene Street, a short distance from the Greyhound Bus Station, in 1971. Today, the Man's World property is a vacant lot.

The 1972 business directory also listed the entire Brown office organization as: James Brown, president; Johnny Terry (a Famous Flame and former prison mate of JB), vice president; Emma Austin (wife of childhood friend Leon Austin), secretary; Deidre Brown, treasurer; Freddie Holmes, road manager; Alan Leeds, tour manager (he later would become tour manager for rock star Prince); Bobby Jackson, booking agent; and Connie Wroolie, receptionist.

Just over three months after his appearance with Joey Bishop, Brown hit a sad time in his life with the death of his stepmother, Olivia Brown, who died June 27, 1971, in an Augusta hospital. Funeral services were held at the First Mount Moriah Baptist Church with the Reverend Arthur D. Sims officiating. Burial was in Mount Olive Memorial Gardens in Augusta.

She was described as a native of Rocky Mount, North Carolina, who had lived in Augusta the previous two years. She had been employed as a licensed practical nurse at University Hospital.

The pallbearers were WRDW radio station employees Mal "Your Pal" Cook, Robert "Flash" Gordon, and William H. "Bill" Berry [the only white pallbearer] as well as Jody Bell, William Dinkins, and Brown's childhood friend, Leon Austin. It's interesting to note that Gordon became the general manager of the James Brown Arena, and his first "job" was to preside over the funeral there of James Brown.

Berry, who became program director of other radio stations in Augusta and director of marketing for the National Barrel Horse Association based in Augusta, recalls that JB was very hands-on with his radio stations and very hands-on about the music played on his stations.

"He pretty much controlled it," Berry told me. "Basically you were to play him and his artists as much as possible." On a typical day when he was home, Brown would come to WRDW about two in the morning.

"That's when he'd get back in town or be up and around," Berry said. "Mr. Brown was famous for staying up late at night and sleeping late into the day. He liked to come to the station and get on the air. He'd find something he needed to talk about such as his new single or a new album or something going on in the community."

As with other WRDW employees, Berry's involvement in management and advertising sales extended often to Brown's concerts both in and out of Augusta.

"I once went with his father, Pop [Joe] Brown, to a concert in Swainsboro, Georgia, in the late '60s," Berry told me. "We were riding in my Oldsmobile and I lost a water pump on the way down. We had to stop on the side of the road in the night to fill the radiator several times until we got as far as we could and couldn't get any more water. This was in the '60s when the Ku Klux Klan was still very active in the state. Joe Brown said to me, 'Mr. Berry, what are they going to do to us finding a black man and white man on the side of the road way down here in rural middle Georgia? They may take us into the swamp and leave us.' But this old white farmer came along and picked us up in his pickup truck. He was nice as he could be and took us straight to the building where they were having the concert."

The rest of 1971 for James Brown was his usual typical life, filled with highs and lows. His father was seen in August in a photograph in the *Augusta Herald* standing amid twelve bicycles outside WRDW. The caption for the photo noted that his famous son had paid for the bicycles out of his own pocket, and they would be given away to local needy children.

Brown performed two sold-out concerts on September 1, 1971, in Bell Auditorium. According to the Augusta police, Telfair Street in front of the building was jammed with people and vehicles as the first show ended and ticket-holders tried to get into the second show. The police added there were no serious problems reported.

On November 2, the Augusta newspapers reported that a petition bearing two hundred and fifteen names was calling for the Augusta City Council to change the name of four-lane Gwinnett in the heart of Augusta's black community to James Brown Boulevard. It was noted the petition had come to the council from Harold Suber of Man To Man, a black youth organization concerned with equal opportunities.

The petitioners stated that the namesake of Gwinnett Street— Button Gwinnett—"owned slaves at the time and after he signed the Declaration of Independence which contradicts his belief in freedom."

Several years passed before the name of Gwinnett Street was changed not to James Brown Boulevard but to Laney-Walker Boulevard in honor of black educator Lucy Craft Laney, who lived just off the street and whose former home at 1116 Phillips Street is the Lucy Laney Museum, and the Reverend Charles T. Walker, who founded the imposing Tabernacle Baptist Church on the street and the first black YMCA in New York City.

Eventually, Brown was honored with a major Augusta street in his name when most of Ninth Street (also known as Campbell Street) was renamed James Brown Boulevard in 1993 during the administration of mayor Charles A. DeVaney, and the remaining two blocks of Ninth Street renamed after him in 2003 during the administration of mayor Bob Young.

On the same day that the Augusta newspapers announced receipt of the petition, it was also reported that James Brown had been sued by Murphy Williams Jr., filed with the Richmond County Superior Court. Williams contended that Brown owed him $1,250 for five bronze portraits he made of the singer.

In late November 1971, James Brown Enterprises presented the Concerned Mothers of Augusta, an organization that provided hot breakfasts for underprivileged children, a check for $500, proceeds from a recent concert by Jackie Wilson.

Once again, Brown was using his influence and talents to help others, just as he did at the close of 1971 by spending two hours on Christmas Eve touring the wards of the U.S. Army hospital at nearby Fort Gordon.

A story that day in the *Augusta Herald* reported that Deidre Brown had persuaded her husband to cancel their two-day Florida vacation to visit with the soldiers in the hospital, many of whom had been wounded in Vietnam where Brown had performed three years earlier. He still would be doing a concert on Christmas Day in Washington, D.C.

"Also in the spirit of Christmas," the *Augusta Herald* reported, "Brown visited the site of a house fire Thursday on Tate Alley off Stevens Creek Road where a woman and her son had lost everything.

"The singer noticed that the son of Mrs. Lily Mae Overton was about his size and placed his jacket on the young man. Brown also made a contribution and started a fund to help the Overtons back on their feet financially. Donations of food and clothes for the stricken family may be made at the Martinez Fire Department."

Living on Walton Way Extension and having his business office on Greene Street put Brown very close to the International Recording studio at the Surrey Center shopping place at Hickman and Wheeler roads, not far from the Augusta National Golf Course where the Masters Tournament is held annually.

But it wasn't golf records that Brown had on his mind. It was records that would revolutionize the international recording industry as he became the undisputed grand funk master.

NINE

National Politics and Funk Music

Jesus Christ got mad didn't he? I've got a right to get mad. I think he once got angry. I didn't even go that far. I'm not as great as Jesus Christ. I got frustrated. Frustrated is different. When you get things going down—when liberty and justice for all is dissipating—you've got a problem.

—James Brown
March 25, 1991
Augusta Chronicle

In 1972 James Brown was plunging more and more into active political involvements and using his music for his messages. His crusade against drugs almost bordered on an obsession, which was quite ironic in light of the drug addiction that would befall himself in coming years, even though he often denied using drugs.

In May 1972, he translated that crusade into his single "King Heroin." The same month the single was released, about two hundred fans and state government workers packed into the office of Georgia governor (and future U.S. president) Jimmy Carter to see JB present Carter with a check for $5,000 for the governor's drug treatment program.

"Any man concerned with this country would do the same thing," he told reporters.

Two months later he would take his anti-drug campaign to California where he was honored in Sacramento with "James Brown Anti-Drug Week" and in Compton, which made him an honorary citizen and proclaimed July 5 as "James Brown Day."

California governor (and future U.S. president) Ronald Reagan commended JB as an entertainer who has "made our young people aware of the danger to their minds and bodies which accompanies drug experimentation and abuse."

Just weeks after JB was honored by Reagan, he was back performing in Augusta at "The Soul Bowl" in the stadium of Butler High School on Friday, August 11, 1972, featuring Bobby Byrd, Lyn Collins, Solomon Burke, the Detroit Emeralds, the Independents, and Z. Z. Hill. Proceeds from the show were to benefit Paine College's Build It Back campaign to replace burned Haygood Hall and to fight drug abuse. The admission fees were advertised to be "coming to you at the People's Prices: 99 cents for children under 12; $4 in advance; $5 at the gate."

JB continued his attempts to become "an average guy" in Augusta among his hometown friends and business associates. He dropped by Silas X. Floyd school on May 2, 1972, to visit with his favorite teacher, Laura Garvin, who had announced her intentions to retire.

The caption under the photo of him and Garvin in the *Augusta Chronicle* read, "Miss Garvin was given a lot of persuasion by the singer to change her mind. He credits her with the inspiration which helped him on the road to success."

As he would continue to do many, many, times over the years, JB began his regular ritual in the early 1970s of dropping into Augusta area restaurants and nightclubs and singing at the drop of a hat. My father, Ollen Rhodes, recalls being in the nightclub at the Partridge Inn in early 1972 when James Brown came in alone and sat at a table.

"When the band finished the song they were singing, the guy with the mike held it out toward James with a nod of his head," my father said. "James went up onstage and put on a show for us for about an hour, and there were only about a dozen people there. He was a showman, and he loved God and he loved all people."

My father and JB became very close, especially when my dad became a building inspector and subcontractor in Aiken County, South Carolina. JB would get my dad to help with repairs and improvements on his Beech Island house, and—since my father was a member of the Gideons—they often talked about the Bible.

I cannot recall anytime in his final years when JB saw me that he didn't ask, "How's your father?" That's the kind of person he really was.

Perhaps one of the strangest tours that JB ever conducted in Augusta was in October 1972 when he led a delegation of federal officials to visit the local alcohol and drug abuse center and the sickle cell anemia centers. Brown—always conservative in his political and social beliefs—had declared himself to be a supporter of Richard Nixon who was seeking reelection as president at the time.

The Washington, D.C., officials who came to town included Stanley Thomas, deputy assistant secretary of the U.S. Department of Health, Education, and Welfare; Dr. George Riley, the department's sickle cell anemia clinic; Norris Sydmor, a Nixon staff assistant; and Connie Mack Higgins, administrative assistant at the Small Business Administration.

They spent only fifteen minutes at the Augusta-Richmond County Alcohol and Drug Abuse Center and ten minutes at the Sickle Cell Anemia Center on Gwinnett Street.

When JB was asked by a reporter how much good that group could really do in just the two hours they spent in town, JB retorted, "Can you measure motivation?" During the visit, the federal officials presented Brown with a letter from President Nixon thanking him for his support.

However, 1972 ended with some very high points and very low points for James Brown. Even his powerful friends in Washington, couldn't keep him from being arrested in Knoxville, Tennessee, on December 10, 1972, following a concert in Knoxville's civic coliseum. JB, as always, was trying to satisfy his fans and, apparently, was lingering too long after his concert as far as the Knoxville police officers on duty were concerned.

The police contended that JB and his aides refused to clear the area after the concert when told to do so. Brown countered that he and his two employees were attacked by the police in the same town where he owned the radio station WJBE-AM.

Either way, the police arrested Brown—apparently his first arrest since the 1950s in Augusta—and charged him with disorderly conduct. They also arrested his road manager, Freddie Holmes, and his aide, Oliver Dyers, and charged them with disorderly conduct and assault.

Brown's attorney in Augusta, Albert G. Ingram, flew to Knoxville and met with mayor Kyle Testerman. Ingram later told reporters that a human error had occurred and Testerman explained, "The whole incident was a combination of misunderstandings."

Robert J. Booker, a columnist for the *Knoxville News Sentinel* and former executive director of the Beck Cultural Exchange Center, was administrative assistant to Mayor Testerman at the time. He recalls being frantically summoned to the city coliseum on the night of the incident. He quickly investigated what were the facts in the case. Booker recalled in his *News-Sentinel* column after Brown's death, "I talked to the officers there and then called the chief of police and the safety director. I thought the charges against Brown and his men should be dropped, but I was alone in my opinion."

In that same column, Booker said Brown's WJBE listeners' angry calls were broadcast by the station; saying if that kind of police harassment could happen to someone as famous as James Brown, it could happen to anyone else.

Just a few days after the incident, Mayor Testerman sent Booker to Augusta to pick up the vice president of Brown's organization and bring him back to Knoxville for negotiations in the matter. Brown wanted the policemen involved to be fired and the medical bills paid for his two injured men.

Booker told *News-Sentinel* readers the mayor apparently had reached an agreement with Brown and his representative, and a final talk was set for the day after Christmas, but by the close of the business day, Brown's representative had not reached city hall. Mayor Testerman finally ordered the charges dropped on December 27 but not before angrily firing off some verbal ammunition accusing Brown of ungentlemanly conduct.

The mayor also accused Brown of using his radio station to incite the black community over the incident, and he promised that the FCC would be looking into that when the license for WJBE came up for renewal the following January.

The Associated Press reported that Brown responded with a seven-minute, tape-recorded broadcast over WJBE in which he said, "I was very much surprised because I thought the mayor was the kind of man who wanted to bring it to a head. . . . I feel very sad and very sorry for him. . . . I feel very, very sorry for the white people and the black people who are poor because this is not justice. . . . They don't intend to give no black man justice, or a poor white man. Racism is worse than Communism. . . . You're dealing with racism in Knoxville."

The Knoxville incident reignited just over a month later when Phillip Bowling, one of the Knoxville policemen who allegedly took part in the attack on Brown and his aides, was suspended from the force after a suit was filed in federal court by James William McCraw of Asheville, North Carolina. McCraw, who was allegedly beaten by Bowling and other policemen in a Holiday Inn parking lot on October 21, requested $175,000 in damages. The Holiday Inn incident with McCraw occurred about two months before JB's altercation.

McCraw contended in his suit that his civil rights were violated by Bowling when Bowling and other police responded to a call about a fight on the premises.

A guest on the second balcony of the Holiday Inn filmed the whole thing and turned the film over to the *Knoxville News-Sentinel,* which in turn passed the film on to the city of Knoxville authorities who then suspended Bowling.

Immediately following Bowling's suspension, James Brown filed a $1 million civil rights lawsuit (seeking $500,000 each for Holmes and Dyer) in U.S. District Court in Knoxville in February 1973 naming as defendants Mayor Testerman, "former patrolman Phillip Bowling," safety director Duane Ausetts, police chief Joe Fowler, and secretary of the city civil service board Preston V. Phelps.

Brown contended that his civil rights had been violated and his career had been damaged by the unfavorable publicity over the Knoxville incident.

On April 16, 1974, the U.S. District Court jury of four men and two women ruled that the rights of Brown and his aides had not been violated, and the suit was dismissed. Brown, of course, was disappointed by the decision and told reporters it was a bad law system that would allow "police to beat up a black man" and get away with it.

As for former mayoral aide Robert Booker, he told readers that among his "prized possessions" is the subpoena ordering his appearance in U.S. District Court in the case of *James Brown v. the City of Knoxville.*

In spite of everything going on in Knoxville that December between JB and the mayor, there was a bright moment in the Brown household in Augusta when Deidre gave birth to the couple's daughter, Yamma Noyola Brown, at St. Joseph's Hospital (now known as Trinity)—the same medical center off Wrightsboro Road where wrestler Hulk Hogan, gospel-country singer Amy Grant, professional golfer Larry Mize, and Tony Award winner Faith Prince had first seen the light of day.

And not too far away in the front yard of the Brown homestead at 3056 Walton Way Extension, the black Santa Claus and black Wise Men smiled amid the Christmas lights.

Throughout 1970, 1971, and 1972, James Brown had continued to rack up hit after hit singles, including "(Get Up I Feel Like Being a) Sex Machine," "Super Bad," "Hot Pants," and "Get on the Good Foot." All of these reached either number one or number two on *Billboard* magazine's rhythm and blues chart and climbed into top twenty positions on *Billboard*'s pop/rock music chart.

Brown's masterful recordings and legendary performances continued to make him a musical God overseas, but his personal and legal troubles continued to grow in his hometown and home country.

His deep feelings came to the surface at a concert in Rio de Janeiro, Brazil, in April 1973 when he told reporters at a press conference that the only thing that set him apart from history's greatest musicians was the color of his skin. He added at a press conference, "I have sold more records than Bach, Beethoven and Brahms put together, but because of the racial problem in the United States, nobody emphasizes this."

Additionally, Brown expressed bitterness that white performers who had sold far less records than he had been given television opportunities that he was denied. He said, "It is tough to see a white, who has sold [just] a half-million records have this opportunity. I have sold more than 40 million, and I feel I can look this white in the eyes and say I'm better."

Two months after that concert in Brazil, Brown's feelings about being denied equal opportunities in show business were overshadowed by the loss of his nineteen-year-old son, Teddy Lewis Brown, who was killed with two others in a one-car accident near Elizabethtown, New York, on June 14. Teddy was a passenger in the vehicle.

According to New York state police, the car carrying Brown and Arthur Rosemund, eighteen, and Johnny Young, thirty-one, both of Toccoa, on a Thursday drifted off Interstate 87, crashed into a bridge abutment, and overturned. All three were dead on the scene.

James Brown was in Augusta when he got the news. He immediately left that Thursday night for the upstate New York town to identify his son's body. Teddy left behind a young widow.

An unidentified friend of Teddy's told the Augusta newspapers, "He was a warm and considerate person; the kind you don't run across too often. His ambitions were to become a businessman, and he was very close to his father. He admired what his father did, and he was working in his dad's company [Man's World Enterprises in Augusta]."

Teddy's funeral was held in Mount Zion Baptist Church on West Whitman Street in Toccoa, the same church where his parents first met and where Velma still attends services today.

Bad news continued to follow James Brown throughout 1973 with the mysterious fire at his large Third World nightclub in Augusta only three months after it opened and with the Internal Revenue Service filing tax liens totaling $94,555 against three of his radio stations.

The Third World nightclub, then at 34 East Gwinnett Street (now Laney-Walker Boulevard), was a combination nightclub and snack bar with a radio broadcasting booth. It was one of the best night spots ever opened in Augusta, with seating attendants looking sharp in black tuxedos and white gloves.

In its short three months of life, it brought into town some of the nation's top black talent, including Ray Charles who performed for an entire week in the building less than two months before the fire. I spent some time with Charles in his room at the Holiday Inn on Gordon Highway and at a rehearsal with his orchestra at the Third World.

Charles talked about the closeness of soul and country music—which JB also loved—and said, "Both are played by the ear and from the heart. I think a better name for country music might be 'white soul music.'"

When asked if soul music really is just black country music, he replied, "To tell you the truth, if you wanted to give it a title

like that, I think it is true. Both are about plain, everyday people
. . . about the common place. They're both not glossy, and you
don't have to be a scholar to understand it. I think people who
love country music love the blues, and that people who love the
blues love country music.

Like James Brown, Charles also grew up in the South listening
to country music on the radio. They both recorded country music
albums and appeared onstage at Nashville's Grand Ole Opry
House. Charles even played briefly with an all-white country band
in Tampa called the Florida Playboys.

"When I was seven or eight years old, I used to listen to the
Grand Ole Opry on the radio every Saturday night," Charles told
me. "I wouldn't miss it for the world—just like I wouldn't miss
The Shadow [radio drama]. I remember loving to hear all those
people like Grandpa Jones, Roy Acuff, Ernest Tubb, and Minnie
Pearl."

Among those in the house band at the Third World was Walter
Jowers, a white bass guitarist who later settled in Tennessee. He
started playing electric guitar in 1965 after being inspired by
JB's "Papa's Got a New Bag." Jowers recalls legendary session
musician Cornell Dupree telling him at the Third World, "You are
the funkiest-playing white boy I ever heard."

Investigating officials later reported that the Third World fire
began about 1 a.m. on Wednesday, October 17, 1973. The first
firefighting unit to arrive on the scene came from East Augusta
followed by units from West Richmond County and suburban fire
departments. Roughly fifty firemen were involved in trying to stop
the blaze.

When all was said and done, the damage was estimated at
$125,000, and arson was suspected. Firemen discovered a glass
jar near the front of the club containing nearly a pint of gasoline.
No definite cause was ever determined.

The club's manager, Charlie Reid Jr., told investigators
the Third World was closed every Tuesday night, and no one

was supposed to be in the building when the fire started early Wednesday. JB was in Augusta the night of the fire.

The irony of the nightclub saga is that the James Brown–owned nightclub eventually became a funeral home after the building was restored by Charlie Reid Jr. and his father, Charlie Reid Sr., who owned the Paramount Country Club. The C. A. Reid Sr. Memorial Funeral Home was where James Brown's body was taken after his death.

And former Third World manager Charlie A. Reid Jr. officiated over Brown's funerals in New York, South Carolina, and Georgia thirty-three years after the Third World fire

As if the fire wasn't bad enough news for JB as 1973 came to a close, the Internal Revenue Service on December 13 filed federal tax liens on Brown's radio stations totaling $94,555 on unpaid payroll taxes from several years involving employees of the stations before Brown became the owner.

But bad news rarely kept Brown down for long, and—even in the face of his son's death, the destruction of his nightclub, and the liens filed by the IRS—James Brown continued to carve out new musical frontiers, transforming his raw, gospel-inspired sixties sounds into the funkadelic, new groove music of the seventies.

He had released the instrumental single "Ain't It Funky Now" in November 1969 that went to number three on *Billboard's* rhythm and blues chart and to number twenty-four on *Billboard's* pop/rock music chart. That was followed by the singles "Funky Drummer" released in March 1970, "Make It Funky (Part 1)" released in August 1971, "Make It Funky (Part 3)"—apparently he skipped Part 2—released in October 1971, and "Funky President" released in October 1974.

And in that period, he released other JB single classics such as "Brother Rapp" in May 1970, "(Get Up I Feel Like Being a) Sex Machine" in July 1970, "Super Bad" in October 1970, "Hot Pants" in July 1971, the crowd-pleasing "Get On the Good Foot" in November 1972, and "Papa Don't Take No Mess" in October 1974.

Allan Slutsky, cowriter of the book *The Funkmasters: The Great James Brown Rhythm Sections* (Warner Brothers Publications, 1997) points to JB's 1965 "Papa's Got a Brand New Bag" as the turning point for JB's getting down and getting funky.

The Reverend Al Sharpton told the MSNBC network, "He made soul music a world music. What James Brown was to music in terms of soul and hip-hop, rap, all of that, is what Bach was to classical music. This is a guy who literally changed the music industry. He put everybody on a different beat, a different style of music. He pioneered it."

Little Richard likewise told the MSNBC network, "He was an innovator. He was an emancipator. He was an originator. Rap music, all that stuff, came from James Brown."

It was especially amazing that James Brown and his super cool musicians were not laying down their funky sounds in a recording studio in a historic blues town like Memphis or a musically creative town like Los Angeles but in a small, virtually unknown studio in Brown's hometown of Augusta.

Lowell Dorn, information technology manager with Morris Communications in Augusta, clearly recalls the day JB showed up unannounced at the International Recording Studio in the upscale, fashionable Surrey Shopping Center, where Dorn was a recording engineer. He told me:

> *Our studio was set up backwards. You came into the office and then went through the studio and the control room was all the way in the back. We were working on something one afternoon—Bruce Dees and some other staff musicians— when our secretary, Bonnie Peterson, came back and said, "You'll never guess who's up front."*

I looked at her and said, "OK, who?" And she said, "James Brown." I said, "What does he want?" She said, "He wants to talk with you." I left the control room and went up front. I shook his hand. He was dressed in a suit and looked very nice. He had a gentleman with him, whom I later found was named Freddie [road manager Freddie Holmes]. Freddie had a box under his arm, and I could tell immediately it was a master two-inch tape.

After the pleasantries, he said that he had this tape he wanted to put some vocals on. I said, "OK, we'll try and schedule some time," cause we stayed real busy then recording covers. I looked at my schedule book and came up with a day and handed him a rate card.

He looked at the rate card and said, "What's this?" I said, "It's a rate card. That's what we charge for our services." He looked at me funny and said incredulously, "You're going to charge a big star like me?" I said, "Yes I am." He said, "Man, I'll make this place!" I said, "Mr. Brown, this place is already made. As a matter of fact, your first visit is cash in advance." He huffed up, and they walked out the door. Bonnie looked at me and said, "I can't believe you ran James Brown out." I said, "If he ain't going to pay, I'm not going to do stuff for free, I don't care who it is."

I didn't think I'd ever hear from him again, but the next day about the same time of day, the same two guys came back, with one having the tape under his arm. James said to me, "Man, I've got to get a vocal on this thing." I said, "Mr. Brown, do I need to show you a rate card?" He said, "No, Freddie, pay the man!" Freddie reached in his coat pocket and pulled out a wad of cash, and he paid me and we set up a recording time.

Dorn said it wasn't long after that JB started showing up on a regular basis at the Surrey Center studio. One of the first sessions

84

was with JB producing his solo vocalist Lyn Collins singing "Mama Feelgood."

"I remember that night in the studio like it was yesterday," Dorn said. "It was one of the funkiest tracks. We didn't cut all of the tracks to 'Mama Feelgood' there, but we did do the vocal and most of the rhythm section tracks. It was a funky, funky tune, and she was dynamite. That whole session had so much energy. It was a hit record, and you knew it. You just knew it."

The song did become a major hit single for Collins and also ended up being included on the movie soundtrack of *Black Caesar*.

The way *Black Caesar* came about pretty much began when Isaac Hayes created film history by composing the music score for the movie *Shaft* in 1971. The enormous popularity of that movie among black and white celluloid fans led to Curtis Mayfield's composing the score for the film *Superfly* in 1972, and to James Brown's composing the score the following year for the movie *Black Caesar*.

Fred Williamson, the star of *Black Caesar*, played the character of Tommy Gibbs, a tough, ghetto-reared kid angry at the racist society around him who sees criminal power in Harlem, as the solution to his rage.

The movie was promoted with the advertising tag line, "Hail Caesar, Godfather of Harlem . . . The Cat with the .45-Caliber Claws!" That supposedly is what led James Brown to begin calling himself the "Godfather of Soul."

When James Brown went into the International Recording Studio to record the *Black Caesar* album, he had with him one of the most powerful musical aggregations of his career with vocalist Lyn Collins; Jimmy Nolen on guitar; Fred Wesley on trombone; St. Clair Pinckney, a former Augustan, on bass guitar; Jabo Starks and Steve Gadd on drums; and with other musical assistance from Fred Thomas, Buster Williams, Marvin Stamm, Joe Farrell, Randy Brecker, and David Spinozza.

Dorn specifically recalls the emotional recording of "Mama's Dead," which is on the *Black Caesar* soundtrack.

> *James usually would come into our studio anywhere from about four to six o'clock. He had called me before this session and said he wanted some recording time and didn't want anyone else in the studio, just me and him.*
>
> *When he came in, I told everyone else to go and that I'd see them tomorrow. James came back in the studio, and we put on a tape of the instrumental tracks which had been recorded somewhere else. He said, "I want just one light on the microphone in the studio, and that's all I want." I went to put the tape on, and he said, "Just roll it." He started on the emotional vocal part and got choked up and that got me crying too. It took several takes until we got the vocals down. He cried a good bit.*

JB's real mother, Susie, was very much alive then, so apparently Brown's emotional state must have come from thinking of the death that year of his son, Teddy.

Dorn remembers a funny story about the recording of "Doing It to Death," which most fans know from its key phrase, "Gonna have a funky good time."

> *When we got through with the session, James asked me for a four-track radio cart tape of it that radio stations then used. Bruce Dees [who later toured with country star Ronnie Milsap and recorded with Milsap, Barbara Mandrell, and other Nashville heavyweights] and I cleaned up the studio and shut things down and then went out to Bruce's car to smoke some cigarettes. We had the doors open and were listening to the radio station that James owned in Augusta.*
>
> *We heard the disc jockey say, "After this commercial, we've got James Brown's new hit coming up!" So we sat there*

listening, and five minutes later we heard him come back on and say, "This is James Brown's new hit, and it's number three in Chicago and number two in New York," and he put on the song, and it was the one we had just finished recording thirty minutes earlier! Nobody outside of us had even heard that song!

Asked how a typical session with Brown went, Dorn replied:

The band, usually led by Fred Wesley, would come about three thirty or four o'clock. We'd put everybody in the studio, rhythm section, drums, bass, piano player, and all that, and we'd set the levels, and they'd start rehearsing and we'd wait until he got there. Sometimes he'd get there early. Sometimes he'd get there at nine or ten o'clock.

If he said he was going to be there at seven, he was never there at seven. He was either there early or late. He was never on time for anything. Not one time. That was just not in the cards, because he just got sidetracked with so much stuff going around him in his world. But they'd get that song down so tight, and Fred was a fabulous leader for that group. Maceo Parker was kind of like the assistant director for the band, and he and Fred ran things.

When they got in that studio, it was all business. There was no clowning around; no joking around. And when James walked in, it was tight, and it was ready. A lot of times, he had no idea what he was going to do.

He came in one time with some lyrics written on a paper bag, but most of the time he just came in with an idea in his head and nothing on paper, and he would create whatever he wanted in the studio. There would be minutes or a long length of time when nothing was really happening, and then all of a sudden this genius lick or vocal or something would come out of him and—boom—that was it. You knew when it happened.

Brown's monster hit "Get On the Good Foot" was another one that Dorn helped engineer. Dorn said part of it was recorded by Jerry Reeves at Reeves's Soundcraft studio on Buena Vista Avenue in North Augusta (where International Recording would later move) and part of it was done at the Surrey Center studio.

The *Black Caesar* album led to an even more important album in James Brown's musical career, *The Payback,* recorded in Augusta's International Recording Studio in 1973. The album lists JB as producer and Lowell Dorn and Bob Both as engineers. It is regarded as the most successful of JB's albums from the 1970s and reportedly is the only gold-certified album of Brown's career, selling more than five hundred thousand copies.

The Payback album included James Brown on vocals and electric piano; Jimmy Nolen and Hearlon Martin on guitars; Maceo Parker, flute and alto saxophone; St. Clair Pinckney, tenor saxophone; Darryl "Hasaan" Jamison, Isiah "Ike" Oakley, and Jerone "Jasaan" Sanford on trumpets; Fred Wesley, trombone; Fred Thomas and Charles Sherrell on bass guitars; John "Jabo" Starks, drums; and Johnny Griggs and John Morgan on percussion.

On September 1, 1974, Brown scored another personal high by appearing in a show with B. B. King, Etta James, Bill Withers, and the Spinners performing for more than 120,000 people at a music festival in Zaire, Africa, just before the legendary "Rumble in the Jungle" boxing match between George Foreman and Muhammad Ali.

Brown's trombonist, Fred Wesley in 1997 recalled his flight to Zaire to the *Seattle Times* saying, "I, along with the James Brown band, had flown to Kinshasa, Zaire, on the same overloaded DC-8 as Muhammad Ali and his crew. The plane was so overloaded because the organizers had tried to get all the people who participated in the music festival on that same airplane. I don't think they had properly anticipated the amount of equipment the performers carried with them. I bet the wardrobe for the Pointer

Sisters alone took up an entire bin. The plane barely got off the ground."

Brown himself, the year before he died, humbly told BBC news reporter Yve Ngoo, "I was surprised at the outpouring of love from my African brothers and sisters and it [Africa] was so vast. I saw children in the bush, walking with records underneath their arms, but nothing to play them on, walking to gather at someone's house who had a record player."

As Thanksgiving of 1974 rolled around, the citizens of Augusta were treated to hometown hero James Brown on "The Payback" tour in Bell Auditorium starring James Brown and "The Shades of Soul" featuring Lyn Collins, Fred Ashley and the J.B.'s, Maceo Parker and the Macks, and guest star Benny Lattimore. Tickets were $4 in advance or $5 at the door. A "Best Dressed" contest offered a $300 prize for the male and female winner.

It was a great time for JB as Augustans and others around the world were paying back the Godfather of Soul himself by showering him with the praise he so richly deserved.

TEN

Big in Europe, Failing in America

*People around Augusta have no idea how popular
James is overseas.*

—Anne Weston, backup vocalist
December 1, 1989
Augusta Chronicle

In the mid-and late seventies, James Brown's star was rising everywhere in the world except in America where disco music was keeping a lot of his singles from rising to the top of the charts and where his concert draw was slipping.

But the rest of the world continued to see JB for the music legend he was and continued to pay homage to him in overwhelming numbers.

"He was like a god in Europe," Brown's former comptroller Fred Daviss told reporter Phillip Ramati of the *Macon Telegraph*. "It was unbelievable. The crowds there were scary."

Among those who had a first-class seat for the Brown phenomenon overseas was Canadian Anne Weston who spent five years with Brown as a backup vocalist. During that time she met her future husband, David, a New Yorker who played bass guitar in Brown's orchestra for seven years.

The two married in 1981 and decided to get off the road, taking traditional jobs in Augusta, raising two sons—Dane and Taylor—and creating music on the side with their band, Word of Mouth. The band settled into a restaurant/nightclub in the 700 block of Broad Street called Goldsmith's where one of their frequent customers was their former boss, James Brown, who often joined them onstage.

"We were with him [Brown] in Africa, South America, Australia, New Zealand, Hawaii, Kuwait, Spain, Italy, England, France, Norway, Holland, Finland, Sweden, and lots, lots more places," Weston told me in 1989. . . . "I'll never forget one time we landed in Africa. The runway was lined with hundreds of thousands of people as far as you could see. They just wanted to get close to James. The pilot couldn't even taxi the plane to the terminal because there were so many people."

In August 1977, British-born director Adrian Maben brought his film crew to Augusta as part of a two-year project trying to visually record how James Brown did what he did. The film was a joint venture of RM Productions in Munich, Germany, and Swallowdale Productions in England.

Before filming in Augusta, the production crew already had done some filming in Mexico City and Mexicali in Mexico and Senegal and Dakar in Africa. The crew expected to do additional filming in the Virgin Islands. The filming in Africa had taken James Brown to Gorée Island in Senegal where many slaves had been kept before being shipped to America.

"The film's a musical insight of James Brown, about what I've done and what I'm going to be doing," Brown said to reporter Gregg Steinle of the *Augusta Chronicle*. Brown revealed that he had just received authorization to perform in the Soviet Union and of the filming taking place in his hometown, he said, "It's great, just great."

Maben, who directed the musical documentary *Pink Floyd Live at Pompeii* three years earlier, observed, "We're really here to try and film the way in which he puts his music together. . . . Some performers spend a week in a studio trying to record half a song. James sometimes records three songs in one day."

Eventually the film was released under the title *soulconnection* with many of Brown's fans regarding it as the best documentary created during his lifetime. One fan on the Internet even described it as "a true FUNK BOMB!"

Because of JB's international connections, he was made an honorary citizen of the African republic of Liberia in December 1978. He was performing two nights that month at the "Freedom Festival" in Monrovia, Liberia, sponsored by The Committee for the Liberia Fund for the Liberation of Southern Africa, and the next week, on Tuesday afternoon, telling reporters in Augusta about his new honor.

The formal document read:

> *Upon recommendation of the governing council of the Order of the Star of Africa, I, William R. Tolbert Jr., president of the Republic of Liberia and Grand Master of said order, in consideration of meritorious and distinguished service to the Republic of Liberia do hereby confer upon James Brown the Order of the Star of Africa.*

While he was at it, Brown took the opportunity to tell Augusta reporters that the U.S. Army had asked for his help in combating drug abuse by American soldiers. He added, "It is so crucial at this point. They [Army officials] can't put them out of service knowing they're addicts."

While accolades were coming from Europe in the mid-seventies, Brown's troubles continued to mount on the home front with two lots he owned—one at 1501-1505 Walton Way and the other at 1507-1509 Walton Way—that were being put up for public auction in May 1977 to collect a debt on default of payments.

On June 8, 1978, Brown's Augusta radio station WRDW-AM received $70,000 in damages when the station's transmitter blew up.

The following month, on an order from U.S. District Court Judge C. Stanley Blair in Baltimore, Maryland, JB was arrested on Monday morning, July 17, in New York City for contempt of court. He was brought to Baltimore and put in jail to make sure he appeared before Judge Blair in a hearing involving the WEBB radio station Brown had purchased in Baltimore.

Brown was held in contempt for missing court hearings and depositions in connection with his purchase of the station. The station's former owners claimed Brown had not paid them in full, and they wanted it placed in receivership.

The day after the initial hearing in federal court, Judge Blair sent Brown back to jail saying he had failed to provide sufficient financial information on charges that he owed $170,000 toward the purchase of WEBB. Brown had bought the station in 1969 for $270,000 but had only paid the owners $100,000 as of mid-1978.

Attorneys for the former owners wanted Brown to submit financial records regarding the station from 1969 to 1975, and when Brown failed to do so or appear in court, he was held in civil contempt.

Judge Blair told Brown he would either have to post a $100,000 bond or spend another night in jail. Brown refused to let his attorney, Ellis Parker, post the bond, because Brown said Parker would lose the $100,000 if he did not provide the requested financial data within forty-eight hours. Parker called the demands "nonsense," saying that the requested documents would fill six file cabinets and half a dozen boxes.

Brown's comptroller back in Augusta, Fred Daviss, said in a UPI wire service article published in the *Augusta Herald* that Brown had agreed to pay too much for the station and added, "Here is a man trying to perform a service to the black community [of Baltimore], and he is getting his tail kicked."

Brown's vice president in charge of operations, Al Garner, said the station never had made money, and that there were sixty-nine FCC violations against the station at the time of its purchase by Brown.

As the problems with the Baltimore station swirled around, the news wasn't good that same July for WRDW in Augusta. where a Richmond County superior court judge had ordered that "all office furniture, business machines, fixtures and broadcasting equipment located at 1840 Eisenhower Drive" be sold at the courthouse on the first Tuesday in August to satisfy a claim brought against JB Broadcasting Ltd. by the Employment Security Agency in Georgia.

The auction of the property, authorities said, was because Brown's company had not fulfilled all the requirements of the agency that business firms must pay taxes to fund unemployment compensation.

The following March in U.S. District Court in Augusta, JB Broadcasting of Augusta Ltd.—doing business as WRDW-AM radio—filed a petition for financial relief under Chapter 11 of the U.S. Bankruptcy Act. Brown's company, in a three-page document, claimed it was "unable to pay its debts as they mature."

According to the document, the station had thirty-two creditors, including the National Bank of Georgia, United Press International news wire service, IRS, Richmond County tax commissioner, Georgia Power, Southern Bell, an Augusta lawyer, and several station employees.

But no matter how intense his personal troubles were, he still found the time and the means to keep on creating and to keep on trying to improve society and race relations whenever he could.

Such was the case in July 1975 when Brown announced he was launching a nationally syndicated TV show called *Future Shock* that would be filmed in the studio of WAGT television station at Broad and Ninth streets in downtown Augusta.

He told the *Augusta News-Review* that initially the show would be broadcast regionally, but he expected it to become one of the most watched shows in the nation. That's the way JB always was: he was his best drum beater. No one could ever accuse James Brown of not believing in himself.

Brown saw his show not only as a way of promoting bands from the Augusta area but also as a way to promote dancing and artwork. He said, "It kind of gives the kids some hope. They now know that they can get on national television."

In an interesting side note, Brown said that he had cut down on his concerts and would have time to produce the show, even though he may not always host it. The question, of course, was: Did Brown really cut down on his concerts, or had a lot of his concerts disappeared in the changing music scene?

Brown may have written the black inspirational anthem of the decade with "Say It Loud—I'm Black and I'm Proud," but the truth is JB wanted all races to be proud of him and his good deeds. JB in December 1978 told me he once had been asked to be the grand marshal for an Augusta Black Festival Parade but had declined. He added, "I wouldn't do it because that would be a step backwards. I don't want to be a part of anything all-black just as I wouldn't want to be a part of anything all-white."

In that same conversation in December 1978, Brown told me, "I never worried about hating a white man. That would have been stupid on my part. Old people around Augusta thought I was crazy for demanding my rights here. I wasn't demanding them because I am black. I was demanding them because I am an American."

He apparently even had some regret about recording his black anthem song telling David Hinckley of the *New York Daily News* in 1984, "Now, 'Say It Loud—I'm Black and I'm Proud' probably done more for the black race than any other record, but if I had my choice, I wouldn't have done it, because I don't like defining anyone by race. To teach race is to teach separatism."

Through his association with Richard Nixon, Jimmy Carter, Ronald Reagan, Hubert Humphrey, and other politicians, James Brown astutely realized that he could have a positive influence by using his close relationship with elected officials.

As a political reporter for the *Augusta Herald* afternoon newspaper, I came to know this firsthand when I happened to be with Brown and South Carolina gubernatorial candidate Dick Riley in late 1978 at a Democratic rally in the Augusta Hilton Convention Center.

I was talking with Riley and happened to ask him if he knew Brown, who was a resident of South Carolina. Riley said, "No, but I would love to meet him." So, I hauled Riley over to JB, and introduced the two and told JB that Riley was running for governor of South Carolina. They immediately bonded and engaged in a very in-depth conversation.

"I've listened to your conversation, and I think the best way to look at a man is in the face and eyes," JB later told Riley. You're one of the most solid men I've seen." Riley equally was impressed with Brown and told him, "I need you on my cabinet." Brown responded, "I don't think you need anyone to sing or dance for you in the [South Carolina] Capitol." Riley then said, "You'd swing up the place a bit."

The two men discussed their backgrounds and learned that both of their families came from Barnwell and Williston, South Carolina. Riley then quipped, "Me and you are blood brothers." Riley and Brown agreed that whether the subject is politics or music they must stay on top of what is happening to communicate with the people they're trying to reach.

After Riley left to talk with some other people, JB turned to me and said, "He's an unusual man. So straight. I believe in him. I'm sure I can give him help, because when I do, I give it to myself."

Brown also told me that the gathering that night of Democratic leaders and Democratic hope-to-be leaders showed him "another side of Augusta." He added, "I'm very much pleased by what I have seen and heard tonight. It is a side I have always wanted to see here. There are just regular brothers and sisters here. I don't like the words 'black politician.' I think to think of politicians who may be black."

As it turned out, Brown ended up making several campaign appearances for Dick Riley, who became governor of South Carolina from 1979 to 1987. He was U.S. secretary of education (1993–2001) before settling down in civilian life as a senior partner at Nelson, Mullins, Riley, and Scarborough LLP in Greenville, South Carolina.

When Riley did achieve his political dreams and was elected to the governor's office, JB was a "special guest" at the Inaugural Gala Celebration Homecoming in Township Auditorium in Columbia on Tuesday night, January 9, 1979, honoring Governor-Elect Riley and Lieutenant Governor-Elect Nancy Stevenson.

The evening was basically a showcase of South Carolina cultural talents, including Brook Benton, the Columbia City Ballet, the Drifters, Snuffy Jenkins and the Hired Hands, the Palmetto Cloggers, and the University of South Carolina Brass Ensemble.

And I ended up that night sitting on the front row next to JB—a guy even more famous than the guy being sworn in as the new governor of South Carolina.

I caught a ride that afternoon from Augusta to Columbia, about an hour's drive on Interstate 20, with Al Garner, Brown's vice president of operations and had left my car at Brown's worldwide headquarters at Executive Office Park on Stevens Creek Road just off Interstate 20 near Washington Road. But when JB offered me a ride back to Augusta, I quickly accepted.

JB drove his black Lincoln Continental wearing his black tuxedo, with me riding shotgun seat, and Brown's father, Joe, and his cousin and best friend and office manager, William "Willie" Glenn, in the backseat.

JB and I got into a lively discussion about women's rights, with JB taking the conservative side and yours truly being far more liberal. It was my contention that women should be allowed to achieve whatever their talents and education could let them achieve. But JB argued that it still was a man's world, and that even women singing stars took away from the paychecks of male singing stars.

Our discussion got very intense; JB was paying more attention to me and less to his speedometer. We were about halfway home

97

when I saw JB stare into his rearview mirror and tell us there was a South Carolina state patrol trooper coming up close behind. I glanced over and saw the speedometer was reading about eighty miles an hour when the limit then on that stretch, I believe, was sixty miles per hour.

Most people in that situation would immediately drop their speed down to the limit and pray for the best. Ah, but not James Brown! He kept going eighty miles an hour. I said something like, "James, don't you think you need to get down to the speed limit?"

He said sternly back to me, "No, I'm not going to give him that satisfaction."

That was typical James Brown stemming from the days when he walked through tough Augusta neighborhoods as a kid refusing to bow down to bullies. That same attitude would persist throughout his life including his refusal to bow down to the white music establishment.

James Brown simply didn't back down from anybody.

He wasn't trying to act like James Brown, the music star who was better than anybody else. He was just being James Brown, a man like any other black or white man who wanted and demanded equal treatment. He had no intention of backing down to anyone, period. And that's just the way it was.

Sure enough, the inevitable happened, and the South Carolina state patrolman turned on his flashing lights and siren. Brown immediately pulled the car over on the right shoulder. He didn't wait for the patrolman to approach the side of the car but got out to talk with him.

JB's father, Glenn, and I all looked back to see what was happening. The state patrolman was black—something you rarely saw on South Carolina state and federal highways in the late 1970s. It was an interesting sight with JB in his black tuxedo pulling out his wallet to show the patrolman his license, and the state patrolman in his spiffy uniform writing JB a speeding ticket.

Not long afterward, Brown got back in the driver's seat with a glum look on his face, clutching the speeding ticket he just had been issued. "Well, I guess you shouldn't have a hard time getting that ticket taken care of by the new governor," I said jokingly, trying to lighten the now very somber mood in the car and feeling somewhat guilty about distracting JB with our argument.

JB didn't think it was funny, but he still wished me good night when he dropped me off at my car at his office. And not another word about that incident was ever said between us.

ELEVEN

Hello, Grand Ole Opry

My own daddy told me that I'd never make it by
singing. My own daddy told me that.

—James Brown
February 3, 1980
the Augusta Chronicle

Anyone who thinks that James Brown didn't love country music apparently never talked to Brown, who in 1979 eagerly accepted an invitation by country music superstar Porter Wagoner to perform on the world-famous Grand Ole Opry radio show.

The Pointer Sisters, had appeared on the Opry program broadcast live over Nashville's WSM-AM radio station singing their country-flavored hit single "Fairy Tales" when it was near the top of the music charts. And after Brown's appearance, Motown Records legend Stevie Wonder also sang to the Opry House audience with little fanfare in the national media.

But between those shows, James Brown performed on the Opry stage on March 10, 1979, setting off a spark that flashed from Nashville and traveled around the globe.

Brown later told me, "They treated me like I was a prodigal son. They treated me so nice I felt guilty. I felt I got as much praise as a white man who goes into a black church and puts $100 in the collection plate."

JB continued, "I always have loved country music ever since I was a kid and listened to the radio in Augusta. Country music really is just the white man's blues."

Brown said he had been invited to appear on the Opry by Porter Wagoner, former singing partner of Dolly Parton and the inspiration for Parton's gigantic hit single "I Will Always Love You." The visit was arranged through Wagoner's recording session piano player, Mike Lawler, who had been keyboard player for Brown for more than two years, and through Brown's longtime band leader Hollie Ferris.

Brown sang "Your Cheating Heart," "Tennessee Waltz," "Georgia on My Mind," and a medley of his soul music hits. Brown said of his host, "Porter used to walk behind the mules plowing up the fields and singing to himself. He told me that a guy heard him announcing himself like he was on the Grand Ole Opry and told him, 'That's the closest to the Opry you'll ever get.'

"I can relate to that," JB told me almost a year after that Opry appearance. "My own daddy told me that I'd never make it by singing. My own daddy told me that."

Speaking of his Opry appearance, Brown said, "I thought it was one of the best things I have ever done in my life. It was definitely a high point."

Almost four years after the Opry show, Brown took an even bigger plunge into country music when Oklahoma country music impresario Jim Halsey officially announced in March 1983 that Brown had signed an exclusive recording contract with a Halsey company called Churchill Records and Video Ltd.

Halsey formed the Tulsa-based Churchill Company the previous year and had signed eight artists to the label, including county stars Roy Clark (whom Halsey had long promoted), Jimmy Dean, and Hank Thompson. I became the first reporter to interview Churchill artist Ronnie Dunn of Oklahoma eight years before he would make recording history teaming up with Kix Brooks to form the mega hit country duo Brooks and Dunn. Halsey also had an entertainment booking agency that handled the Oak Ridge Boys, Don Williams, Tammy Wynette, Lee Greenwood, Terri Gibbs [another Augusta-area talent], and Roy Clark. Halsey had personally traveled to Augusta in late February to finalize the contract with Brown.

"He will have total creative control from the album cover to the final product. That's the secret of what we're doing." Halsey told me in a telephone call from New York City. "Respect is a key word to me. I respect the artists I work with, and I still get excited about my business. I'm very excited about being able to work with Mr. Brown."

Halsey and Brown confirmed a new record label had been created called "Augusta Sound," which was a division of Churchill/Augusta Inc. Records produced on the label would be distributed by the powerful MCA Distributing Corporation, which also was the distributor of MCA records and cassette tapes.

Already in mid-March, the Augusta Sound label released its first single, Brown's original composition, "Bring It On, Bring It On." Then Halsey and Brown announced that Brown had recorded a country music album for the Augusta Sound label called *Country Funk,* which would be released in the coming months. Halsey and Brown were also already planning a duet album with Brown and country music superstar Roy Clark, known especially for cohosting the popular syndicated *Hee Haw* TV comedy series with Buck Owens.

"I think we can get Mr. Brown and Mr. Clark together for an album," Halsey said. "They both want to do it."

Brown agreed, telling me the same day by phone from his Augusta office, "We're going to do it. We feel that the respect for each other is there, the chemistry is there, and, most of all, the love is there; the love for humanity that we both have. I've always connected soul and country music. They've both told the truth. They're just from different parts of the city."

The pairing was not that far from strange. Clark, in 1979, had joined musical forces with jazz and blues great Gatemouth Brown to record the Grammy-nominated *Makin' Music* album. It was very successful and earned an unheard of five-star rating from *Down Beat* magazine.

Tommy Martin, president of Churchill/Augusta, also commented on the Brown signing in a press release saying,

"Churchill/Augusta wants to keep the timeless James Brown style that made him a star. We're not changing him. We're hoping to broaden his following. To me, he's the most dynamic performer in the business, and we're releasing a product that his fans want: both his longtime fans and the young people who are just discovering the James Brown brand of soul."

Halsey, the crafty entertainment guru, also was aware that Georgia native soul and pop singer Ray Charles had recently signed with Columbia Records. Music insiders were saying a duet album was being discussed between Charles and country legend George Jones. Charles and Jones did eventually record the hit country single "We Didn't See a Thing."

Brown's duet album with Roy Clark never came about, but in 1983 he did release a wonderful album called *Bring It On* (apparently the title *Country Funk* must have fallen by the wayside), based on his earlier single release. It contained one of the best versions I've ever heard of "Tennessee Waltz" (the classic written by Pee Wee King and Red Stewart), as well as a rocking, country-flavored version of "The Night Time Is the Right Time," and a long and nostalgic version of Jerry Butler's hit "For Your Precious Love."

In spite of the thrill of being on the Grand Ole Opry JB was going through some tough times personally. It was a few days before his appearance in Nashville that his radio station, WRDW, had filed for bankruptcy.

JB could be going through tough times, yet he almost always held his head high and kept on smiling and joking around his friends, family, and the media. He had an amazing ability to bounce back from troubles that would break lesser men and women. But even James Brown had to reach out for help when the weight of the world was just too much even for him.

On November 1, 1979, I found myself at Augusta's Bush Field airport with Brown and Bob Young, then a news reporter for WBBQ-FM radio station and later mayor of Augusta, waiting for the arrival of New York lawyer William Kunstler.

Brown and Kunstler greeted each other with a hug, although Kunstler later would say that they were meeting each other for the first time. Kunstler had come to Augusta to help Brown with some legal problems concerning record royalties and with his WRDW radio station in Augusta. When Brown was asked specifically what he needed Kunstler's services for, Brown replied, "For help! I need help very, very bad!"

Kunstler told us at the airport that Brown's problems "are common to many people who reach his status in the entertainment world. . . . I suspect any black businessman in the United States today is going to have problems with the white world."

In return for Kunstler's assistance, Kunstler said Brown would be making appearances on behalf of Kunstler's clients. Kunstler hoped that it would "give us another person in the entertainment field who could make a difference [in a court trial] between victory and defeat." He said that the appearances of superstars such as singer Harry Belafonte and actor Marlon Brando on behalf of his clients had been greatly beneficial in controversial cases such as the time Brando went to South Dakota while Kunstler was defending the Native Americans at Wounded Knee. The extent of what Kunstler eventually did for Brown is unclear.

Also on that day at Bush Field, Brown revealed he was going to California in December to film his part as the minister of the Triple Rock Baptist Church in a movie titled *The Blues Brothers,* costarring Dan Aykroyd and John Belushi. Brown's vice president of operations, Al Garner, said the script called for Brown to sing two songs in the Universal Pictures production.

Surely neither Brown, nor Kunstler, nor Garner, nor future mayor Bob Young, nor I could ever have guessed the impact of Brown singing those two songs in *The Blues Brothers.*

And yet, in the long run, those two songs probably did as much in helping Brown get back on his feet than anything William Kunstler was doing for him.

TWELVE

Singing with the Blues Brothers

If you start letting people define who you are, people will then decide what is credible and what is not. And you never give them that, Reverend. You may suffer, but you never give them that.

—James Brown to Al Sharpton in
Al On America (Dafina Books, 2002)

The first three months of 1982 was an indication that it very likely could be one of the best years of James Brown's life.

On January 15, Brown met with president Ronald Reagan and vice president George H. W. Bush. He told me the following April, "The president and I talked about bringing up the economy and working with the private sector. . . . I endorse the human rights concepts of Jimmy Carter, but I also endorse the no-nonsense approach of Ronald Reagan. It is time we clean up areas that have a lot of fat."

When I asked Brown if blacks feared that Reagan might cut off federal funding for programs that help them, JB replied, "He's going to cut off the programs of both blacks and whites. Black people shouldn't think they are the only people in the world. They are not the only people in the world who are hungry."

While JB went on to say that he was not a "lover of welfare," he added that he believed welfare subsidies were needed for handicapped people, the elderly, and mothers unable to work and who needed help in feeding their children. He further told me that he had created the "James Brown Foundation" to put money into communities to help young, unskilled workers.

Further talk about politics led Brown to remark, "Recently a reviewer came down on me because he didn't want me to work with politics. I'm not working with politics. I'm working for the people. I've gone beyond politics. I think people are more important. Out of the three P's, I've dropped politics, but I have kept people and pride."

The same week in mid-January when Brown had met with Reagan and Bush, he was an honored guest at the inauguration of Augusta's first black mayor, Edward Marlowe McIntyre. McIntyre's inauguration was the first to be held in the Augusta-Richmond County Civic Center (renamed James Brown Arena in 2006), where twenty-four years later the third funeral service for James Brown would take place.

Also in the first three months of 1982 JB was profiled in *Rolling Stone* magazine; he received a standing ovation when he was introduced with Tina Turner as a presenter on the Grammy Awards televised program; and he got rave reviews for concerts in February in Los Angeles.

In mid-March, he met with the prime minister of the Bahamas and recorded an album in Jamaica with the studio band of the late reggae star Bob Marley. (Unfortunately, it would seem that this album was never released although different people have told me they have heard bootleg copies.)

Also in early 1982, James Brown addressed the congregation at the March 11 memorial service in the Cathedral of Saint John the Divine in New York City for John Belushi. The thirty-three-year-old actor and singer had been found dead of an overdose of cocaine and heroin on March 5 in his room at the Chateau Marmont hotel in West Hollywood, California.

Brown always gave credit to Aykroyd and Belushi for revitalizing his show business career when they brought him into their 1980 hit movie *The Blues Brothers* as the singing and dancing reverend, Cleophus James.

Brown only had a cameo role that lasted just a few minutes singing and dancing to "(Let's All Go Back to) the Old Landmark" in the pulpit of a church, backed by the Reverend James Cleveland Choir. But he truly lit up the screen with his vivacious personality and emotional singing.

"It took a Chicago guy [Belushi] to give me my true identity," Brown told me. "It boosted my career as well as that of Ray Charles, Cab Calloway, and Aretha Franklin. Belushi told me he felt I never had a fair shake in show business. He was one of the funniest men onstage, but he was a serious man off. He was warm, touching, and very nice. I think *The Blues Brothers* is a classic movie like *Gone With the Wind,* and I'm glad I was a part of it."

The same year *The Blues Brothers* was released, Brown performed on *Saturday Night Live* singing "Rapp Payback" and a medley of his hits on the December 13, 1980, episode hosted by actress Jamie Leigh Curtis.

Although Belushi was gone, Aykroyd and Brown remained friends in the years to come, and Aykroyd performed at Brown's "Birthday Bash" in May 1997 in the Augusta-Richmond County Civic Center.

While *The Blues Brothers* movie had a dramatic, positive affect on James Brown's performing career, it also had a dramatic, personal affect on his friend, Al Sharpton who recalled that incident in his book, *Al On America*, coauthored with Karen Hunter.

Sharpton was on the movie set watching JB being filmed doing his famous slide to the pulpit, dancing around, and singing. He remembered that director John Landis stopped the filming and told Brown to calm down some. According to Sharpton, JB responded, "If you wanted Frank Sinatra, you should have booked him. If you want James Brown, this is what you get."

Sharpton called that incident a "defining moment." He later asked JB why he stood his ground that day, and JB replied simply but profoundly, "If you start letting people define who you are, people will then decide what is credible and what is not. And you never give them that, Reverend. You may suffer, but you never give them that."

Another major incident happened in James Brown's life in the first three months of 1983, but it's up for debate on whether—in the long run—it was a very good thing or a very bad thing. It definitely would change his life as nothing else had before.

Brown, by that time, was a single guy again. His second marriage of ten years to Deidre Jenkins officially had ended on January 10, 1981. He was a guest artist on the TV music series *Solid Gold* when he first met the show's hair stylist, Adrienne Modell Lois Rodriguez. He was forty-eight and she was thirty-two.

JB loved many things in life, including good food, good music, and good sex, and near the top of that list was a good hairstylist. He kept the best ones with him over the years including his childhood friend Leon Austin and his housekeeper Ella Overton.

So it was that JB would take the marriage plunge again two years later with hair stylist Rodriguez. Their union would become one of the most tumultuous relationships in entertainment history, producing headlines worldwide.

She was like few women he had ever known, and, to borrow a title from a JB hit, Adrienne, like papa, "didn't take no mess." Many of his other relationships were with submissive women who took his abuse, but that certainly was not the case with Miss Adrienne.

In March 1983 the IRS in March auctioned off Brown's Lincoln Continental, Mercedes-Benz, customized Dodge van, furniture, television set, and other items to pay off Brown's reported $2.82 million debt in federal taxes.

The rest of that year for James Brown was typical of his extreme highs and lows. The high was being inducted into the Georgia Music Hall of Fame in September in the performing artist category. The low came two months later proclaimed in a headline in the November 4 *Augusta Herald,* "James Brown Singing 'Blues' as He Hears Child Support Charge."

The story reported that JB had been ordered to appear in a courtroom in Sacramento, California, to answer a charge that he had failed to pay $500 a month to support a fifteen-year-old son born out of wedlock to Mary Brown, the former president of James Brown's California fan club. She contended he owed $29,500 in back payments.

Sacramento fans packed the courtroom just to see the famous entertainer. One excited observer exclaimed, "I can't believe you're here," to which Brown replied glumly, "I can't believe I'm here either."

On November 18, Judge Carol Miller sentenced Brown to seventy-five days in jail but suspended the sentence on the condition that Brown pay $10,500 in back child support within ten days.

Brown must have done so with whatever cash he could round up, because on Wednesday, November 30, the *Augusta Herald* reported that Brown's band did not have the money to pay for gasoline to get their bus back to Augusta from California. The singer apparently had decided to make use of his indefinite stay in Sacramento on the child support charges to book some Thanksgiving weekend concerts.

"The cream and green bus with Brown's name on the side and 13 passengers aboard left the parking lot of the Woodlake Inn [in Sacramento] late Tuesday in search of a place to camp until money arrives from Brown," the Associated Press account related. "The singer and manager Henry Stallings reportedly boarded a plane Monday for Los Angeles in search of funds."

The story reported, "A member of the band, the JB's, said the concerts were organized too hastily and lacked promotion."

If you asked any former member of James Brown's bands at any stage of his career what it was like on the road with the Godfather of Soul, they most likely would tell you that life on the road with JB certainly was never dull. And apparently neither was life at home with JB.

THIRTEEN

The Saga of Adrienne Brown

The demand [being on the road] was too great. Me
and my wife worked so much that we couldn't look
at each other. We didn't know who we were. It took
these two years in prison for me to realize this. The
good Lord knew what he was doing even though
the courts imprisoned me unjustly. The good Lord
turned it around in my favor.

—James Brown
March 18, 1991
Jet magazine

On the night of August 30, 1984, JB let me attend a rehearsal
of his band in his suite at Executive Office Park on Claussen
Road near the intersection of Washington Road and Interstate 20.
Brown and his troupe were to perform the next night in Atlanta's
massive Omni coliseum with opening acts B. B. King, Wilson
Pickett, and Bobby "Blue" Bland.

From Atlanta on a Friday night, the Brown revue headed for
New Orleans for two shows on Saturday night before traveling to
Wilmington, Delaware, for a Monday Labor Day show, then back
to Augusta on the next Tuesday.

Just a few weeks earlier, a review in *People* magazine of two
of Brown's new albums proclaimed, "Brown is not just a singer.
His voice is an instrument enmeshed with and leading his band in
a way that has never been duplicated."

One of those albums was *Unity*, which many music critics
called "his best record in years." The album on the Tommy
Boy Records label teamed up Brown with young rapper Afrika

Bambaataa; with the duo recording a six-part, 12-inch single titled "Unity" with its theme being peace, love, unity, and no drugs.

Brown told David Hinckley of the *New York Daily News,* "I'd heard Bam's stuff, and he was moving in the right direction toward world peace. It's a long cut broken up into six sections because we wanted to get a lot of concepts in. It's spiritual as well as musical. . . . People ask me how long it took to record, [and] I say, 'My whole life.'"

Bambaataa told Ted Greenwald for the August 1984 issue of *NY Talk,* an alternative arts and entertainment magazine, "Anyone who deals with hip hop music credits James Brown and Sly Stone as the true kings, lords, gods, whatever you want to call them, of funk. James Brown made funk, which was a dirty word, into a human, get-down, nitty-gritty word that meant something. Sly Stone crossed it over so whites could understand it. So we credit those two with bringing the funk on and building it up. And then we credit George Clinton with making it an empire, a religion and a way of life."

For the band rehearsal at the Executive Office Park that August night, Brown was dressed in the country-and-western-style clothes that would be a trademark of his down home life in Augusta: black cowboy boots; white straw, cowboy hat; western-looking scarf; and a large, silver and turquoise bracelet around his right wrist. "You gotta hear this," Brown told me, as he led the way to his black, Econoline van parked near his office suite. He opened the driver's door, reaching over the steering wheel, and turned on the ignition and cassette system.

As he and I stood outside the van in the warm night air, the speakers began blaring Brown's unique, musical sound with his unmistakable voice boasting, "Every time I think of two, all-beef patties with special sauce, lettuce, cheese, pickles, and onions on sesame seed buns, I get on my good foot, and I do the James Brown all the way down to Mick-a-dees—Big Mac! Tastes so good!"

Brown told me that "Mick-a-dees" is what many people, at that time only in northern states, called McDonald's, and that he had filmed a national television commercial for McDonald's in Chicago with the commercial showing a bunch of his fans running into him in a McDonald's restaurant.

Besides the TV commercial, he also was happy about an upcoming banquet of the Black Music Association in Washington, D.C., where he was to receive another award. And he'd recently made another cameo appearance in the now cult-classic Dan Aykroyd film, *Dr. Detroit.*

JB also mentioned that he was going to be featured in another major motion picture. That movie, released in 1985, was the Sylvester Stallone boxing classic *Rocky IV* in which JB would be seen in the unforgettable flashy production of *Living in America.*

At fifty-one James Brown wasn't recording the hit singles of his peak years, but he was a long ways from being forgotten by his fans.

He also wasn't forgotten by his newest main squeeze, Adrienne Rodriguez, who—if you believe her later accounts—was the chief architect behind JB's show business rebirth. She told reporters about how they met and their subsequent life, "We fell in love. James Brown was as much as retired at the time. Together we brought him back. We went on the road. It was just the two of us, booking dates, carrying baggage, no entourage. We made our dreams come true. It was the happiest three years of my life."

About a month after my conversation with Brown in the parking lot of his office complex, he got married for the third time on September 21, 1984. Several of Brown's relatives, including his mother, Susie, packed into the office of the Aiken County, probate judge to witness Brown, marrying Rodriguez. He wore a nice suit. She wore a beige chiffon dress with hat to match.

Following the ten-minute ceremony, Brown signed autographs for fans who had learned of the momentous occasion. And, as the new Mrs. Brown would say, the first couple of years for JB and Adrienne were happy ones.

Near the end of 1985, I wrote a lengthy, full-page profile about JB that was published on December 4 in the *Chronicle* with the large headline, "James Brown—Soul Brother No. 1 Claims No Glory in His Own Hometown."

In the lead paragraphs I wrote, "He is billed worldwide as Soul Brother No. 1, The Hardest Working Man in Show Business and The Godfather of Soul. But in Augusta he is James or Mr. Brown to his friends and business associates.

"Where his musical career is concerned, James Brown is a citizen of the world, whose legendary public life frequently is reported. Where his private life is concerned, he remains a mystery to his hometown folks, who seem to think Brown stays one step ahead of his creditors and the tax collectors."

JB would spend about three days a week in his Augusta office, working from late afternoon into the night. He was on the phone most of the time making calls to or receiving them from radio station disc jockeys, concert promoters, magazine and newspaper writers, talent agents, and celebrities from all over the United States and the world.

He gave me a glimpse of his frenzied love of phone calling when I visited his office in late 1985 and one of his office assistants interrupted our conversation to say a disc jockey was calling from Milwaukee.

Brown grabbed the phone and shouted, "Papa's Got a Brand New Bag! It's a Man's World! Try Me! Night Train! Payback! Hot Pants! If we go to Milwaukee County Stadium, we'll have to run after the show. . . . If you're a firm believer and a God-fearing man, you have no problems! God is the boss, and I'm the hoss!"

Brown started naming some of his early recordings and started softly and passionately singing into the phone, "Alone from night to night you find me. / Too weak to break these chains that bind me." "A cigarette that bears some lipstick traces." He broke off and asked, "You remember that?" Then he resumed singing, "Again, this couldn't happen again." He stopped singing and asked again, "You remember that?"

Those few minutes of listening to him talk with that disc jockey was another example of the true and classic Brown that I would see repeatedly through my long association with him. He loved music so much that he frequently would sing to people at the drop of a hat and would give them their own personal, mini-concert.

Although he often was prone to self-praise, JB made it very clear that his religion was more important than himself. He told me that when he accepted God and when God accepted him for the second time, it was the best thing to happen in his illustrious life.

"When I accepted him [again] as my Savior. That was my greatest thing," he said. "I was baptized for the second time in St. Peter's Baptist Church in Elko, South Carolina, one hundred yards from where U.S. Senator Strom Thurmond married his first wife. My father and all of my family went to that church. When I was baptized for the second time my whole life changed."

On race, he said, "I'm not black or white. I'm people, and people have no color. That's why I love President [Ronald] Reagan so much, because he said he's color blind. That's probably the greatest statement a president ever made." Brown said he last visited with Reagan in the White House about a year and a half earlier.

At the conclusion of our conversation that day in his office, Brown was in a very reflective and sensitive mood. Even though his climb to fame had happened three decades earlier, Brown said softly, "It seems like yesterday."

When asked about the best advice he could give kids today, he replied, "Honor thy father and thy mother that their days be long upon the land that the Lord thou God gives them. That's one of the Ten Commandments." And, typical of his caring nature, he added, "How's your father doing? A sweet fellow. I love him. Tell him I love him."

Much to my pleasure, that in-depth profile meant a great deal to JB. He had a framed copy of the full-page article on a wall near his desk, and it was visible in many subsequent photos and television reports.

But the best thing about that article was that it inspired two young fans, Terrence Dicks and Greg Peterson, to spearhead a movement to bring about local recognition of JB in his hometown. That public recognition came when then Augusta mayor Charles A. DeVaney proclaimed June 28, 1986, as "James Brown Day." The celebration took place outdoors at the Augusta Riverfront Marina on the Savannah River.

"Throughout the years, James has never failed to recognize Augusta as his home," DeVaney wrote in a letter for the special day. "Therefore it is only fitting that Augusta recognize one of its most famous citizens."

In the week before that special day, Brown talked with me on the phone and said, "What a beautiful city Augusta has become. When God recognizes you with his blessings, that is the highest honor a man can receive. When your fellow man recognizes you, that is the second highest honor you can receive."

Speaking of high honors, earlier that year in January, Brown was one of the first ten inductees into the Rock and Roll Hall of Fame during a ceremony at the Waldorf=Astoria Hotel in New York City.

And to top it off, Brown and his new wife, Adrienne, were granted a private audience with Pope John Paul II in Rome, at the Vatican. Brown said—for a poor kid from rural Barnwell County, South Carolina, then regularly attending a small Baptist church in Elko, South Carolina—that meeting with the pope was the highlight of his life.

"I thought God has brought me far to deliver me to such a highly recognized spiritual leader. People were there from all over the world coming together and worshipping God," Brown told me of the Vatican gathering. "God is the greatest hit maker in the world. I'd rather be a poor man with religion than a rich man without it."

James Brown Day at the Riverfront Marina was to begin at 3 p.m. with a free concert by three bands followed by the awards ceremony at 4 p.m. Brown, for some reason, didn't show up until 4:45 p.m., even though his house was just a few miles away, which caused some anxiety.

The word was out also that Brown had been hospitalized in New York just the week before because of "a simple case of exhaustion." His longtime backup vocalist Martha High said, "He just needed a little rest because we've been on tour for six or seven months."

An estimated four thousand to five thousand people attended the start of the ceremony, but the bottom fell out when a lightning-powered rainstorm scattered a lot of the crowd back to their cars. But the turnout was still large by the time Brown's limousine pulled into the marina.

"The rain is here, but it's also needed to calm my nerves and let us know that there is someone more powerful than all of us," Brown told the crowd in remarks broadcast by a local radio station. "This is James Brown Day in Augusta, but it also is your day today." Sharing the special day with JB were his childhood friend, Leon Austin, and their former Silas X. Floyd schoolteacher, Laura Garvin.

Alabama governor George Wallace, Georgia governor Joe Frank Harris, and President Reagan all sent congratulatory messages. U.S. Representative D. Douglas Barnard Jr. of Augusta remarked, "James is indeed our number one ambassador." That statement later would come back to haunt him, when Adrienne got in trouble with the law and declared "diplomatic immunity" based on Barnard's public proclamation.

Unfortunately, most of the audience couldn't tell what Brown and the distinguished guests were saying because of the poor public address system and people in the crowd shouting that they couldn't hear. Those at home listening to the proceedings live broadcast on WCKJ-AM radio had a much easier time.

As if 1986 couldn't get much better —his induction into the Rock and Roll Hall of Fame, his private meeting with the pope, a Top Ten single with "Living in America," and being honored in his hometown—he ended the year with the release of his autobiography with Bruce Tucker [*James Brown: The Godfather of Soul*] (Macmillan, 1986) and a concert on Saturday night, December 27, in the Augusta-Richmond County Civic Center with Wilson Pickett as the opening act.

The day before the concert, JB and Adrienne went to the Augusta-Richmond County Museum (later to be known as the Augusta Museum of History) and presented one of JB's suits for a museum exhibit to John Reynolds, president of the museum's board of trustees.

"My book is selling as hot as a 45 rpm record," Brown told me. "Paramount Pictures is talking with us about making it into a movie. I would be playing myself for most of the movie. The girls say I look so good I could play all the parts."

There was one little weird incident near the end of 1986 when Brown told Richmond County Sheriff's Department deputies that someone had entered a Plymouth van parked in front of his Executive Office Park suite and removed $7,000 in cash from the glove compartment. Investigators could not find any signs of a forced entry.

William Glenn, vice president of operations for James Brown Enterprises, told officers he was unsure why Brown had stored the cash in the vehicle and that nothing else had been touched. He added, "Mr. Brown just said the money was in the van, and it got taken (between 6:30 and 7 p.m.) Friday night."

Everything else seemed to be so right at that time in James Brown's personal life. And everything seemed to be so right with his public life as once again he assumed his rightful place as an important and influential musical figure. But, just seven months later, the cracks started showing, beginning with a simple traffic accident and escalating seriously from there.

On July 8, 1987, JB was backing his van out of a driveway in the Fairington subdivision in south Richmond County just before midnight and backed into a westbound car driven by thirty-three-year-old Carolyn H. Harvey. Brown was ticketed by a sheriff's deputy for failure to show proof of insurance. He later paid a $25 fine. The van was in the name of a Brown company called Living Productions, apparently named after his "*Living in America*" hit single.

It was Adrienne's turn to be in the news on September 3, 1987, when Richmond County sheriff's deputies stopped her for speeding on Washington Road and charged her with driving under the influence, speeding, and criminal trespassing. The case came up in Richmond County State Court on January 23, 1989, at which time Adrienne pleaded no contest.

Judge Gayle B. Hamrick sentenced Adrienne to twelve months on probation, fined her $600, ordered her to perform two days of community service and attend an alcohol and drug education course, and pay $75 restitution for "a small amount of damage" to the upholstery of the sheriff's patrol car Adrienne was placed in after the incident.

Next it was JB's turn again to be in the police news.

Just after 4 p.m. on Saturday afternoon, September 12, 1987, Brown was speeding on the four-lane, limited-access John C. Calhoun Expressway when an Augusta police officer started chasing him.

Brown exited right off the Calhoun Expressway onto 15th Street and headed south a few blocks before turning right onto four-lane Walton Way. He then turned right into the parking lot of the International House of Pancakes and then out onto two-lane Chafee Avenue, which he followed to the parking lot of a

Kroger's grocery store, and then turned back onto 15th Street heading north. He went over the Butt Memorial Bridge and turned right onto Greene Street where he finally stopped in the 1400 block.

Officers K. S. Hydrick and R. L. Joyner charged Brown with speeding, fleeing, and attempting to elude police. He was said to have been driving 71 mph in a 50 mph zone and was weaving in and out of traffic. JB gave his residential address as 2506 Parkway Drive, which actually was the home of his father. He was taken into custody and later released, according to news accounts.

Almost two months later, Brown was jailed in the Aiken County Detention Center after being arrested on November 7, 1987, and charged with leaving the scene of an accident, property damage, and resisting arrest. Adrienne Brown told an inquiring reporter that the man in jail wasn't the singer James Brown and added, "You've got the wrong man."

Unfortunately, it was the right man making some wrong life choices.

According to the police accounts, Brown had been driving across the Sand Bar Ferry Road bridge that spans the Savannah River and connects Georgia and South Carolina. It was a route Brown took thousands of times from his nearby Beech Island, home. Brown rear-ended a car with his van, pushing it into a guard rail on the bridge, and then left the scene.

Aiken County Sheriff's Department deputies said, that when they located Brown, he resisted arrest and a deputy reportedly broke a finger in the scuffle. Brown spent one night in jail and was released on a $10,118 bond. Brown's attorney, Bill Weeks, the following March managed to get the resisting arrest charged changed to one case of simple assault and one count of disorderly conduct. The charges were remanded to the jurisdiction of Aiken County magistrate Al Bradley, who later became a close friend of Brown's. Brown ended up forfeiting a $436 bond without having to appear before the magistrate.

About a month after Brown's attorney got his resisting arrest charge reduced from the November traffic incident, sheriff's deputies were charging Brown again: this time with assault with intent to murder and assault and battery of a high and aggravated nature.

Those dire charges resulted from a domestic dispute between JB and Adrienne at the couple's home on Easter Sunday night, April 3, 1988. Aiken County Sheriff Carol Heath told the *Augusta Chronicle*, "He beat her up real bad. She's got bruises all over her. He also shot up her car." The sheriff's department report said three bullets hit the rear of the car and one hit below a headlight. The Lincoln Town Car was on loan from an Augusta car dealership.

Adrienne, then thirty-eight, also said that Brown took her $35,000 Black Diamond mink coat, laid it outside on the ground, and fired shots into it from his .22 caliber rifle.

"I didn't do anything to provoke him, no sir," she told investigators. "This is not the first time he's done this. He's knocked out all my teeth." Sheriff Heath would confirm that his deputies had been out to the Brown's ranch home "half a dozen times," and that Adrienne filed complaints but dropped the charges before they got to court.

Attorney Bill Weeks described the JB and Adrienne marriage as "stormy," to which another Brown attorney, Albert H. "Buddy" Dallas, told the *Chronicle*, "Stormy would be a mild adjective. Mr. and Mrs. Brown make a very exciting couple. May I suggest that everybody has overreacted? When I was called about this, my comment was, 'What else is new?'"

Adrienne later told reporters, "James Brown is a big hypocrite. The Godfather of Soul is not what he pretends to be. He warns young people to stay off drugs, but he doesn't practice what he preaches to children." She affirmed her role in helping resurrect Brown's career, saying, "We brought him back from nothing. I worked with him, and we built him all the way back up. Now he's big and thinks he's on top of the world."

Brown himself would later say that the argument was because he was heading out on a tour of South America without her. He added, "I never laid a hand on her. I can tell you it's over now. She's not coming back to my house. She's just mad because I won't take her to Brazil, and she's not going to go. She's never going to go."

Adrienne again asked that the assault charge be dropped, but this time officers had seen the bruises and were going to press the charges on their own.

Just days after the domestic dispute, Adrienne was back in the news, charged with possession of the illegal drug PCP (angel dust). Augusta policeman D. R. Brown (no relation) somehow received information that Adrienne would be at Bush Field airport receiving a shipment of PCP from New York. The officer and Augusta police detective T. C. Walker approached Adrienne at the airport with another woman, Ranell T. Wright, twenty-five, of the Bronx, New York.

The officers confiscated nasal spray bottles full of a "brown, leafy" substance mixed with what tested to be PCP. According to reports, Adrienne also tried to hide a cigarette that also tested positive for PCP. Adrienne and Wright were booked into the Augusta-Richmond County Law Enforcement Center and each was charged with one count of possession of PCP. They were released after posting bonds.

A few weeks later I called JB at his Beech Island home to talk about his most recent ups and downs. Some headline writer at the *Chronicle* put at the top of my May 14, 1988, story in the *Augusta Chronicle*, "Despite His Problems, Brown Feels Good."

JB said in the conversation for that article that he still loved his wife in spite of her accusations and her own drug problems. "The National Enquirer paid my wife $15,000 for those photos," he said about color shots of Adrienne showing marks on her face that she claimed her husband had caused. "My wife is a real stinker," JB added. "She sets rooms on fire. She's a brat."

He was referring to the latest domestic dispute involving the Browns when Adrienne set some of his clothes on fire the previous week in the couple's room at the Sheraton-Wayfarer Hotel in Bedford, New Hampshire. Adrienne was charged with arson and criminal mischief and was free on bond with an arraignment set for May 25.

JB denied his wife's charge that he used drugs and said, "I've never been on drugs in my life. She just was mad because I wouldn't take her to Brazil." As for the accusations that he beat her and shot at her car, Brown simply replied, "No comment."

When I asked JB if he still loved his wife, he exclaimed in mock surprise, "Are we still in love? You know I love my wife. I love you, too, as a brother in friendship."

Just five days after our conversation, Aiken County sheriff's deputies were heading back to the Brown residence in South Carolina after yet another reported assault on Adrienne.

Ellen Smith, a neighbor of the Brown's, called the Aiken County Sheriff's Department about 1:30 p.m., on Wednesday, May 18, 1988, and said Adrienne had come to her home for help. Jim Strader, South Carolina bureau chief for the *Augusta Herald* and *Augusta Chronicle* would quote Smith saying, "She came up to the house and asked me to call Mr. Hartman [investigator William Hartman] and say that James was beating her again," the neighbor said. "It's very nerve-racking. It just goes on day and night."

Just as deputy Scott Gofoth and investigator Hartman were approaching the Brown house, JB headed out from his long driveway at a high rate of speed. Captain James Whitehurst of the Aiken County Sheriff's Department later said, "He was letting that Lincoln sail," bureau chief Strader quoted Whitehurst in the *Herald*. "They thought it was a B-17 coming out of there."

The officers finally stopped Brown on U.S. Highway 278 at Lewis Road about a mile from his Beech Island home on Douglas Drive. Brown apparently tried to resist arrest, leading the officers to tackle him. His 1983 burgundy Lincoln Town Car was towed to the sheriff's department. The drug PCP was found in the car and in his blood and urine. Brown spent the night in the Aiken County Detention Center and was released the next morning on a bond of $24,218.

Brown pleaded no contest on July 21. Judge James E. Moore sentenced him to two and one-half years of suspended jail time, fined him $1,200, and placed him on probation until he performed a benefit concert for the local Fraternal Order of Police and Helping Hands organizations.

It was pretty clear to local observers and to Brown's friends that he was headed down a self-destructive path, when on Saturday, September 24, 1988, things spiraled out of control at his Executive Office Park office suite.

According to the court testimony of the case published in the *Chronicle*, Brown said the sequence of events began when he was on his way to visit a man who helped take care of his father. However, that really didn't explain why he went into a suite near his own carrying a shotgun and a pistol and confronted attendees at an insurance seminar. He began talking into the seminar's microphone using "threatening and abusive" language and demanded to know who had been using his restroom!

A woman at the seminar phoned the police, and Brown fled the office complex with his shotgun and the restroom keys in his red and white pickup truck. Richmond County Sheriff Department's lieutenant Larry Overstreet was the first to respond, and he tried to stop Brown on Washington Road.

Overstreet followed Brown onto the interstate highway but stopped his pursuit about a mile later at the state line. Brown apparently took the first exit after crossing the Savannah River and passing the South Carolina Welcome Center and turned right onto Martintown Road. That's when North Augusta, South Carolina, police officers Ronald L. Delaughter and William C. Luckey picked up the chase, later testifying that Brown's pickup reached speeds in excess of eighty miles per hour on the four-lane, heavily traveled, highway in a residential area.

Brown pulled into the parking lot of a gasoline station on Martintown Road at Atomic Road but became frightened by the actions of the North Augusta police officers. He later testified, "I was getting ready to get out when he [an officer] started beating on the door and the window." He said his window glass was broken.

"Glass went everywhere, and I knew he was enraged," Brown testified. "I was scared to death. I went to Vietnam, and I wasn't that frightened." He said when shots were fired at his tires, he had never been so scared in his life. Officer Delaughter testified that he and Luckey did shoot out the front tires of the pickup because they thought Brown was trying to run them down.

Brown's pickup then continued on Martintown Road about a mile to its intersection with Gordon Highway. He exited right onto Gordon Highway, crossed the Savannah River again, heading back to Georgia, and exited right onto Broad Street. He then took a left at Broad and sped down the tree-lined, Old Town section of Augusta with Broad feeding into Sand Bar Ferry Road, which leads back to South Carolina. There was no question Brown was trying to get to his home.

By that time, as officers later testified, the disabled pickup truck was leading a procession of fourteen police cars, all with their blue lights and sirens on, at speeds less than thirty miles per hour! It sounds like something out of a redneck comedy movie. But this wasn't funny at all—to the officers or to Brown.

For some reason, Brown turned left onto Courtland Drive into a residential area and then onto Fairhope Street where his pickup ran into a ditch. Augusta police said Brown did resist arrest but only minimum force was used to subdue him. He was taken to the Augusta-Richmond County Law Enforcement Center and charged with having no state license tag, reckless driving, driving with a suspended license, attempting to flee and elude police, carrying a pistol without a license, carrying a deadly weapon to a public gathering, and simple assault.

Brown had $7,978 in cash on him. He used $4,100 to pay his bond for release from the Georgia authorities. Then he waived extradition and was taken to Aiken County Detention Center where he was booked on two counts of assault and battery with intent to kill, failure to stop for blue lights and sirens, and driving under the influence. Bond was set at $21,268 with JB eventually being released to await trial on the South Carolina and Georgia charges.

You would think all of that excitement that Saturday, September 24, 1988, would be a full weekend for most people, but not for James Brown. The very next day on Sunday he was stopped in Augusta by city police and charged with driving under the influence. Arresting officer T. J. Taylor would say, "He was incoherent. He just had his hands up in the air while he was driving down the street."

"He didn't mean no harm," was Adrienne's take on the whole thing. She said that Brown was taking medication for surgery that recently had been performed on his jaw and added, "He's in pain. He's not in his right mind."

For William Glenn of James Brown Enterprises, the weekend of events had posed a real concern as JB's latest European tour was due to start on October 5. Glenn told a reporter, "A million and a half dollars down the drain!"

As it turned out, the courts in Georgia and South Carolina allowed JB to honor his European dates, with the tour actually starting October 11 and ending back in the United States with a concert on November 27 in Boston. Before heading out, he met with reporter Linda Day of the *Chronicle* in his office on September 28 and told her, "Yeah, I have a problem. We all have problems. I need some help."

JB said he would be seeking some professional help but never said during that interview that he actually had a drug problem. He referred to it as a "stress control problem and remarked, "I'm only human. I'm not going to say the devil made me do it. Stress made me do it—S-T-R-E-S-S."

Late on the night of October 14, Adrienne, home alone, called me at the *Chronicle* with the news that she would be checking into an Atlanta hospital the next day to be treated for stress.

"I've got chest pains, and I've got terrible migraine headaches. I can't go on like this," she said. "If they want so say I did something wrong, then let them get it over with and stop using me as a public example because of who I am. . . . The news media has been unfair to me. I couldn't get a fair trial here if I want too. They're making a mockery of me and James. . . . and I've never been in trouble in my life."

She concluded, "All this looks bad what James has done, but nobody should have to be put under this kind of public pressure. My husband is out of surgery [for his teeth] and doing his tours. I'm worried about him. He's worried about me. It's hard on our marriage."

When JB returned from Europe, he was back in the Augusta-Richmond County Civic Center on Sunday, December 4, 1988, for an entertainment disaster called Wrestle-Rock '88, which had been intended to satisfy his South Carolina sentencing from his May 18 assault on Adrienne and possession of PCP by performing a benefit concert for two local nonprofits. (Circuit Judge James E. Moore had imposed as part of the sentence having Brown perform a benefit concert for the local Fraternal Order of Police and Helping Hands organizations.)

The proceeds from the $10 ticket sales to Wrestle-Rock '88 were intended not only for the two organizations but also for Toys for Tots and the Leukemia Society. For a variety of reasons, only four hundred people showed up in the nine-thousand-seat civic center. Reportedly only about sixty of the four hundred seats were paid for. The huge place looked virtually empty, and Brown said he had pumped $40,000 of his own money into the event.

Show promoter Jean Daughtry blamed the civic center

management including difficulties with ticket sales and event scheduling. The show's date was changed several times during the initial negotiations, she said.

The Wrestle-Rock '88 event started about 2 p.m. with a slate of wrestling matches that included the Freebirds and the Rock and Roll Express. Then about 4 p.m. the music began with musicians from the bands of Chicago, Atlanta Rhythm Section, and Lynyrd Skynyrd coming out onstage and jamming for about an hour.

At about 5 p.m. out came JB wearing a white suit, black shirt, and a black bow tie. He thanked the crowd for showing up, launched into "I Got You" and then sang just one more song before telling the sparse crowd good-bye. Apparently, he felt that he had satisfied his sentencing requirement.

Brown tried to be upbeat about the whole thing saying, "The thought was the message. The turnout didn't bother me." The *Chronicle* headline the next day, of course, read, "James Brown 'Feels Good' Despite Turnout." Headline writers just loved to say how good Brown felt.

Someone must not have told Brown he was feeling good, because he was in a South Carolina courtroom less than two weeks later answering to the charges from his September 24 two-state chase.

FOURTEEN

Funeral in the Imperial

When I was in prison, I had all the time to serve God. I'm very deep into the Bible. That's why my songs are about good things, positive things. . . . I organized a choir in prison and showed them how to be professional singers. I found several good voices there. I taught them "God Smiles On Me," "Pass Me Not Oh Gentle Savior," "Jesus Keep Me Near the Cross," and "I've Got Victory in Jesus." Even in my darkest days, I thought that God smiles on me / He has set me free / God has smiled on them / He's been good to me.

—James Brown
December 4, 1984
Augusta Chronicle

In mid-December of 1988, James Brown was standing before a circuit court judge in Aiken, South Carolina, asking the judge not to send him back to jail as the judge was about to recess the court for the day.

Dressed in a light gray suit, dark red shirt, and patterned dark tie, JB had sat through all of the proceedings on Tuesday, December 13, 1988, conducted by Judge Hubert E. Long. Brown, who sat silently with his legal team throughout the day, apparently had been told that the custom of anyone on trial in a South Carolina courts was to be kept in prison during the trial period.

"I don't know the court procedures," Brown was quoted in the *Augusta Chronicle* as saying. "I trust my attorneys to speak with you, but I would request something of you. I only ask that you let me go home. I ask that you trust me to go home, and I'll come back." Unfortunately, Judge Long explained that state law required him to be detained during the trial period once a jury had been sworn in.

"We've got a jury, and we're ready to go to trial in the morning," Long told the entertainer. "If you're not here in the morning, whose fault is it? Mine! You're supposed to be in jail until your trial's completed." Brown's legal team had tried without luck to get the trial moved to another county citing local media coverage that might make a fair trial impossible. But Judge Long noted, "I looked at the [video] tapes, and Mr. Brown does a lot of the talking," referring to the many interviews Brown granted radio, TV, and newspaper reporters between his September arrest and December trial.

Then, Brown's primary defense attorney, Bill Weeks, made several motions trying to get the trial postponed or the charges dismissed, but Judge Long stood firm and eventually told Weeks, "You're asking for the world, and you ain't going to get it."

On Thursday, December 15, 1988, Brown's world of past arrests, PCP drug usage, and running from the law came crashing down with his conviction in Aiken County General Sessions Court for aggravated assault and failure to stop for police. Several people during the trial had testified that Brown's actions were uncharacteristic of him. Al "Sonny" Miller, uncle of Brown's wife, according to the *Augusta Chronicle,* told the court, "He's not really a bad person. It's just the drugs. When he takes the drugs, he gets crazy." Brown's attorney "Buddy" Dallas said, "James Brown—the real James Brown—is a kind and humble man. This is certainly not the rational personality of Mr. Brown."

Before his sentence was imposed, JB—dressed in a brown suit, suede vest, bright blue shirt, and green cowboy scarf around his neck—addressed the court for fifteen minutes. He carried a Bible as he walked back and forth before the judge's bench, and he talked about his humble beginnings, his fame, and his family problems.

"I respect police," he was quoted in the *Chronicle*. "Without them, we have nothing. . . . I didn't see the blue lights when I should have. When I saw them, I said, 'What have you done James Brown? Let it be known that James Brown is a man who wants to do right. [To Judge Long] I just want you [Judge Long] to give me a chance."

The jury's guilty verdict was handed down about 6 p.m. on Thursday, December 15, 1988, but the sentence was not pronounced until about two hours later. Adrienne Brown also had appealed to Judge Long for mercy. She broke down crying and sobbed, "He's all I've got. I'm all he's got."

His attorney, Weeks, appealed to the judge saying, "Your honor, he's not Public Enemy No. 1 (apparently a reference to a James Cagney movie) as the press and people would have you believe. I don't think a substantial sentence of incarceration is going to benefit anyone. Any length of time in jail is going to destroy his career."

It undoubtedly had to be the lowest point in the life of the fifty-five-year-old superstar, and yet in the "long run" it turned out to be one of the best life-changing moments for James Brown. He himself admitted in later years that his time in prison probably saved him for his family and friends.

On Friday, December 16, 1988, JB was taken from the Aiken County Detention Center to the Broad River Correctional Institution in Columbia, South Carolina, about an hour away, for two weeks of "reception and evaluation" before being assigned to his regular prison facility.

Brown subsequently was deemed to be a "suitable candidate" for the minimum security State Park Correctional Center north of Columbia, which mainly housed elderly and handicapped prisoners. Brown, at age fifty-five, was in fact a senior citizen.

In January of 1989, Brown was taken from the center to Richmond County where he received a second, six-year sentence before State Court Judge Gayle B. Hamrick for the September 24 charges against him in Georgia; to run concurrent with the South Carolina sentence.

Brown's attorney, Bill Weeks, had asked Hamrick to consider the sentence imposed by South Carolina along with Brown's age and the fact that all of the September 24 incidents in Georgia and South Carolina had happened within an hour.

"Sometimes it takes a knock on the head before you can get somebody's attention," Weeks told Judge Hamrick. "Well, South Carolina certainly gave him a knock on the head. . . . Very honestly, I think they laid a heavy hammer on him." Before Hamrick's sentencing, JB told the judge, "My life has always been a model [for others], and I just don't feel good about it now."

After his sentencing, Hamrick allowed Brown, under guard, to visit an Augusta dental office where his Atlanta dentist checked to see how he was healing from reconstructive jaw surgery. He then was returned to the State Park Correctional Center. Hamrick later said he allowed the dental visit as it was paid for by Brown and was not a burden to taxpayers.

Brown's other attorney, "Buddy" Dallas, said in spite of the two concurrent six-year sentences in Georgia and South Carolina that Brown remained upbeat. Dallas added, "After twenty-five years without a break," the *Chronicle* quoted him as saying, "he's thoroughly enjoying just coming out of the fast lane. James Brown is just reintroducing himself to James Brown."

One of the most shameful episodes involving the South Carolina correctional system happened on April 27, 1989, when JB was summoned by Circuit Judge Frank Eppes and driven eight miles from his minimum security center to the Richland County Courthouse to sign autographs for about forty people, including Eppes!

"Somebody asked me if I could get him up here to get his autograph and I said I would try," Eppes was quoted as saying in a Knight-Ridder story published on the front page of the *Augusta Herald*. "He was dressed up nice and neat, clean-shaven and bright-eyed—seemed full of life to me." Eppes apparently did not ask Brown to sing or dance.

"I was flabbergasted," said Parker Evatt, South Carolina Department of Corrections commissioner. "What happened is totally irregular."

One of the loudest protests came from Al Sharpton, who had been working tirelessly for Brown's release from prison. He told reporters, "James Brown has done six months, and I think he's done enough. I think this judge has underscored the point I've been making for six months; that this is a judicial joke to continue to hold James Brown."

JB did end up to be a model prisoner during his fifteen months at the State Park Correctional Center and pretty much disappeared from the limelight except for a couple of mentions in the press that Adrienne had visited him in Columbia twice a week or that Sharpton still was fighting for his release. He spent many mornings working in the prison's kitchen and spent many evenings working with the prison's choir.

Then came the news that JB had arrived at the Lower Savannah Work Release Center on Wire Road in Aiken, South Carolina, on Thursday, April 12, 1990, to begin serving out the rest of his incarceration in a work-release program. He was dressed in white wraparound sunglasses, alligator skin cowboy boots, and a black leather outfit.

According to the *Chronicle*, Brown's transfer from the Columbia facility brought him within fifteen miles of his Beech Island residence, but when Brown was asked if he was happy to be home, he threw up his hands and said, "Home?"

Adrienne put it more specifically in saying, "This is not a victory. Changing him from one place to another—from one jail to another—is not a victory. The only victory is when I know James is coming home. He's served too much time for a crime he did not commit."

Ah, it is amazing how much that PCP can erase memory.

The *Augusta Chronicle* told readers that Brown would be assigned to the Aiken-Barnwell Counties Community Action Commission, a social services agency that worked to improve the lives of poor citizens. He also would be speaking to local young folks on the need to stay away from alcohol and illegal drugs.

William Glenn was less than enthusiastic about the news saying in the same article, "I don't see where it's going to do a lot any good. He won't be able to leave and go to work here and put his people back to work, such as the band and hairstylists who are out of work."

Although he was still a prisoner, in early June 1990 Brown was admitted to Aiken Regional Medical Center for extensive dental implants surgery. The South Carolina Department of Corrections said the medical treatment was "beyond the scope" of what the department normally provided for its prisoners and that Brown would be paying for the surgery himself.

The same week that JB was having his surgery, Adrienne was admitted to Roosevelt Hospital in New York for an undisclosed procedure. She asked the hospital to refer all questions to her spokesman, Al Sharpton, but phone calls by the media to Sharpton's office were not returned.

By August 1990, Brown was taking weekend passes to visit his Beech Island home, and by all accounts his relationship with Adrienne returned to the loving one they had when they first met.

On Wednesday, February 27, 1991, James Brown was introduced in a public forum to an important audience, but it wasn't his usual emcee, Danny Ray, doing the introduction before a packed auditorium. His attorney, "Buddy" Dallas, introduced him to the South Carolina Parole Board in Columbia.

"It is my distinct pleasure to introduce you to James Brown; a man that is known locally, nationally, and internationally," Dallas was quoted as saying in a front page story in the *Chronicle*. JB then rose from his seat and spoke into the microphone promising the parole board that, if released, he would be a positive role model for young people.

He said, "I would like to go around to schools and preach about drugs and staying in school. I realize I have more than a normal obligation to humanity, to my country, and last but not least to myself. . . . I respect the law more than a lot of people respect the law."

For about twenty minutes, the parole board heard from Brown; his attorney, Dallas; and another of his attorneys, Reginald Simmons. Then the board endorsed his release. Board chairman, Raymond Rossi, announced that JB was a free man after two years and two months in custody. His parole officially would not expire until October 23, 1993, after which he would be on probation for five years.

He would have to take periodic drug tests, enter a treatment program, and he would have to clear his concert dates with a parole officer as well as obtain permission to leave the United States.

Immediately after hugging his wife, Adrienne; daughter, Deanna; and other family members and friends, JB went to an adjoining room for a press conference with the media from South Carolina, Georgia, North Carolina, and New York who had packed the parole board's hearing room. JB was, of course, asked how he felt, and he replied, "Should I be repetitious? I feel good!"

As to his future, JB said he would rest about three weeks at his Beech Island home before resuming his concerts and other show business activities. He said, "I've got more tours now than I ever had in my life. I just need more James Brown to keep up with it. We've got a lot of plans, recordings, movies." The headline on the front page of the *Chronicle* the next day read, "James Brown Says Freedom 'Feels Good.'"

Back at his Beech Island home after his release, Brown granted an interview with the owner of *Ebony* and *Jet* magazines, Robert

E. Johnson, who later quoted Brown as saying, "My wife stood by me when nearly everybody else deserted me, and I love her for this. We are definitely going to make more time for ourselves."

Adrienne responded, "There's one thing that I've learned from all of this: there ain't no bridge I can't cross and there's nothing I cannot handle that God puts before me and my husband now. . . . Do you realize deep down the humiliation that this man had to go through and how he had to hold his head up and he had to hold back the tears and wave to his fans and the people in prison and show them that he was James Brown."

Just as his arrest in Augusta in the late 1950s had led to an incredible and wonderful period in his life, so it was that his conviction in that same Aiken County courthouse would eventually lead to the rebirth of the Godfather of Soul.

Throughout those prison years, many people would ask me what JB would do when he got out. My response always was the same: He would be huge! I knew if anyone could stage a successful comeback, it would be James Brown. I knew the prison time would just make him more legendary than ever. And that's exactly what happened. For, you see, it was pretty clear that fans of JB's music could not care less about his domestic problems or his prison time.

Brown announced his first major comeback appearance to the world with a press conference in New York City at 11 a.m. on Tuesday, March 26, 1991. But he would talk about it with me the day before at Augusta's Bush Field airport before boarding the private jet sent by the Time-Warner Inc. entertainment conglomerate, which was producing a live, pay-per-view concert to be broadcast on June 10 from Los Angeles's Wiltern Theater, arranged by boxing promoter Butch Lewis.

"It's going to be a very exciting thing," Brown said with a huge smile. He looked absolutely incredible and happier than I had seen him in a long, long time. His entourage also boarding the private jet included his wife, Adrienne, his attorney, Reginald

D. Simmons of Aiken, his friend, Aiken County magistrate Al Bradley, and Bradley's wife, Carol.

The next day in New York City, Brown—wearing a gray suit with a black silk shirt and red tie—would bask in the spotlight again at the news conference before twenty television film crews, lots of photographers, dozens of reporters, and former Heavyweight boxing champions Joe Frazier and Michael Spinks.

He told those attending that he soon would resume touring and that he would begin working on a self-produced album. He added, "I've had two years of not rest but a chance to regroup in my head. I'm gonna have a new sound musically when I come out. It'll be Brown, but it's gonna be some things happening that I never took time to think about," he continued. "In two years [in prison], you can think of a lot of things."

Brown further noted that the jail time didn't get him down and added, "I stayed in shape. . . . I did the one thing we all do when we're in trouble. I went back to God. I found my way to God, all day, every day."

Before leaving on his New York City journey, Brown had been in a very talkative and reflective mood with me at Augusta's airport, the place that in years past had been the starting point for his many world tours.

"We're going to come up with a foundation to help schools a lot," he said. "We're going to help South Carolina, because it's fourth in illiteracy. You know, that's my pet project. We're going to do a scholarship drive to send kids to school. . . . We've got to find ways to help young men who can't go through the regular process because there is no sign of entrepreneurship in their families. We've got to create the *want* again.

"You see, that's the hope factor—a lot of kids don't *want* to be anything. They turn their hats backwards, put on their sneakers, and cut their dungarees and do whatever they feel. . . . There's no church in their lives. They don't even go to that. We've got to bring all of those good values back."

He spoke of the great plans for the future and said he most likely would perform that summer in a benefit show before Great Britain's royal family. "I'm to be there, I believe, with Princess Dee [Diana] and Princess Fergie [Prince Andrew's then wife, Sarah Ferguson] and the Queen Mother—something like a command performance. It's going to be for charity. They need a lot of help over there. We've got a lot of world poverty problems. We've got to help everybody. I don't mind doing it."

He said, on the day before his pay-per-view concert in Los Angeles, he finally was to get his "star" on Hollywood Boulevard, and he was looking forward to a Liberty Festival concert on July 13 at Robert F. Kennedy Stadium in Washington, D.C.

"We're going to brag on the things that are good about America, "cause I see all the things that's happening that's not too good," he said. "We're going to recognize the Kennedys and the Kings. We're going to represent the people that fought and made America more of a better place to live. Hopefully, we'll all join together and make our country something we love instead of something we doubt. We want the young people to know they can be what they want to be, but they first have to want to be something."

Brown was less than enthusiastic about the news that PolyGram Records would be coming out in May with a four-CD box set called *Star Time* containing seventy-one of his songs recorded between 1956 and 1984. It was to have a sixty-eight-page booklet detailing his career with a suggested retail list price of $59.98.

"There's only one thing about PolyGram," JB told me at the airport. "They don't pay me for the new records except songwriting royalties. I hear the new box set is fantastic, but PolyGram hasn't sent me a copy. I recorded over 5,700 songs for PolyGram and wrote over 4,500 of them."

Besides the PolyGram box set coming out in May, Brown got some national TV exposure that same month by appearing on the popular NBC comedy *Amen,* staring Sherman Hemsley (who is known to do his own James Brown impression) in the role of Deacon Frye.

"*Amen* is one of the last of the clean shows the public can watch on television," Brown said. "I'm proud to be doing it. The people on the show are very, very nice and made me feel very, very good doing it." He told me on the phone that he had never met Hemsley, who earlier starred on the TV series *The Jeffersons.*

"My wife knew him, because he's been trying to get me on his show for a long time," Brown added. "He's been getting the musical people on. He had [MC] Hammer on a while back and that was good. Then Hammer was bragging on James Brown, and Sherman wanted me to do the show too. Sherman has been a good supporter. He has done my song *Living in America* on his show and gave me a lot of support when I was in trouble."

Brown told me that he wanted to be positive about the future and put his troubles in the past. "We're too close, Don, for some things that I don't have to try and justify in the past," he said. "I know you and your family, and I think we've known each other long enough that we've been square and you've always tried to broaden that gap. You know what's missing. You've been to Vietnam. You know what we need to do as a people. You know what a family needs to do to come back together, 'cause the American family has slipped apart. We've gotten away from that. We've got to get back to those good old values."

On June 24, 1991, Augustans were treated to the amazing sight of James Brown gleefully dancing and singing in front of the old Silas X. Floyd school and in front of the in-ground fountain in the Eighth Street plaza on the Riverwalk. The occasion was the filming of the music video *Movin' On* for Fragile Films of Los Angeles and Scotti Brothers Records. The video, directed by Jules Lichtman who had directed MC Hammer's *Pray* music video, featured four horn players, three gospel singers, six dancers, and many local Augustans.

That same month, Robert Sandall wrote a long and super complimentary article for the Sunday edition of the London *Times* on June 30, 1991. The article was headlined, "Return of a Soul Survivor," with Sandall noting, "Brown's music is still mainly about live performance. He wrote the book about pop stagecraft, and everybody who is anybody has read it. Carefully.

"In the early 1960s, Mick Jagger sat at his feet at Harlem's Apollo Theater studying his every wiggle and purple cape routine. Today's newest superstar, MC Hammer, shamelessly plagiarizes Brown's choreography. Prince has tried hard to emulate his funk master's hyperactivity theatrical style of presentation. And Michael Jackson has spoken, sort of, about his awed fascination for the frenzied trance states into which Brown works himself on stage."

JB's first American concert after the pay-per-view was on July 20, 1991, for the first "Georgia Festival" in Atlanta-Fulton County Stadium, reuniting him with his friend Little Richard who had guided him on his musical path through that fateful meeting at Bill's Rendezvous Club in Toccoa, Georgia.

One press release stated, "The Georgia Festival marks James Brown's return to the music industry after a series of clashes with the law. Also it's James Brown's first American concert [since being released]. James Brown is Back on the Good Foot as a crusader for a drug-free America."

A few days before the festival, JB was in the office of Georgia governor Zell Miller who presented him with a proclamation praising Brown's "unique brand of funk" that mixes "the sounds of the sacred with the profane and the country corn with the big city hustle."

The Morris News Service story in the *Augusta Chronicle* said Miller called Brown a close personal friend and added, "You've had a wonderful past, and the best is yet to come." The governor was asked if he was surprised to be honoring a man Georgia authorities had jailed, and he replied, "I'm not surprised because I knew the inner man of James Brown, and the inner man is compassionate and a man that's strong and a man that's not going to stay down and that's going to come back. And here he is, bigger and better than ever."

Brown's musical star would continue to climb the rest of 1991 with the release of his back-to-basics, critically praised album *Love Over-Due* containing the notable cuts "(So Tired of Standing Still We Got to) Move On" and "Standing On Higher Ground." Tom Moon wrote in the *Philadelphia Inquirer*, "He's back, he's saying it loud, and he has every reason to be proud."

He also teamed up with MC Hammer to appear on the HBO cable TV show *Influences* aired in September, and the CBS network show *A Party for Richard Pryor* that aired in November. He also was back on the international concert scene with a concert in London's Wembley Arena on Sunday, December 1.

The first Christmas after JB's release was a good one, and I was invited to the annual party JB and his wife threw for his staff, family, and friends at the Sheraton Hotel near Wheeler Road and Bobby Jones Expressway. The roughly one hundred attendees included Al Sharpton and his wife, Kathy Jordan Sharpton, who had been a backup vocalist for Brown, Augusta mayor Charles A. DeVaney, state representative George Brown (no relation), and Atlanta police chief Eldrin Bell.

Also present were three astronauts—Fred Gregory, Marsha Ivens, and William Readdy—and the daughters of Georgia-born astronaut Sonny Carter who passed away the previous April. They were there to honor Brown and his music, which was used to wake up the astronauts in space. Gregory recalled on a recent space mission being awakened to Brown's recording of "Put a Little Love in Your Heart."

Although everything had seemed to be so right in the Brown household during that Christmas season, that proved just the opposite the following year when Brown's staff, family, and friends gathered for the annual holiday party in the ballroom of the Sheraton Augusta Hotel on December 16, 1992.

Among those in attendance would be the Reverend Sharpton and his wife, Kathy, Augusta Mayor Charles A. DeVaney, Georgia state representatives George Brown and Henry Howard, former Augusta Mayor Edward McIntyre, future Augusta mayor Bob Young, Atlanta Police Chief Eldrin Bell, Fort Gordon Commander Major General Robert E. Gray, NASA astronauts Marsha Ivens and William Readdy and musical guests The Chi-Lites.

Guests first noticed something very unusual: JB was there but Adrienne wasn't, and JB seemed to be in a more somber mood than usual; even though he was still smiling as he greeted his Christmas party guests including me.

Key guests were seated at a long table, which was covered with an elegant white tablecloth, placed on a raised platform at one end of the room. It was very noticeable that the place reserved for Adrienne was empty.

Just after midnight as Representative Brown was speaking with the spotlight on him, the door on his left side opened. All eyes turned to the bright light of the open door leading to a hallway as Adrienne walked in wearing garish-looking purplish makeup, a sparkling gold and black dress, and a huge head of hair that looked as if it needed a good combing.

She did not look happy and neither did her husband. She was the focus of all eyes in the room as she stepped up to the higher table level and made her way down to her chair. She ended up sitting between Kathy and Al Sharpton, with Sharpton sitting between her and James.

For a good while, they didn't even look at each other. There was no doubt that something serious was up, and, to Brown watchers, this was a major deal; it was the first public indication since his joyous release from prison that all was not happy in the Brown household.

State Representative Brown, presented James with a proclamation from the Georgia General Assembly honoring him. Atlanta Police Chief Bell also announced the Atlanta city council had voted to make Brown an honorary major on the Atlanta police force. Mayor DeVaney told Brown, "My job tonight is to say thank you. You have indeed overcome a lot of adversities, and you have represented this community in just ways that few people really do, and even though folks have not always been perhaps as nice as they should have been, you never forgot home."

When JB took the microphone, he said, "There's two people a man always has a problem pleasing, but he always tries, and that's God and his wife."

Then Adrienne got up and went to the microphone and said, "I wasn't going to be here tonight, nor was I going to speak, but since I am, ladies, would you mind standing? Wives, mothers . . . They [she said gesturing to the seated men] would be nothing without us." She then went into detail about how, when she met JB on the *Solid Gold* TV show set, his career was at a low point and how she had built him back from nothing. She even said he was "retired" when they met.

> *"I want to say to you," Adrienne continued, "that none of us would be here tonight if two people—I'll take that back, number one, God who brought me and my husband together— resulted in an effort saying, "Well, now, here is a woman who can help me and knows about show business. Maybe we can do it this time.*
>
> *"I always felt he was cheated—cheated because of his color. The man had fought to become the first black man in history, before many of you were born, to get his picture on an album cover. We've come a long way. We have Eddie Murphys. We have Arsenio Halls. We have a mixed room here tonight [white and black guests] with love, and none of this could have taken place without somebody who wouldn't give in or who believed in him. I believed in him. I believe he can make it with or without me now.*

142

"We didn't have money [starting out]. We had to take money with us to pay the band off. We didn't have an entourage. We didn't have dancers. We didn't have a whole lot of things. In fact, a lot of times we couldn't pay for our own plane tickets. But we started this thing back up. Because you know why? Because this man had too much gift to give. I thought to myself, 'If there is a God in Heaven, I want to give him a push.' I hope I didn't push him too hard.

"But I want to say to you, I remember when I was doing everything from packing bags, lugging bags, checking bags, doing hair ten to twelve times a day, ironing clothes, doing everything and the woman remains in the background as her husband goes out, neat as a pin, and ready to take his bows.

"Men, gentlemen, please, I'm just giving you the other side of the story here tonight, and I want to say to you that I want to thank you for being here and seeing how far our family has grown thanks to the effort, every time someone comes aboard, one more believes in us, one sticks by us.

"But throughout all of this, as I had the ladies stand, [and] as the song goes, it's a man's world. You can buck all you want. You can buck all you want, but they're going to do what they want to do. Am I right? Thank you, I'm not preaching, but in order for this story to be told tonight, there is only one thing I have to say. There must always be, from the beginning of time, be a nucleus. The nucleus grows off and separates, separates, separates, and tries to multiply.

"We have tried to multiply, and you know, tried to bring on as many good people that are willing to work as possible as we can handle. I hope with God's help and my husband's success and all of you should be commemorated for sticking in there. Some of you packed your bags when times were hard [saying], 'Oh my God. What's going on here?' But I want to say to you . . . that there's always a story to be told.

"There are always the hard times. It's not as glamorous a life as so many people think it is. There is a lot of hard work. While many of you are sleeping, we're out there working and trying to get to the next gig. And where we find the energy sometimes I don't know. But as Mrs. James Brown or Mrs. Adrienne Brown, I'd like to thank all of you—ladies, gentlemen, distinguished guests—for through the hard times, through the good times, and that's what a family is about. And number one, of course, for Mr. James Brown, my husband, for carrying the load when it sometimes was unfair and me in the background—but you know I'm there."

She ended her remarks to loud applause, cheers, a standing ovation, and a bright, white, toothy smile from her husband who apparently felt another family crisis had passed in that moment.

Even though I was a guest at a private party, the dramatic evening had put me in a very precarious position. I could ignore it and hope that no one in that packed dining room would say anything about that night to anyone outside of that room. But, of course, considering how many politicians and others were there who loved gossip I knew that it would be the main topic of discussion around town the next day.

And, I knew if my bosses at the *Chronicle* learned that I had been there and had observed something newsworthy concerning the Browns and had ignored it, I could be fired. After all, if someone had become very sick in that room and a doctor was present, the doctor could not have ignored it. And, if a crime was being committed in that room, Atlanta Police Chief Bell could not have ignored it.

So, I wrote a brief account of the incident that appeared in the *Chronicle* on page two in the first section on Friday, December 18, 1992. Brown's limousine chauffeur, a friend of mine, reported to me that he had taken the article to Brown in Atlanta and that Brown had laughed. But Adrienne not only didn't laugh, she

▲ The horse-drawn carriage carrying James Brown's casket arrives at the front of the Apollo Theater along 125th Street in New York City on December 28, 2006. *Andrew Davis Tucker*

▲ In this photo reprinted and Web posted around the world, emcee Danny Ray puts a cape over James Brown for the last time on December 30, 2006, at the James Brown Arena. *Chris Thelen*

▲ One of Augusta's largest parades happened on Broad Street on February 4, 1969, when JB returned to the city for a concert benefiting Paine College. He announced that he had enough of living in New York State and planned to return to Augusta. *Lee Downing.*

▶ On May 2, 1972, JB swung by Silas X. Floyd Elementary School in Augusta to try and persuade his favorite teacher, Laura Garvin, not to retire. He always gave much credit to Garvin for inspiring him and included her in many of his proudest Augusta moments. *Lee Downing.*

▲ JB and his wife, Adrienne, on December 26, 1986, donated one of his suits to the Augusta Museum of History. It was accepted by John Reynolds, president of the museum's board of trustees. *Margaret Moore*

▲ JB was playful on his Beech Island property posing for photos on May 13, 1988, in spite of going through domestic problems with his third wife, Adrienne. When I asked him if he still was in love with his wife, JB replied, "You know I love my wife. I love you, too, as a brother in friendship." *Jeff Barnes*

▲ During one of his darkest hours on December 15, 1988, JB leaves the Aiken County, South Carolina, courthouse through a security area with an unidentified officer to begin his jail term. *Steve Thackston*

▼ In his successful hearing before the South Carolina Parole Board gaining his freedom on February 27, 1991, JB sat between his lawyers Buddy Dallas, left, and Reginald Simmons. *Ron Cockerille*

▲ On March 25, 1991, JB shook hands with Bush Field airport employee Robert Bell in Augusta. He was fresh out of jail and bound for a press conference in New York City announcing his comeback Pay-Per-View concert. *Walt Unks*

▶ It was a touching moment when JB leaned over the podium at Augusta's Barton Chapel Elementary School on February 18, 1992, to speak with 7-year-old Brantley Burley. Brown was at the school to deliver an anti-drug message. *Michael Mulvey*

▲ At his annual Christmas party for friends, family, and staff members, JB on December 16, 1992, greeted then Augusta Mayor Charles DeVaney and his wife, Nancy, while the Reverend Al Sharpton stood nearby. *Matthew Craig*

▶ JB's grandson, Jason (Deanna's son), sits in his famous grandfather's lap at the dedication of James Brown Boulevard in Augusta on November 20, 1993. *Eric Olig*

▲ JB performs in the Augusta-Richmond County Civic Center at his "Birthday Bash" on May 3, 1994. Actress Sharon Stone was among the guest stars present at this one. *Blake Madden*

▶ On May 3, 1995, one of JB's guests at his annual "Birthday Bash" in Augusta was rapper/ dancer superstar MC Hammer. The entertainer-turned-preacher would be at JB's third Augusta funeral 11 years later to pay him final tribute. *Carol Cleere*

▲ Country music star and South Carolina native Aaron Tippin on May 3, 1995, hugs JB after inducting him into the South Carolina Music and Entertainment Hall of Fame during the annual James Brown "Birthday Bash." JB's wife, Adrienne, applauds the latest honor for her husband. *Carol Cleere*

▲ Rehearsals, for the privileged few who could get into them, were almost as good as the shows themselves, as JB demonstrated in the Imperial Theatre on March 12, 1996. *Blake Madden*

▲ Who would have expected "white bread," '60s pop singer Pat Boone to record "Papa's Got a Brand New Bag" with the King of Soul at Studio South in Augusta on April 13, 1998. *Brant Sanderlin*

▲ James Brown hugs Augusta Mayor Bob Young on Bell Auditorium's stage on January 4, 1999, to kick-off the mayor's Unity Celebration following the mayor's inauguration. Bob and his wife, Gwen, would be sitting with me at JB's fourth marriage ceremony to Tomi Rae Hynie and at JB's Augusta funeral. *Jeff Janowski*

◀ Children loved JB, and he loved them. Latoya McNeil, 7, of Augusta, ran up and gave him a hug before the start of his toy giveaway on December 23, 1999, at the Imperial Theatre. *Patrick J. Krohn*

▲ JB doing his thing on October 12, 2000, at the Augusta-Richmond County Civic Center (later renamed James Brown Arena). *Michael Holahan*

▼ During another fiery rehearsal, JB danced on October 3, 2001, in the Imperial Theatre with his backup singers, The Bittersweets: from left, Sheila Wheat, Kelly Jarrell, and Candice Hurst. *Andrew Davis Tucker*

▲ One of the blessings of JB's life was his annual toy giveaway before Christmas at the Imperial Theatre. Here, he hands out a basketball on December 19, 2001. The sign promotes JB's radio station WAAW-FM. *Andrew Davis Tucker*

▲ There were times in their lives when James Brown and original Famous Flame Bobby Byrd were on the outs. But mostly they were great friends, as shown during this rehearsal in Augusta's Imperial Theatre on October 4, 2001. *Jeff Barnes*

▲ James Brown loved to have the legendary gospel group Swanee Quintet sing with him. Here he and his wife, Tomi Rae, on November 27, 2002, joined Swanee lead vocalist Percy Griffin during a turkey giveaway at Dyess Park in Augusta. *Annette M. Drowlette*

▲ James Brown II at the Augusta Common on November 15, 2003, shows off some of his own moves watched by his father. Others looking on are his father's road manager Charles Bobbit (red tie) and childhood friend Leon Austin (holding sign). *Michael Holahan*

▼ JB laughs as the crowd cheers for him during James Brown Day festivities at the Augusta Common on November 15, 2003. *Michael Holahan*

▲ One of the happiest and proudest days for James Brown was the unveiling of his statue in the 800 block of Broad Street on May 6, 2005. Standing near him is the Reverend Al Sharpton. *Michael Holahan*

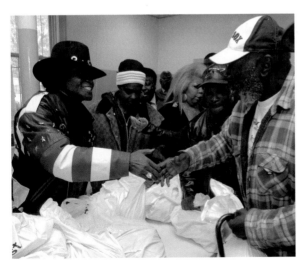

◀ JB loved giving away turkeys before Thanksgiving and toys before Christmas. Here he hands a turkey to Billy Jackson, right, of Augusta at Dyess Park on November 22, 2005, on James Brown Boulevard. *Andrew Davis Tucker*

◀ During his last Augusta performance on May 27, 2006, JB listens to the sax player for Tony Wilson's James Brown Tribute band at the James Brown Soul of America Music Festival at the Augusta Common. *Michael Holahan*

▼ The Augusta Convention & Visitors Bureau contacted me about helping provide information for this 2006 pamphlet showing visitors locations in the Augusta area that are identified with the Godfather of Soul. Pamphlet cover photo: *Robert Seale*

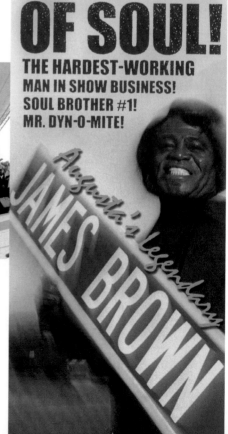

▲ JB's last performance in Augusta came on May 27, 2006, at the James Brown Soul of America Music Festival at the Augusta Common seven months before his death. He looked great even then. *Michael Holahan*

▲ JB returned to the Apollo Theater in Harlem in New York City for a final time on December 28, 2006, for the first of his three funerals. *Andrew Davis Tucker*

◀ Tomi Rae Hynie Brown and her son, James Brown II, arrive at JB's second funeral service (private) on December 29, 2006, at the Carpentersville Baptist Church in North Augusta, South Carolina. *Chris Thelen*

▼ At the third and final funeral for JB, Michael Jackson spoke briefly, flanked by the Reverends Jesse Jackson (to his right), and Al Sharpton at James Brown Arena in Augusta Saturday afternoon December 30, 2006. *Michael Holahan*

◀ This is thought to be the last photo taken of James Brown at his final public appearance on Friday, December 22, 2006, for his annual toy-giveaway at the Imperial Theatre. He is wearing a favorite Western hat that he wore frequently in his final years. *Michael Snyder*

▼ Me visiting JB's statue on New Year's Eve, December 31, 2006, the day after his final funeral. Fans, by this time, had covered it with personal notes, flowers, candles, photos, and other items. *Bennie Brown/Bennie Brown Photography & Video*

▲ Many Augustans who had seen JB in person over the years were among those in line to view his body for the last time at James Brown Arena on December 30, 2006. *Michael Holahan*

pretty much banned me from being in her or her husband's life over the next three years until her death.

Even worse, the black-owned *Augusta Focus* newspaper raked me over the coals with a headline reading "Pimping Mr. Brown." The paper's editor, Frederick Benjamin Sr., wrote in a front page article, "In the world of pimpdom, the *Augusta Chronicle-Herald* wins the title of Mack Daddy Number One. Their tasteless item of December 18 highlighting Adrienne Brown's rambling diatribe against men at Mr. Brown's annual Christmas party missed the point entirely and failed to properly document a grand affair on the local society scene.

"The *Chronicle* pimps [referring to me and my guest, local educator Connie Frierson Ryals] sat on their behinds, ate Mr. Brown's caviar, sipped his fine wine, salivated over all of the genuine attention he was getting and then proceeded to pimp the Godfather of Soul by airing a minor moment of melodrama. Fine journalism!"

Benjamin's article concluded, "It is sad that it is only the black press in Augusta that feels the need to give the brother his due. To the media pimps among us, we can only hope that they grow up and learn some manners."

I suppose Benjamin had missed all the dozens of articles lauding Brown's accomplishments I had written that led to several good things in Brown's life including the special day at the Augusta Riverfront Marina. Years later, I found myself sitting next to Benjamin at another gathering and ended up joking with him about what he had said in his article. He definitely had the right to say what he did, just as I had the right to report the first after-prison crack in the Browns very public marriage.

The cracks continued to grow larger as the Browns' marital problems escalated and became even more public since that initial Christmas incident. Other close friends of JB's also found themselves being cut off from his company as they fell out of favor with Adrienne.

The early part of 1992 found Brown reaping huge honors by receiving the distinguished "Award of Merit" at the nineteenth annual American Music Awards on January 27 in Los Angeles, and the "Lifetime Achievement Award" at the thirty-fourth annual Grammy Awards on February 25 in New York City.

MC Hammer, the American Music Awards show host that year, presented Brown with a trophy that read, "When this unique artist exploded on the scene, his energy and originality captured the music public and inspired so many of his fellow artists. Now, over three decades later, the Godfather of Soul continues to excite the world with his vibrant performances."

Brown later told me, "I tell you, Don, what it did do was make me thank God that people now recognize we are the base of all the music in the world today. The music is American music. We had a diamond in the rough and didn't know it. All these classic acts are more valuable today than they were twenty years ago. They are now putting a stamp on it and saying this is ours, because now it is valuable, valuable, valuable. So it made me feel proud I was around when America finally realized we've got the goose that laid the golden egg when it comes to music."

In the summer of 1993, James suffered a major personal loss with the death of his father, Joseph "Pop" Brown, at the age of eighty-one. His final address in his obituary was 430 Douglas Drive—the home of James and Adrienne—but he died at the U.S. Department of Veterans Affairs Medical Center in Augusta where he had spent his final years.

One can only speculate on what James Brown's life would have been like had Joe Brown not moved his family to Augusta where a better life awaited them all

Pop Brown's funeral was held at 2 p.m. on Wednesday, July 14, 1993, at Trinity Christian Methodist Episcopal Church in Augusta, with the Reverend Aaron Bush officiating. He was buried in Walker Memorial Park in Augusta on Laney-Walker Boulevard.

Although Joe Brown had lived to see his son starting his

comeback, he missed out on seeing "Junior," as he called him, being honored on November 20, 1993, when part of Ninth Street was renamed James Brown Boulevard.

An estimated five thousand people turned out in cold weather for the renaming ceremony, including JB's wife, Adrienne; his mother, Susie; and his childhood friend, Leon Austin. Brown told the crowd, "I thank God for the history to be made here today. I thank God for you, who bought my records, attended my shows and supported me in so many ways. . . . I'll live as long as I can and die when I cannot help it."

About that same time, he told Chick Hernandez of WRDW television station, "America's music is the world's music. I'm an American first. I'm a man. I'm a human being, but I'm an American. Music comes out of America. We control music around the world in the English language. I can't tell you how I got here, and I don't why I'm here, but I know I'm here and I know that I can do good things for other people."

In that same interview he alluded to his past troubles with the law, and said,

I thank God for Augusta being so fair, coming back and recognizing the wrong. . . . I think we understand that all people are not judged by the color of their skin but by the conscience of their character. . . . I don't hold our city or our country responsible, because people are people. If God can forgive, we've got to forgive. . . . If you're being arrested, try and have as many people around you as you can. Do what the officers say. Give them all the cooperation in the world, because there's good and bad in everybody. . . . Let's go forward. May Augusta be proud of itself, proud of the people here. There is a lot of talent here. Let's do it. James Brown represents [that] you can start any place and go as far as you want. I have no bitterness in my heart because I believe in God. I know that God will take care of anything that is not right.

147

He later added,

I'm not a perfect man. Only Jesus Christ was perfect, but I'm a man who wants to do right. And I get on my knees at night and say, "God, forgive me for what I've done wrong and give me another chance at righteousness." I love you out there [television audience]. I love Augusta. I love the CSRA [Central Savannah River Area], and I love the country. I'll always will. I'll keep fighting for those who don't have, the have-nots—white, black, blue, purple, red or orange.

I'm not going to be with you because you're black, or because you're white or because you're Mexican or Italian. I'm going to be with you because you're a human being and if I can help, I want to help, because that's what I'm here for.

Four months after the street was renamed, Adrienne and JB were at it again on Easter Sunday 1994 with the Aiken County sheriff's deputies receiving an anonymous request to respond to a domestic dispute at the Brown's Beech Island ranch home. They found Adrienne suffering from an injured collarbone but unwilling to talk about what had happened. She was treated at Aiken Regional Medical Center and released. No charges were filed in the incident because deputies were unable to find evidence of a fight.

Just a few days later, however, on April 21, 1994, Adrienne reportedly threatened JB with a gun, and Aiken County Family Court judge Larry Inabinet issued a restraining order that directed her to stay away from the Godfather of Soul. Inabinet gave JB sole use of the Beech Island home and ordered the couple to have no further "contact or communication of any disturbing nature." That, of course, had about as much an affect as telling a male hunting dog to stay away from a bitch in heat.

The couple must have gotten back together yet again, because on December 8, 1994, Aiken County sheriff's deputies were back at the Brown household where Adrienne was bleeding from her lips and saying JB had hurt her. She said that he had thrown her to the floor, and that she had hit her face on a chair. He subsequently was charged with domestic violence but told reporters he was innocent.

Brown said his wife has spent most of his money, and that much of their stress was because she wanted to move to Hollywood. Adrienne, in turn, told reporters, "I've taken his womanizing. I've taken his beatings. I can't keep taking the rap for James Brown. I don't want him in jail, but I have drawn the line this time."

She also said, "I've been standing by him all along. I've always dropped the charges in the past when he beat me so now no one believes me any more. Only battered women understand."

Reporters asked a South Carolina parole board spokesman if JB had violated his probation with the latest incident, but the spokesman said it would be unlikely that JB would have to return to prison for the misdemeanor domestic charge.

The following January, the *Chronicle* published a front-page article under the headline, "Browns Nearing Reconciliation, Attorney Says." It quoted Robert Harte, Adrienne's attorney, who said, "She has instructed me to say that she recants anything she said detrimental to him. She is very much in love with James Brown and wants to get to work on restoring their relationship."

In spite of all his troubles, JB still could find the time to be nice to his hometown fans as was demonstrated on August 28, 1994, when he was involved in a minor traffic accident with a bicycle rider in Augusta's upscale Hill residential section. Brown's car, according to the *Augusta Chronicle* report, knocked 42-year-old rider John Nixon to the pavement on Monte Sano Avenue at Henry Street. Nixon refused medical treatment at the scene, police said.

The accident happened near the homes of Maureen and Patrick Claiborne. Their two daughters, Mary Kate, 9, and Megan, 7, and their daughters' across-the-street friend, Mary

Vincent, 8, recognized the singer and all three decided to get his autograph. "The police were asking him questions, but he still couldn't have been nicer to us," Mary Kate told me. "He even signed my autograph 'To Mary Kate, From James "I Feel Good" Brown.' He seemed mad about someone in his family, and he said, 'She'll never get another red cent from me.' I remembered that because I didn't know what a red cent was."

Three months after the traffic incident, Augusta judge Carl C. Brown [no relation] dismissed the traffic charge of failure to yield right of way after JB settled out of court with the bicyclist. Augusta attorney Sam Nicholson, who represented Nixon, said the settlement covered medical expenses and damage to his client's bicycle, but declined to disclose the amount. Nixon did not receive any permanent injuries, the *Chronicle* reported.

In spite of JB and Adrienne having filed for divorce for an uncountable number of times over the years, the Browns got back together. At 4 a.m. on October 31, 1995, Aiken County sheriff's deputies woke up Brown at his Beech Island home, let him get dressed, handcuffed him, and took him to jail on yet another charge from Adrienne that he had beaten her.

In a news conference called the next day, Brown said he was shocked to learn he was going to be taken to jail and even more shocked to learn that deputies were going to handcuff him.

"I started thinking about Rodney King," he said, referring to a black Los Angeles motorist beaten in 1991 by four white policemen. "I felt they would have tried to kill me if I resisted."

Brown was taken to jail and then released on a $940 bond and ordered to appear in court on November 27. He told reporters at his news conference that he had awakened about 4 a.m. on Halloween to the sound of dogs barking and found his wife lying on the floor of her room with her eyes glassy. JB said that he revived her by holding alcohol under her nose. He claimed that he told her if she didn't check into the Betty Ford Center for drug abuse in California within twenty-four hours that he would divorce her.

Nevertheless, it was JB's turn to be hit with a restraining order telling him to stay away from Adrienne. JB also told reporters at the news conference that the incident with the Aiken County deputies had shaken him up so much that he was going to move from Aiken County. Asked where he might go, he replied, "I don't know; somewhere where you're respected."

And as if that wasn't enough fun that week, there was more to come on Thursday, November 2, when forty-five-year-old Adrienne showed up about 4 p.m. at Brown's office complex, which had moved to 1217 West Medical Park Road, near Doctor's Hospital.

The account that JB gave reporters was that he was going through his mail and planning personal appearance dates when he heard that his wife was banging on a back door of his office complex wanting to see him. He said that she was wearing the same nightgown she had on two days earlier on Tuesday morning when she called the deputies to their home. Someone let Mrs. Brown in the back door, and she subsequently locked herself in a bathroom. She was talked into coming out and was taken to Aiken Regional Medical Center.

JB said he never saw his wife while she was inside the building before being taken away to the hospital. Douglas Meltzer of the syndicated TV show *A Current Affair,* however, was present and later said that he [Meltzer] did see Adrienne in the nightgown looking disheveled.

"I think she felt bad because of what she said [in Tuesday's charges], and she probably came back to say she was sorry," JB told reporters. "She was trying to make amends. But now the only amends she has to make is to save her life. She's very ill, and the marriage is over."

He further said that his wife was addicted to drugs and added, "Any time she needs those drugs, she will do anything to get them. Once when I was combing my hair, she slapped me across the face with a razor. The 911 system gives her control over me." He explained much of her drug addiction by saying that Adrienne had undergone surgery seventeen times and was taking twenty different pills.

When asked why didn't the Browns just divorce and be rid of each other, JB replied, "Love has a way of trying to justify any wounds that can't be treated. That's what happened. . . . It's love between us."

Brown's longtime lawyer, "Buddy" Dallas, put in his two cents, telling reporters, "We saw today the condition of Mrs. Brown, and the problem he has had to contend with. He has tried to cover this up and protect her. But he can't protect her anymore. No man should be found guilty on the word of a person who is sick."

Later in November, Adrienne did enter the Betty Ford Clinic in California and was subsequently reunited with JB. The two seemed happy once again at their annual Christmas party in the Sheraton Augusta Hotel that December.

The Reverend Larry Fryer, pastor of Augusta's Trinity Christian Methodist Episcopal Church, remembered JB sitting in Fryer's office at the church and saying, "Reverend Fryer, I love my wife, and I want to do whatever I can to better my marriage. With God as my helper, I will." Fryer saw the Browns kissing, hugging, and talking at their Christmas party and remembered them looking "different from any other time I saw them."

Fryer said, that near the end of the evening, he knelt beside Adrienne's chair. She took his hand and said, "My husband and I will be all right," and she added, "I'll talk with you later." But she never did.

On New Year's Eve, James and Adrienne danced onstage at his concert in Greenwood, South Carolina, about an hour from Augusta and their Beech Island home and sang "Auld Lang Syne." The next day she flew from Augusta to California for elective cosmetic surgery scheduled on January 4 in a plastic surgeon's office in Los Angeles. After the surgery she went to the Hidden Garden, an upscale after-care facility in Beverly Hills, where she suffered cardiac arrest and died on January 6. She was transported to Century City Hospital where she was dead on arrival.

JB immediately flew to Los Angeles where a private service was held in the Old North Church at Forest Lawn Memorial Park in Hollywood Hills. The brief service included a message Brown wrote that said, "Dear Adrienne, Honey my life will never be the same, wait for me. I want to be the first guest on your TV show in heaven. Yours always, James."

Among those attending the service was Little Richard Penniman, media personalities Casey and Jean Kasem, actress Ja'Net DuBois, and actor Dan Aykroyd. Penniman was quoted in *Jet* magazine as saying before going into the church, "James is hurt, but he is a believer in God. I started him in the business. I met Adrienne when she was doing makeup on *Solid Gold*. James is a survivor. I'm sure he's leaning on God."

Brown escorted his wife's body back to Augusta where her public funeral was held on January 16, 1996, in the Imperial Theatre on Broad Street with more than eight hundred people in attendance. Adrienne's casket was placed on the center of the stage, surrounded by gold, purple, and red flowers. Her portrait hung in the center of the stage over it. C. A. Reid Sr. Memorial Funeral Home, which eleven years later would handle JB's own service, handled the Augusta funeral arrangements for Adrienne.

Nancy Thurmond, estranged wife of U.S. senator Strom Thurmond, from Edgefield, South Carolina, spoke at the service, saying Adrienne "had as big a heart as anyone." Al Sharpton remembered Adrienne as one of the few people around Brown who "didn't want anything from him except [for him] to be James Brown."

Adrienne's uncle, Al Miller, said after the funeral that he had seen his niece the day before she died at the center where she was recovering and she was very happy. He told the *National Enquirer* that her last words to him were, "I love James, and I want to look beautiful when I leave here."

The Swanee Quintet was approaching the edge of the Imperial stage singing "One Day at a Time," when JB threw his right arm into the air and slumped in his front-row center seat. Several people jumped to his aid, with some offering him handkerchiefs and others fanning him with the funeral programs.

After the service, the funeral procession left the Imperial Theatre—where JB in later years would continue to rehearse his world concert tours—and proceeded to Walker Memorial Park cemetery on Laney-Walker Boulevard near Bobby Jones Expressway. And there Adrienne was laid to her eternal rest on the right side of JB's father.

The large, flat metal gravestone says a lot about how James actually felt about Adrienne:

ADRIENNE LOIS BROWN
MARCH 9, 1950
JANUARY 6, 1996

She was a native of Los Angeles, California, and the wife of the Godfather of Soul, James Brown. She was a dedicated fighter for humanity, a lover of all people, a person who was not given the world on a silver platter but one who had to work very long and hard for everything she accomplished in life. She was a diligent partner, a lady, a lover and a friend.

Because of the love and affection she had for her father-in-law, Joseph "Pop" Brown, she requested to be buried next to him here in Augusta to be joined by her husband, James Brown, and everyone in his family.

"I will always have everlasting love for you, and I will never forget you. I know one day we will meet each other again, me, you, Pop and all of our family. We will be together again forever. With tears in my eyes and pain in my heart, I say so long."

Your "Woggar"
James
I love you, sugar!!!

154

FIFTEEN

The Godfather Gets Respect

You can't beat the system. Get an education and
work hard. That's the only way to do it. I don't call it
show biz. I made it in show b-u-s-i-n-e-s-s. My act is
10 percent show. The rest is business. You always
know, regardless of what they say, when something
really bad happens, you can always count on God.
. . . Don't let anybody put you down. Just sit down
and keep trying hard.

—James Brown
February 10, 1993
Augusta Chronicle, in a talk
to Youth Development Center inmates

James Brown's dark period of grieving after Adrienne's death
began lifting with noticeable public appearances at which he
seemed to rediscover the personal happiness that had eluded him
for so long.

On Sunday night, April 7, 1996, while the golfing world was
turning its attention to the Augusta National Golf Club for the
annual Masters Tournament, Brown was turning his attention to
a small, jazz-themed, restaurant/nightclub at 1855 Central Avenue
called Le Café Du Teau owned by self-taught chef Don du Teau.

Playing there was a talented jazz-country-rock pianist whom
Brown enjoyed for a long time named Buzz Clifford with his Last
Bohemian Quartet members David Heath on bass guitar, Ricky
Channin on drums, and Steve Mitchell on electric guitar. Brown
frequently told friends, business associates, and media members
how he wanted to help Clifford achieve his own level of fame.

Clifford and his band, Wildlife, had been a featured group at the James Brown Day celebration at Augusta's Riverfront Marina.

It was places like the Word of Mouth Café (formerly Goldsmith's) on Broad Street or the Green Jacket restaurant on Washington Road where Brown felt comfortable when he was at home. Usually he was seen at those places in a relaxed mood.

At some point during his evening at Le Café Du Teau, according to the *Augusta Focus*, JB decided to get up onstage and sing. He sang the ballad "Time after Time" (that he usually performed at private occasions) and the more upbeat "Route 66," which he played on the piano complete with throwing a knee in the air. He also sang a medley of his hits including "Cold Sweat" and "Bewildered." Clifford later called Brown's impromptu performance his "finest appearance ever!" in a small venue.

As it is for a lot of people, music was a healing tonic for James Brown who had made it through his two years of incarceration leading the prison choir in classic hymns.

The next month James Brown was back in his element in the Augusta-Richmond County Civic Center for his annual party celebrating his sixty-third birthday on May 3. The Birthday Bash '96 events had started in 1994. Tickets for the 1996 celebration were $12 and $15 for general admission seats, and $25 for VIP reserved floor seats that included a reception with the guest stars. Leading the main band onstage that night would be keyboardist Buzz Clifford.

Sawyer Brown, the country music group that first hit stardom on Ed McMahon's *Star Search* TV talent show, was there, with keyboardist Gregg "Hobie" Hubbard saying, "We're really just flattered he asked us to be here. That's wild to us that he knows who we are."

Isaac Hayes, who had been inducted into the Georgia Music Hall of Fame two years earlier, was another guest star at the '96 bash. Talking about Brown, Hayes told reporters, "He's the greatest entertainer I've ever seen. The first time I saw Mr. Brown

in concert [in Memphis in the early 1960s] I was in awe. My mouth
was hanging open. He had two drummers, and he did the tricks
with the microphone and the robes."

Rock guitarist Slash of Guns 'N' Roses heavy rock band also
was there and commented on being onstage with the Godfather,
"Just getting up and playing with him, I'm intimidated as hell.
He's where I got my guitar style from."

Hosting the '96 Birthday Bash was WFXA-FM radio personality Minnesota Fats and Brown's daughter, Deanna, along
with nationally know comedian Steve Harvey, host of the TV
program *Showtime at the Apollo*. They introduced JB who came
out onstage and launched into a bilingual version of "Georgia
(on My Mind)" with Brown singing and dancing with Taiwanese
Augusta businesswoman Sho-Ane, owner of a dress-making shop
on Broad Street.

The song was followed by Reverend Larry Fryer who read
a brief tribute to Adrienne Brown. JB performed several of his
hits, including "Living in America," "Try Me," and "Get Up Offa
That Thing" before introducing his former bass guitarist Bootsy
Collins wearing his trademark star-shaped sunglasses.

"He's like Elvis, but he's our black Elvis and he's still here,"
Collins had said before the show.

Another unusual part of the evening was when several
professional football stars joined Brown onstage to record live the
song "NFL James" that was to be a track on a CD called *NFL
Jams*, featuring songs performed by National Football League
players and rhythm and blues singers. The CD eventually did
come out, but, if a track was recorded with Brown that night, it
was not included on that CD.

Brown's star continued to rise in 1996, and he continued to
seem extremely happy. The brand new Georgia Music Hall of
Fame building opened in downtown Macon on Saturday night,
September 21, 1996. Brown did not attend, but his spirit definitely
was there that night along with many people who had crossed his

path in some way such as former WIBB-AM announcer Charles "Big Saul" Greene, who forty years earlier was the engineer for Brown's first and history-making session of "Please, Please, Please" at WIBB.

Also present that night were Ramblin' Tommy Scott from Toccoa and original Famous Flame, Bobby Byrd, and the guy who told Brown and Byrd they needed to go to Macon—Little Richard.

Brown ended 1996 by doing something that gave him much pleasure each year for the rest of his life: distributing Thanksgiving turkeys to needy citizens at Dyess Park on James Brown Boulevard on Saturday afternoon, November 26. He was wearing a red, white, and blue, American flag-style jacket that he loved to wear, and he often gave huge hugs to his hometown supporters who truly loved and respected him.

On January 6, 1997, the first anniversary of Adrienne's death, James Brown was in his Augusta radio station talking with reporter Lori Weichman of the *Augusta Chronicle* about his upcoming appearance that month on January 26 at the Super Bowl in New Orleans. "You don't get a show bigger than the Super Bowl ever," he said. "The good thing about it is, they all know James Brown."

He told Weichman that he had observed Adrienne's death by placing flowers at her grave. JB added, "All the things I accomplished in the past 15 years, she had something to do with it."

On a brighter note, he said that it appeared a movie about his life would be in the works with three production companies—Universal Studios, Walt Disney Studios, and another headed by producer Brian Grazer—expressing interest. Brown said he wouldn't mind if Eddie Murphy portrayed him as a young man, but he wanted to portray himself at the end of the film.

"I'm not James Brown," he told Weichman philosophically. "James Brown is a condition over the years. James Brown is a religious atmosphere that has been to create good will. James Brown is showing that everybody can do it."

On Friday, January 10, 1997, JB finally got his "star" on the Hollywood Walk of Fame. He told reporters that he would be kicking off his fortieth anniversary tour on his birthday, May 3.

During the Super Bowl halftime show, Brown appeared with the Blues Brothers duo, consisting of Dan Aykroyd and actor John Goodman, known for his father role on the *Roseanne* TV comedy, who took the Blues Brothers part of the late John Belushi. The two also joined Brown on May 2 at the new House of Blues nightclub in Myrtle Beach, South Carolina, of which Aykroyd was a part owner. They were also with JB again the next day for his Birthday Bash '97 in Bell Auditorium

Jim Belushi, actor and brother of the late John Belushi, also was dressed in Blues Brothers dark glasses, hat, and dark blue suit. He and Goodman clowned and danced with soul legend Eddie Floyd who came onstage to join them in singing Floyd's classic hit "Knock on Wood."

Aykroyd told the *Chronicle* that he was grateful that JB always gave them credit for resurrecting him from a low point in his career. But Aykroyd added, "He's always been very gracious about crediting us with some kind of help, but I kind of think a talent like James Brown never goes away."

Before launching into the Blues Brothers trademark song "(I'm a) Soul Man," Aykroyd told the audience, "We would like to dedicate this next song to the Godfather of funk, R&B, soul, hip-hop, and all great music. He truly is a Soul Man."

One interesting guest at Brown's party was TV talk show host Rolanda Watts, whom James had proposed to—possibly jokingly, possibly not—on her TV program. She appeared onstage with Brown's daughters, Yamma and Deanna, and teased the crowd asking "Do you think I should marry James Brown?" The audience, as signified by their yeas and nays, apparently were divided on the subject.

It was the last of Brown's Birthday Bashes, as Augustans would learn the next year in April when Brown's attorney, "Buddy" Dallas, revealed that the event had been costing Brown between $50,000 and $100,000 each year since it began in 1994.

It was also revealed that the 1997 bash was a financial and personal disappointment with only 1,246 people attending the roughly half-full auditorium that had been the scene of so many Brown sold-out concert triumphs in the 1960s.

"A man's never a legend in his hometown," Dallas said, even though that really wasn't true considering how many times Brown had been honored in the past in Augusta and how many times he would be honored in the future.

On March 26, JB dropped by the Georgia State Capitol in Atlanta where he met with governor Zell Miller (who profiled James in his book, *They Heard Georgia Singing*). He was introduced to the state representatives in the Georgia House chambers by representative Henry Howard of Augusta (who today is buried a few feet away from Adrienne and Joe "Pop" Brown) and was introduced to the state senators by senator Charles Walker of Augusta (who later found himself in prison serving several years after being convicted of mail fraud, tax evasion, and conspiracy.)

During his House appearance, Brown asked the legislators to turn to the left and to the right and tell their fellow representative they loved them. Morris News Service quoted Brown as telling the senators, "I thank God for the fact that we can make up. I'm thankful that we can recognize we're family." Brown reportedly was mobbed by legislators, staffers, and lobbyists who wanted their photos taken with him.

In late October 1997, JB and his entourage left for a ten-day Japanese tour that was to be followed by performances in Chile, Argentina, Brazil, and Canada. He had been rehearsing the tour for several months on the stage of the Imperial Theatre, which must have been a strange, or maybe comforting, feeling knowing that Adrienne's casket had been on that same stage the previous year.

"I've got to get my Japanese [language] together," Brown told *Chronicle* reporter Willie Mae Worthey outside the World Ribs, Wings and Things restaurant on East Boundary then co-owned by JB and son-in-law Shawn Thomas. "All the shows over there are sold out, and that's a blessing. They want the funk, and we're not ashamed to play it and tell them where it's from."

The year 1998 started out rough with Aiken County sheriff's deputies back at Brown's Beech Island home on January 15 where they found marijuana and confiscated a .30-caliber Winchester rifle and a .22-caliber semiautomatic handgun. They took him into custody on a probate judge's order as a "mental transport" but let him check into Charter Rivers Behavioral Health Systems in Columbia, South Carolina, where he stayed six nights.

On Tuesday, January 27, sheriff's officials asked him to come to the sheriff's office in Aiken to be charged with two counts of unlawful use of a firearm while under the influence of alcohol or a controlled substance, and simple possession of marijuana, all misdemeanors.

"We knew where we could probably find Mr. Brown, and we really wanted to make it as convenient for all parties involved as possible," department spokesman Lieutenant Michael Frank said of the arrest procedure. Brown did appear about 2 p.m. that Tuesday, went before the Aiken County Magistrate Court and was subsequently released on bond.

And late that afternoon, Brown was found with his band at the Studio South recording studio on Peach Orchard Road rehearsing for an upcoming world tour. He told a *Chronicle* reporter that night at T-Bonz restaurant on Washington Road that he smoked a small amount of marijuana for medicinal purposes.

"I have bad eyes," he said. "It was just a little tiny bit. It wasn't even a misdemeanor—it should've been in recorder's court." He shrugged off having the weapons saying, "I got to have protection. I have guns, and I'm gonna keep on having guns. Thank God it's a free country."

His stay at Charter Rivers in Columbia was attributed to his becoming addicted to painkillers after suffering a stage injury in Florida. He blamed one of his daughters (who was not named in the newspaper account) for hospitalizing him against his will and for calling the police on him.

"My daughter made a mistake," he said. "She should have just called me and asked if she could come over and check on me, but she called the police. Then they came and asked me if I would go to the hospital, and I didn't want to say no."

On March 13, an Aiken County circuit court judge fined Brown $1,100 on the charges and ordered him to complete a ninety-day drug treatment program. And, about one month after that, who should team up with Brown at Studio South in Augusta but none other than 1960s "white bread" ballad singer Pat Boone!

"Who would have thought?" Brown said in what surely was an understatement. Boone had come to Augusta to record "Papa's Got a Brand New Bag" with Brown for an album of classic, rhythm and blues songs. Boone said he was also recording with the Four Tops, Smokey Robinson, Sister Sledge, and the Temptations. Brown said it was appropriate Boone was including that particular song on the album and noted, "That was the beginning of funk in 1965. That started the whole thing."

One thing Brown still wasn't ready to give up was his annual toy giveaway in the Imperial Theatre. So it was, on Tuesday, December 22, 1998, that his stretch limo pulled up in front of the Imperial in a space that had been reserved for it. Out stepped JB wearing a red leather suit and silver-tipped black cowboy boots. Parents with children, as usual, had been waiting patiently in line for several hours.

Around 11:30 a.m., children were led through the lobby of the theater and handed a plastic bag with a toy and a dollar bill; all the toys were gone thirty minutes later. The remaining children each were given a dollar. It was estimated that toys totaling $5,000 in value and about $400 in cash were given away that day.

162

The toys had been donated by several local organizations, including New Hope Community Center, radio station WAAW, Hobbytown USA, the Augusta Lynx ice hockey team, Shoney's restaurants, Southern Travel, and Georgia Bank and Trust. Those attending his annual Christmas parties at the Sheraton always were urged to bring a gift for the toy giveaway.

It was easy for critics to say that others gave the turkeys and toys that JB handed out each Thanksgiving and Christmas, but, as for the bottom line, it was James's celebrity status and kind nature that prompted those donations to benefit those less fortunate in the area.

"We do it every year because I was once one of those kids out there," Brown said, motioning to the long line that stretched almost a block from the Imperial to Seventh Street. Ten years later in December 2006, he would make his last toy giveaway and his last public appearance in the Imperial, dying three days afterward.

The last year of JB's last full decade again would be filled with lots of highs and relatively few lows.

St. Clair Pinckney Jr., Brown's great tenor saxophonist from Augusta who was part of Brown's great funk period and played on such memorable albums as *Black Caesar* and *The Payback*, died on February 11, 1999, in Atlanta and was buried at Forest Lawn Memorial Garden in the Atlanta area. There was no mention in the obituary that was published in the *Chronicle* that he had played in Brown's band.

The next month on St. Patrick's Day, Brown was back in the Imperial wearing a green suit and rehearsing yet another world tour that would take him to Helsinki in Finland, and Oslo in Norway, with a stop in Spain before heading back to the states for concerts in San Francisco and Las Vegas. He would be doing his usual past hits but also new songs from his *I'm Back* CD released the previous November.

"It's fantastic—it's the biggest album I've ever had," he said to *Chronicle* reporter Jessica Rinck. "The new album, surprisingly,

I thank God for. Would you record somebody sixty-five years old?" He was also happy that the just-released Mel Gibson movie *Payback* took its name from his Augusta-recorded album.

He talked briefly about all the good things happening in his life and said, "I'm real business. With a seventh-grade education and a shoe-shine box, I had to be real business. Since 1965, it's been all about James Brown and thanking God."

Brown really must have been thanking God in June when it was disclosed that New York bond dealer David Pullman had managed to get an undisclosed Wall Street financial institution to lend Brown $30 million in exchange for future royalties earned by his recording catalog. Pullman earlier had arranged a similar $55 million bond transaction for rock star David Bowie.

According to the news account, the Brown bonds were priced to yield the lending institution 7.98 percent a year with the cost to Brown being 8 percent to 10 percent annually. The short end of the story was Brown would be receiving advance funds for the future earnings of his songwriting and other creative royalties rather than waiting several years down the road for them to be paid. In other words, Brown would be set financially for the rest of his life.

That same month Brown performed at the JVC Jazz Festival in Avery Fisher Hall in New York City, with reviewer Ann Powers lauding his performance in the *New York Times* on June 28, 1999. She wrote about his amazing revue with its break-dancing twins, a magician who poured champagne from a newspaper, an interpretive dancer, six backup singers, Brown's fifteen-piece band, and the two onstage appearances of Al Sharpton who did the funky chicken dance during one and led a prayer during the other.

According to Powers, at one point Brown ordered his fans, "Everyone, turn to the person next to you and say 'I love you.' Start loving each other and respect yourself!"

The next month would be another high for James Brown near Rome, New York, as he enthusiastically opened the Woodstock '99 music festival on July 23. It was billed as a celebration of peace and love and intended as a nostalgic re-creation of the original 1969 Woodstock (New York) festival. More than two hundred thousand fans poured into the site with thousands managing to get in for free.

In spite of intense heat, Brown and his Soul Generals band performed "Cold Sweat."

SIXTEEN

More Famous Flames as His Office Burns

God had a special job for me. He gave me a talent
to relate to people of all cultures. I found that the
common denominator among people was love.
Because regardless of all the obstacles we fight,
the social problems and the poverty problems, it
all boils down to the love factor. And I believe I was
able to create that in my life.

—James Brown
January 1991
Introduction to *Star Time*

So many good things that JB tried to create with his fame and
money were just not meant to be, such as the destruction by
fire of his ultradeluxe Third World nightclub in October 1973.
That same sense of loss, of watching a dream and lots of hard
work go up in smoke, happened to him again years later when
firefighters responded to a blaze at his Augusta office complex
about 9:30 p.m. on Friday, April 28, 2000.

And even more crushing for JB than the personal loss was the
fact that arson was behind the destruction of his James Brown
Enterprises offices.

"What has occurred really is an outrage," said his attorney
and longtime friend, "Buddy" Dallas told *Augusta Chronicle*
reporter Johnny Edwards.

Reportedly destroyed in the blaze were master tapes of
unreleased recordings, including sessions taped at Studio South
in Augusta as well as a live concert at the Apollo Theater in New
York City.

Other irreplaceable items was the preacher's robe that JB wore in *The Blues Brothers* movie, capes worn in concerts, gold records, detailed information about his concert tours and the programming of WAAW-FM radio station that he had bought, a photo of the Apollo astronauts who played "I Got You" in space, a pair of boxing gloves from the set of *Rocky IV*, other priceless photos, and a ceremonial American Indian headdress that was given to him by the Connecticut Pequot tribe that made him an honorary member.

Lieutenant G. B. Hannan, an Augusta-Richmond County Fire Department investigator, said in his findings published in the *Augusta Chronicle* that a fire accelerant—"probably petroleum-based"—was found in several places in the halls and rooms. The front door was discovered to have been left unlocked and a burglar alarm didn't go off.

"This will break Mr. Brown's heart," said Colonel Jim Vause, president of Liberty Security, which was handling protection for Brown. "He gives so much to the community. It would break his heart if someone did this intentionally. There was a lot of his life stored in that building." Vause later reported that firefighters managed to save some valuables but he did not know which ones.

Brown was given the bad news as he stepped off a stage from a concert in Virginia. Reportedly, his first question was if anyone had been hurt.

Upon returning to Augusta, Brown looked over the damage and said it wasn't as bad as he expected. Fire investigator Hannan later said—that had firefighters not extinguished the blaze so quickly—authorities might not have discovered it was the work of foul play. Hannan added, "They had planned for us not to see the things that we see now."

Brown offered a $20,000 reward for information leading to the arrest and conviction of the arsonist or arsonists. Brown's attorney, Dallas, had supper at an Augusta restaurant with the singer on the night of May 3 to celebrate Brown's sixty-seventh birthday. Dallas said afterward, "Knowing him as I know him, I have been able to sense the intense personal hurt."

That intense personal hurt would turn into an even deeper emotional experience for JB when he learned a few weeks later who actually had done the horrible deed. His nightclub fire had produced no known culprits even though arson had been suspected. But thirty-nine-year-old Richard Glenn, the head of security for James Brown Enterprises and the son of his cousin, childhood buddy, and vice president of operations, William Glenn, was eventually charged with and convicted of setting the fire.

Major Ken Autry of the Richmond County Sheriff's Department said that Glenn had started the fire to destroy documents connecting him to a forged $75,000 check that Glenn had stolen from his boss.

Investigator Richard Roundtree said Glenn took a check for $75,000 issued on April 7 by the Pepsi soft drink company for an endorsement, opened an account at a Georgia Bank and Trust branch in Augusta, and on April 14 deposited the check. Between the deposit and the fire Glenn withdrew $35,000 from the account and deposited it into his personal account at Regions Bank.

At Glenn's home, investigators seized $35,000. They also seized another $11,000 in two bank accounts. Glenn subsequently was charged with arson, first degree forgery, and theft by taking. It was Glenn's third forgery charge, and he had served time in prison in 1996 and 1997 for violating probation from his 1992 forgery conviction.

"Buddy" Dallas told Johnny Edwards of the *Augusta Chronicle* that Glenn had worked more than five years for Brown as head of security for James Brown Enterprises and, to a lesser extent, for Brown's personal security. "This is incredible," Dallas said, "How does one bite the hand that feeds him? . . . This will be hard for [JB] to believe, but then I'm sure it was hard for Julius Caesar, too."

In late September, Brown announced that he was planning to move his offices into the former First Federal Savings and Loan

Association building on the northeast corner of 10th and Broad streets. The forty-year-old, four-story building in more recent years had been used by the Bankers First Corporation and later by U.S. District Court. Brown was said to have paid approximately $1 million for the building. His radio station, WAAW-FM was located a block away in space leased in the former H. L. Green building.

For whatever reason, Brown never moved into the building.

In mid-October 2000, Brown was planning a triumphant return to the Augusta-Richmond County Civic Center. Earlier in the year, he had taken the same show to France, England, Germany, Morocco, Sweden, and Japan.

Brown told Steven Uhles, entertainment writer for the *Chronicle*, "We go around the world and sell out everywhere we go, but Augusta hasn't seen James Brown's show in a long time." He later added, "I want the people to realize that we do a clean show; a show without vulgarity. This is a show for the whole family. This is a wholesome show, and we're proud to be a part of that."

He talked about his influence on other music stars, telling Uhles, "We started it all. We started hip-hop, disco, all the rappers. Everybody is into James Brown. . . . When Frank Sinatra, God bless him, was still around, George Michael called him and told him he had just cut a James Brown record. Mr. Sinatra told him, 'That's not new. Everybody copies James Brown.'"

But the triumphant return to Augusta was not meant to be. Only seventeen hundred tickets sold for the proposed concert in the nine-thousand-seat facility.

Uhles, in a later article headlined "To Its Shame, Augusta Snubs Musical Legend," noted that Brown's concert was competing that night with a gospel show next door in Bell Auditorium and a rock show at Augusta State University, but, even if all those people had come to the civic center, it still would be only half full.

169

"I have to wonder what was more important to Augustans than seeing Mr. Brown, an artist who sells out much larger venues everywhere he plays and has built a reputation on spirited live performances. Was 'Must-See TV' that important?" Uhles asked his readers.

"Leading his instrument-toting troops into battle like a funky field marshal, the gold bedecked Mr. Brown and his scarlet-clad warriors leave an audience gasping," Uhles wrote. "An artist who recognizes that you are only as good as those around you, Mr. Brown's current company consists of crack players who gel as a band and function admirably when asked to solo. But, of course, we wouldn't know about that in Augusta, now would we?"

Civic Center general manager Reggie Williams also remarked, "I can't figure Augusta out. The crowd at his concert was 75 percent white. The next night, at the Lynx [ice hockey] game, it was announced that Mr. Brown would not be performing the national anthem, and the crowd cheered. I can't figure it out."

In November, Brown's spirits were lifted by his annual turkey giveaway at Dyess Park on Wednesday, November 22, 2000. More than three hundred people lined up by 10:30 a.m. for the more than eight hundred turkeys donated by fifteen organizations and individuals, including Comcast Cable TV, Suntrust Bank, A World of Music instrument dealer, and Augusta Mayor Bob Young and his wife, Gwen Fulcher Young.

Brown told Clarissa J. Walker of the *Chronicle* that his commitment to feeding needy souls at Thanksgiving was more important than whatever some Augustans might think of him. "People need to eat first. It's God's temple, and we need to keep it in good shape. . . . We just love people, and we love what we are doing. We thank God for people are doing good things for us. We can't thank them enough. The more we give, the more we receive."

Joann McBride, a resident of the Sunset Homes housing project, said, "I think that's lovely and it helps people who are in need. I think that [Brown] is a loving person for doing what he is doing, giving to the neighborhood. Regardless of what people say, he is still standing out there, still being strong for us."

Just a few weeks later, JB was wearing a Christmas stocking hat and his red leather suit and cowboy boots in the Imperial Theatre on Friday, December 22, 2000, to pass out toys to needy children as he had done for the past seven years. This time, JB decided to do more than just give away toys. He also wanted to perform for the children, many of whom were seeing the Godfather of Soul for the first time.

The theater's curtain opened and JB broke into a medley of his hits including "Please, Please, Please" and "Merry Christmas Baby." He even brought some of the children onstage to show off their own dancing skills. He loved the attention, as many children ran up to hug him. "God makes me do this," he said. "We've got to raise money so we can keep doing this fine work."

According to estimates, organizers helped Brown distribute toys that day to more than one thousand children. Among those passing out toys were Brown's daughter, Deanna, and his longtime friend, show emcee, and cape thrower, Danny Ray.

Sixty-eight-year-old Brown spent the summer of 2001 heavily touring with show dates in June in Los Angeles, Monterey, and Anaheim, California; Anchorage and Fairbanks, Alaska; Merrillville and Indianapolis, Indiana; Milwaukee, Wisconsin; Sterling Heights, Michigan; and Ottawa, Canada.

He spent the month of August overseas with shows in Brno, Chezkoslavakia; Istanbul, Turkey; Gosport and Aberdeen, United Kingdom; Cologne, Germany; Monte Carlo, Monaco; Colmar, France; Leuven, Belgium; and Ahaus, Germany.

Elif Crawford, Brown's personal office assistant for his last eight years, recalls that JB never let up on his expectations of those working for him and those who had other dealings with him. "There was no room for saying, 'I'm sorry,'" she recalled. "You had to be one step ahead of him for getting things done."

Papa again had a brand new bag that year thanks to the collaboration of a young man who truly loved James Brown and was in obvious awe of his persona and music and —that young man was Derrick Monk, an Oakland, California, native who had moved to Augusta about ten years earlier. His résumé included winning talent night on the televised *Showtime at the Apollo* program; doing production work with rapper MC Hammer and the rhythm and blues group Immature; and producing Brown's 1998 classic funk album *I'm Back*.

Monk produced *The Merry Christmas Album* of seasonal songs that he and Brown cowrote, and, in early 2001, he cowrote and produced Brown recording a song called "School In, Peace" in which Brown repeats the phrase, "Killing is out. / School is in." It was inspired by news reports of students being killed by other students and was intended for an upcoming Brown album called *The Next Step*.

I had a memorable, unexpected encounter with JB that fall. I hadn't spoken to him in several years—not since the Adrienne Brown Christmas blowup.

Then on Tuesday, October 2, I walked behind the buildings of the *Chronicle* and Morris Communications Corporation to put some papers in my car, which was parked in a lot behind the Imperial Theatre. There, near the theater's rear stage door, I saw JB standing with about ten other guys. I impulsively yelled out "JB !!"

He glanced in my direction with a startled look and then broke into a big grin. I headed over to him with a big smile and shook his hand. And do you know what his first words to me after those divided years were? He asked enthusiastically, "How's your father doing?" I told him that my dad was doing well and I just had been with him the previous Sunday.

He then turned to the guys, who were his band members, and said, "This is Mr. Rhodes. He saw me in Vietnam." James never got over that I was there for his Long Binh USO show. He then introduced every one of the band members by name, and told me to drop by his rehearsals that were under way in the Imperial whenever I wanted.

So, about 4:45 p.m. that same day and also the next day, I ended up sitting on metal folding chairs on the stage in the wings, just off stage left, between his show announcer and cape thrower Danny Ray and his longtime childhood friend Leon Austin, who had taught JB, the "right way to play a piano."

They weren't the only cool folks present in the Imperial that afternoon for the band rehearsal. Tomi Rae Hynie was there, looking after her and James's son, James Joseph Brown II, born a few months earlier on June 11. JB told me that he and Tomi Rae would wed soon. "Don't forget to send me an invitation to that," I replied. The sixty-eight-year-old entertainer beamed at the infant sitting in a child's carseat beside his redheaded mother and remarked, "I'm very proud of him."

During the rehearsal, Hynie sang a rocking version of "Can't Turn You Loose" and an emotionally charged version of "This Bitter Earth." Other highlights for me that afternoon was JB doing "Please, Please, Please" and "Killing Is Out" ("for the *Chronicle*," as he would say).

A special surprise at the rehearsal were Bobby and Vicki Byrd. I had not crossed their path since being introduced to them by Little Richard several years earlier on the opening night of the Georgia Music Hall of Fame. Both were looking great and happy and said they were back doing some show dates with Brown's revue.

Also at the rehearsal Bobby sang "I Know You Got Soul" and "Get On Up" (which he had cowritten with Brown). Vicki would sing the Otis Redding-Aretha Franklin classic "Respect" in her wonderful voice that made it clear why JB always said she was the best female vocalist ever in his bands.

"We got our big start in Macon, thanks to Little Richard, whom we met in Toccoa," Bobby told me during a rehearsal break. "I think music has a lot of do with Mr. Brown and Little Richard being so happy and still being so strong today. That's what they live by. I don't think there's anything else they ever wanted to do. Nothing but music."

Emcee Danny Ray even got to rehearse some, saying in that familiar voice of his, "The James Brown Enterprises proudly presents the *Jaaaaaaaymes* Brown Show. Featuring Miss Tomi Rae, the Bittersweets, R. J., Miss Sara Reya, and, of, course, the Godfather of Soul himself, Mr. *Jaaaaaaaaaaaaymes* Brown. Standing in the spotlight are a group of young men who have given the world some of the greatest soul talent. So, put your hands together and welcome the Soul Generals." The band then launched into a funky number.

Brown turned to me several times during that rehearsal and talked directly to me while most of the band members, dancers, and singers watched. It was an odd feeling. And, quite possibly just in my honor, Brown got Byrd to sing some of the old stuff that they sang in their beginning Famous Flames days in Toccoa, including "One Mint Julep" and "Deep Blue Sea."

"This is what we used to do called Do Wop years ago. I mean we really had to sing," Brown said before going into "Don't Do It" with the lines, "If what they are saying is true, / that you and I are through, / if you leave me pretty baby, / I'll have bread without no meat. / Don't do it. Don't do it."

He then added, "That's the 5 Royales. A lot of our stuff came from the 5 Royales 'cause them cats were gospel singers, but they pronounced it different. . . . We're doing these things because I think it's a little nice to explain what we are about. . . . We really had to sing then."

After the rehearsal, JB wanted to talk about his new single that was being referred to in the press as *Killing Is Out, School Is In*. Brown said of the kids against kids violence that inspired the song, "'I've never seen it this bad. I pray for the families.'"

He then introduced me to the song's producer and cowriter, Derrick Monk, who said, "This record is about the violence and

174

terrorism going on in America, but we're focusing more on our future, which is the youth. Mr. Brown has been doing this song everywhere in concert, and the response has been great. People are singing and chanting it back. It's unbelievable the way it's catching on like wildfire."

Just a few weeks earlier, JB had presented President George W. Bush with a T-shirt proclaiming, "Killing Is Out—School Is In—James Brown." The presentation was made during a ceremony in the East Room of the White House honoring Brown and other black musicians. The Imperial rehearsal took place just a few weeks after the September 11, 2001, terrorist attacks on the World Trade Center and the Pentagon, and Brown told me that he had been getting overwhelming responses with his song *Living in America* that he had recorded in 1986.

"PolyGram Records wants me to record it over again," Brown said. "My band, led by Hollie Farris, now plays it better than the way it was originally cut." Farris was standing nearby and he told me, "You should hear him [Brown] sing 'God Bless America.'" Brown turned to Farris and said, "Oh, you liked that the other night? You going to put an arrangement on that for me?"

The bandleader smiled and said, "Sure," to which Brown said, "We've done 'God Bless America' before, but we have become really conscious of what is happening (in this country), and we really did it right the other night. You see, most people in America still aren't conscious of the fact that we're at war. We're at war! W-A-R! War. We've got to change our whole program. What our country did not do, we've got to do it now. Every American— regardless of his origin, where he came from—every American today are kin to each other. And we've got to come together and do something about it."

Before that afternoon was over, Brown as usual told me to be sure and say hello to my Aiken County building inspector father, Ollen. I held up my cassette tape recorder and said, "You tell him," and Brown went, "Mr. Rhodes, this is James Brown saying hello. I've got your big head son here. You know I love him, and I love you and I thank you for all the fine things you did for me and my home."

James Brown ended 2001 with one of the greatest shows of his life, and I was lucky to be there for it: his fourth marriage ceremony. He was sixty-eight and his new bride and featured vocalist, Tomi Rae Hynie, was thirty-two. Their son was six months old and was held by Tomi Rae's mother during the ceremony.

My partner, Eddie Smith, and I were right behind her, and sitting in the folding chairs on our row next to the sunken bar were Augusta mayor Bob Young and his wife, Gwen, and to their immediate left Bobby and Vicki Byrd.

The forty-five-minute ceremony in Brown's Beech Island home was conducted by the Reverend Larry Fryer (remember his role in counseling James and Adrienne Brown in the final years of Adrienne's life?).

Tomi Rae wore a white satin gown with a flowing train, large white bridal veil, and held a bouquet of white roses. She later told the *National Enquirer*, "It was a beautiful wedding. As we made our vows, our baby son looked up at us and gurgled with joy. I'm on Cloud Nine."

JB was dressed in black shoes, a pinstriped black suit with tails going almost to the floor, black vest, dark purple shirt, and black bow tie with two white roses in his left lapel. His hair, as usual, was immaculately coiffed.

The wedding reception at the home was lavish with a large buffet of salmon, shrimp, steak, and other goodies. It was a joyous affair with Buzz Clifford and Derrick Monk performing along with great organ playing by Leon Austin.

Just as he had done at the Green Jacket restaurant years earlier for the anniversary celebration of his friends Flo and Don Carter, JB took the microphone early in the evening and sang to his bride the Sammy Cahn and Julie Styne song "Time after Time," which contains the lyrics, "I only know what I know, / the passing years will show, / you've kept my love so young, so new. / And time after time, / you'll hear me say that I'm, / so lucky to be loving you."

Apparently the marriage did not receive the approval of the entire Brown family. One of JB's daughters was overheard telling another guest, "I hate her. I hate her. I hate her."

Just a few days after the marriage, JB and Tomi Rae were at the Imperial Theatre on December 19 for yet another toy giveaway to needy children. They looked extremely happy and left soon afterward for a honeymoon in Las Vegas, San Francisco, and Los Angeles before heading for a New Year's Eve show with the Soul Generals and other Brown revue members in Honolulu, Hawaii.

Unfortunately, the happiness would not last.

SEVENTEEN

Keeping on the Good Foot: 2002–2004

USA TODAY newspaper reporter:
"What's the best concert you ever gave?"
James Brown: "The last one I did."

At the beginning of 2002, James Brown was back in a courtroom in Los Angeles. This time, he was facing a $1 million sexual harassment lawsuit filed by thirty-six-year-old Lisa Ross Agbalaya, a former model and married mother of three, who had been fired after serving as the West Coast president of James Brown Enterprises.

She contended that, during a business trip to Augusta in 1999, her sixty-six-year-old boss had attacked her in his Beech Island home by grabbing her by the hips and pulling her close to him. She told the Los Angeles Superior Court that, after rejecting his advances, JB closed the California offices where she had been employed for seven years and where she had been making $750 per week.

Her lawsuit filed in May 2000 said, "*Sex Machine* is more than simply a title to one of James Brown's many hit records. It would also appear to be a description of James Brown the man." Brown was present throughout the week-long trial and contended that he was innocent. He told the jury, "She's a married woman, and I wouldn't do that."

He also told reporters outside the courtroom, "I'm trying not to get angry about all of this, but I think the case is crazy, and I am deeply hurt. All my life, I've always tried to be the good guy and help people."

Brown said that he was never alone with Agbalaya at his office in Augusta or home in Beech Island. His legal team called several of his employees to the stand to testify to that. Agbalaya's attorney, Shelly McMillan, later said, "Every one of the witnesses who got up here to corroborate Mr. Brown's version . . . is on Mr. Brown's payroll. Each one has a motive to lie based on their regular paycheck from Mr. Brown."

The jury, however, agreed with Brown's version and cleared him of sexual harassment and infliction of emotional distress allegations. The jury, however, did award Agbalaya $40,000 in damages for wrongful termination. "The bottom line is: I know what James Brown did, and he knows what he did," Agbalaya told reporters after the trial ended. "You know, we can get as many witnesses to say whatever, but he knows and I know."

As if being sued by his former employee on the West Coast wasn't bad enough, in early 2002 Brown's two daughters from his second marriage, thirty-three-year-old Deanna Brown Thomas, and twenty-nine-year-old Yamma Brown Lumar, began proceedings to sue their own father! The two claimed they had a hand in cowriting at least twenty-three of Brown's songs in the 1970s while they still were children but had not been paid any royalties for those songs.

According to the suit their father began retaining their royalties when they were minors but he failed to pay them any of that money or allow the royalties to go directly to them.

Brown's attorney, "Buddy" Dallas, told me that the daughters' lawsuit against their father eventually was settled for $250,000. Three sources very close to JB told me that in the final week of his life, Brown told each of them, "I'll never forgive my daughters for them suing me."

April 2002 was a much better month for JB who was honored in his native state with governor Jim Hodges officially proclaiming Brown as "South Carolina's Godfather of Soul" for his musical contributions to the state's history. Brown celebrated with a brief concert, performing "I Got You" on the steps of the South Carolina statehouse in Columbia backed by a group called the

Sensational Epics, while lawmakers, state employees, and tourists watched.

As his sixty-ninth birthday approached, Brown was back in Europe conquering one city after another.

In March, I received an e-mail from John Havard, development associate producer at Diverse North Ltd., based at Stonyroyd House in Leeds, England. He told me that the company was interested in doing a film documentary about JB and asked some questions about JB's early life in Augusta and what buildings and other places still existed from those days.

In late April, I was allowed to attend three days of rehearsals by JB with his band and dancers and singers in the Imperial Theatre where I was told that the revue was headed the next week for England and Scotland. JB was scheduled to perform on his May 3rd birthday in Brighton. I e-mailed Havard and told him that JB was heading that way, and it would be a good opportunity for his film crew to talk with him.

And I added that I even told JB during the rehearsals about Diverse North's desire; wanting to make the documentary. He replied, "Lots of people want to do one." Filmmaker Havard immediately wrote back, "By a strange twist of fate, JB is playing in Leeds, my home town and where Diverse North our company is based, on May 4th! Who would have thought the links between Leeds and Augusta could be so strong! It would be a terrific privilege if we could have the opportunity to meet JB, even if just for five minutes to make his acquaintance. . . . Leeds isn't a very big place, so it would be a terrific waste to miss the opportunity."

Thanks to JB's friend and road manager, Charles Bobbit, Havard did get to meet with JB in person. Bobbit told Havard the key was having something to offer that really interested JB. Havard and his associates told JB and Bobbit they would present their ideas in writing and get back to them at a stop in London while JB still was on tour in about three or four weeks. The documentary, however, as best I can tell never materialized.

In spite of the federal lawsuit by his two daughters in September, JB ended 2002 doing what he loved to do: giving out turkeys at Thanksgiving and toys at Christmas.

He was back at Dyess Park on James Brown Boulevard on Wednesday, November 27, wearing a brown Western hat with a leather and metal band and grinning from ear to ear as Percy Griffin, lead singer of the Swanee Quintet, sang a traditional gospel song. He was joined at the park by his wife, Tomi Rae, Leon Austin, Elif Crawford, and others.

The only sad note that day was a small story published in the *Chronicle* in which Charles Bobbit, had confirmed to the *Philadelphia Inquirer* that Brown had been suffering from diabetes and circulation problems in his legs that had gone undiagnosed for years.

"He doesn't take insulin, but he does take pills," Bobbit disclosed. He said that at a recent concert in Seattle, Washington, Brown had to be taken by wheelchair from the stage to his limousine because of a prior injury. "He slipped and fell getting off a plane in Augusta, and his ankle really swelled up," Bobbit said.

Nevertheless, on Friday, December 20, 2002, in the front hallway of the Imperial Theatre was JB was shaking hands with four-year-old Christian Daniels who was wearing a red and white stocking cap and had just received a bicycle. Brown had a look of compassion on his face as he bent over to shake hands. The boy had a look of awe even though he could not possibly comprehend who this generous man dressed in his nice suit really was. It was a toss-up on who was the happiest.

On March 3, 2003, James Brown was at Augusta's Bush Field airport but wasn't there to catch a flight as usual. This time he was lending his support to the inauguration of Continental Express Airlines' direct flights between Augusta and Newark, New Jersey. Augusta mayor Bob Young flew up that morning to Newark's Liberty International Airport and returned to Augusta with

Newark mayor Sharp James. And who was there to welcome the Newark mayor to Augusta? James Brown dressed in a black suit and dark red shirt.

"I think this will help bring business back and gives us a chance to be better connected with the rest of the country," Brown said. Now, if any words in the English language best described JB's life work, it definitely was those two: *better connected*, whether applied to people, show business, or new airlines routes.

Over the years in Augusta, I saw firsthand how better connected Brown became in spite of all the nasty headlines, the multiple wives, the suing children, or the record companies that seemed to care less and less.

On April 26, 2003, that was proven even truer when I received this simple e-mail from a fan who wrote: "Dear Mr. Rhodes! I can't give my regards to Mr. Brown by mail 'coz I can't wright [*sic*] in English. Please send my best regards to James Brown on his 70th anniversary [birthday] on May 3. I am his hottest fan in Russia. To be continued further by me, I hope it will be possible directly to Mr. Brown. Yours sincerely, Ilya Schallmann, Russia, Karzan."

My, God! Was James Brown really turning seventy years old? Yes, and he would be celebrating it with a performance at the House of Blues in Lake Buena Vista, Florida. He spent the rest of that May performing in Little Rock, Arkansas; Montgomery, Alabama; at Battery Park in New York City; and in Dover and Asbury Park, New Jersey.

He spent June at the massive Bonnaroo Music Festival in Manchester, Tennessee; and performed in Santa Rosa, and Saratoga, and Del Mar, California; Jacksonville, Oregon; and in Chandler, Arizona.

And in July he would be in Duanesburg, New York, followed the rest of the month by concerts at Royal Albert Hall in London; Kings Dock in Liverpool; and the Pori Jazz Festival in Pori, Finland, where a wonderful, warm photo was taken of

Tarja Halonen, the matronly looking, belly-dancing president of Finland, dancing onstage with James Brown in his Soul Generals suit. The crowd chanted, "Tarja! Tarja! Tarja!"

And more concerts would follow throughout the rest of the year at JB's always unrelenting pace. However, he told *USA Today* reporter Steve Jones, just before his seventieth birthday, "I know my [performing] days are numbered. . . . When you see me on that stage—all that energy lasts just for the time I'm up there. When I get off that stage, I'm in trouble. But I have to do it. These young kids, they like to see me do the things I used to do because they've heard all about it."

No one knew there was serious trouble between JB and Tomi Rae until July 21, 2003, when JB took out a full-page advertisement in the show business magazine *Variety* saying that because of their "heavy, demanding tour schedule," JB and his wife had decided to go their separate ways.

In an odd touch, even for JB, the announcement was accompanied by a photo taken at Walt Disney World of JB and Tomi Rae smiling broadly with their son; JB was standing in the middle with one arm stretched behind his wife and the other behind the Disney costumed character Goofy.

The *National Enquirer* printed the news with a headline reading: "The Untold Story of James Brown's Split with Young Wife—He thinks she's married to another man, sources say." The article contended that Tomi Rae married Javed Ahmed on February 17, 1997, but never obtained a divorce. JB's attorney back home, "Buddy" Dallas, also was caught by surprise with the news and told the *Enquirer*, "The first I heard about a divorce was on TV. If he was divorcing Tomi Rae, he would have had me draw up the papers. He mentioned nothing to me."

As if the troubles with Tomi Rae were not enough, someone else close to him wanted some of the songwriting royalties just as his daughters, Deanna and Yamma, had sought. This time the person seeking money from JB's music was longtime friend and

Famous Flames cofounder Bobby Byrd. Byrd claimed Brown owed him millions from his creative roles in past Brown hit singles and albums.

The efforts of Bobby and his wife, Vicki, to collect the royalties had shifted into high gear in 1987 when they heard Eric B. & Rakim's rap hit "I Know You Got Soul" that "sampled" (used a segment of) Byrd's recording of the song in Rakin's version. The song itself had been co-authored by JB and Byrd. This also is the song I heard JB and Bobby sing in the Imperial Theatre during a band rehearsal.

The Byrds approached Universal Music Group, which had bought the catalogs of the King and Smah labels, but were told that Byrd's royalties were sent to Brown. They talked with Brown, but he apparently denied ever receiving the monies. The Byrds further pursued the affair with Universal Music reportedly offering them $60,000, which they rejected. They filed suit in 2002 against Universal Music Group in federal court in New York City, but the suit was dismissed because of the statute of limitations. The Byrds filed an appeal.

Byrd talked with Nekesa Mumbi Moody of the Associated Press about how he wanted his due in royalties and how his mother had helped Brown after he was released from the youth detention center.

"My mom had five children, and as far as she was concerned, he was the sixth," Byrd said. "He was my brother. I mean, he was really, really, really wonderful. We had some times together. Then we started making records."

Byrd again contended that all of the Flames had a part in cowriting their first recording success, "Please, Please, Please," but only Brown and former Flame Johnny Terry had been given legal credit as the song's writers. Byrd said he didn't protest legally earlier because he was making money touring with Brown and didn't want to "rock the boat."

Byrd acknowledged that he did get writer's royalties from

other hits that he cowrote with Brown, but he was not getting artist royalties from the recordings themselves.

Brown eventually reconciled with Byrd just as he also did with Tomi Rae, and JB and Byrd were back together onstage in Augusta on Saturday, November 15, 2003, at the Augusta Common park in the 800 block of Broad Street.

The city was officially recognizing Brown as one of the 2003 Kennedy Center honorees for his contributions to American performing arts. The official ceremony and tribute show was scheduled for December 7 in Washington, D.C.

It was a beautiful, sunny, pleasant afternoon in Augusta. Brown was joined by Leon Austin, Charles Bobbit, former Atlanta police chief Eldrin Bell, and Brown's family members, including his "wife" and young son.

Several hundred people were waiting at the Common when Brown arrived in a purple two-piece suit. Master of ceremonies, Danny Ray, announced, "Ladies and gentlemen, the hardest-working man in show business, James Brown."

Brown was presented a key to the city by mayor Bob Young, who announced that a statue of Brown's image would be dedicated the following May on JB's seventy-first birthday during a music festival that would also be named for James Brown. The mayor additionally announced that all of Ninth Street would be named for JB (a couple of blocks had kept the name of Ninth Street when the avenue was named James Brown Boulevard in 1993).

I was standing next to JB in a small tent behind the stage when he was shown a small, clay model of the proposed statue for the first time.

JB looked at the figure—standing erect with a big, floor-length cape, huge shock of hair, and its left hand clasped to its chest holding a microphone—and proclaimed, "Looks like Thomas Jefferson! Looks like Thomas Jefferson!" And he was right. It did look a lot like the statue at the Jefferson Memorial in Washington, D.C.

During the ceremony onstage at the Common, Brown announced and he and Tomi Rae wanted to convert his old Silas X. Floyd Elementary School into a training facility for young musicians.

"I thank God for everything," he told entertainment writer Steven Uhles of the *Augusta Chronicle* a few days earlier. "I thank God three times. I thank God. I thank God. I thank God. These are some very good things that are happening, and I have been working very hard.

"I want to see things come together [in Augusta] while I'm still living," he said. "I may not look like I'm seventy, but I am in show business, so I know how to freshen up. I want people in Augusta to take advantage of me while I'm still here. Utilize this face. It's not that pretty, but everyone knows it, and I want to add, to contribute locally."

In talking about the impending Kennedy Center honor, Brown told Uhles, "I was able to give music to the have-nots." He said, "Give them some music to call their own. I was able to take what was once considered ethnic or race music and make it the No. 1 music in the world. And my contribution happened because people accepted me. [My first hit] "Please, Please, Please" let me in."

During the conversation, Uhles wrote that Brown glanced at a photograph of his late father wearing his Navy uniform and remarked, "Let's not forget God, who watches over us while we sleep. Let's not forget our country, who tries to protect us. Let's not forget the people losing their lives abroad, on both sides. Let's not forget these people, who are doing so much."

When Thanksgiving 2003 rolled around, JB could not do what he loved doing almost more than anything else in the world because he was booked for a concert overseas. So he called up his old friend, Al Sharpton, and told him to drop whatever he was doing and be at the giveaway, even though Sharpton that year was a Democratic presidential candidate.

"He never forgot the days when he didn't have a turkey," Sharpton later said at Dyess Park. Sharpton said Brown had approached him backstage at the Apollo Theater about standing in for him. "I said I'd do it," Sharpton recalled. "He's like my father."

While the Swanee Quintet sang gospel songs, Sharpton was observed tapping his foot to the beat. The local Popeye's restaurants assisted for the first time providing 650 turkeys and packages of Cajun rice and biscuits.

Tomi Rae and JB continued to show up together the rest of the year. Tomi Rae was his special guest on December 7, 2003, when he was honored by the Kennedy Center along with violinist Itzhak Perlman, movie and stage director Mike Nichols, Grand Ole Opry star Loretta Lynn, and film, stage, and television comedian Carol Burnett.

For the show tribute that was televised later, the honorees and their special guests sat in the center balcony box with U.S. President George W. Bush and First Lady Laura Bush. Also joining JB and Tomi Rae that special evening was Al Sharpton.

The night before the tribute show was taped in the Kennedy Center, the actual awards ceremony took place in the Benjamin Franklin State Dining Room at the Department of State. The affair was hosted by secretary of state Colin L. Powell.

Nichols was the first to be honored, followed by Brown, with Secretary of State Powell remarking:

> *For five decades, the creative explosions in popular music caused by Mr. Dynamite, James Brown, have reverberated around the globe. I listened to James's R&B hits in the 1950s. So did a teenager named Mick Jagger.*
>
> *In the 1960s, I recall his soul music pouring out of Army hootches in Vietnam. In the '70s and '80s, my kids listened to James and a whole new generation of artists listened, artists whose style and music were sparked by his innovations. And*

now my grandkids and folks such as Eminem and LL Cool J and so many others are into rap and hip-hop. They are only the latest detonations from the global chain reaction that James ignited half a century ago. And who can forget his marvelous dance moves: the spin, the shuffle, the moonwalk. I was going to do it. But [my wife] Alma said no. She said, one, I might embarrass myself, but I also might hurt myself.

James, you know, I really could use you. I could use you on those diplomatic conferences that I have to go to, sitting there all day long as I did earlier this week in the Netherlands and in Brussels, meetings that went on forever and ever. Man, you could have livened up things at the end of a long day, when we're all dying to reach an agreement on something! I can just see you now, jumping up, throwing off the cape. 'Get up! Get up! Get up offa that thing! Please, please, please, let me see it!'

Godfather, I hereby appoint you Secretary of Soul and Foreign Minister of Funk. And I thank you.

Tomi Rae wasn't exactly thanking JB the next month when their marital problems exploded on the morning of Wednesday, January 28, 2004. The Aiken County Sheriff's Department received a 911 call at 10:48 a.m. from Tomi Rae at their Douglas Drive home in Beech Island.

Aiken County sheriff Mike Hunt later said that two deputies opened the front door when they couldn't get an answer and encountered Mrs. Brown, who said her husband had pushed her to the floor during an argument. Tomi Rae had scratches and bruises on her right arm and hip. She was taken by ambulance to the Medical College of Georgia hospital in Augusta. The sheriff said JB was cooperative when he was arrested.

He was taken to the Aiken County Detention Center and charged with a single count of misdemeanor criminal domestic violence. He spent Wednesday night in the center before being released the next day on bond.

Sheriff's department spokesman Lieutenant Michael Frank said the nature of the couple's argument "was personal and not something we will disclose." The *Chronicle* noted that JB in 2003 had received a full pardon from the South Carolina Department of Probation, Parole, and Pardon Services for his 1988 weapons and assault convictions.

The *Augusta Chronicle*'s editorial page subsequently published its opinion of the latest Brown episode noting, "People all over the globe love Brown's music and idolize his persona. They don't understand why this beloved figure isn't more revered in his own hometown. The answer is, although he's done much to make our community proud of him including many personal and generous kindnesses, he's also done much to bring shame on himself: weapons and assault convictions, domestic violence arrests, problems with drugs, more than two years in prison. Whenever Brown is on top of the world, he does something to knock himself down."

The editorial observed that a statue was being made of JB and added, "Before we go and put his image in bronze, it would sure be nice if he'd sculpt that image a bit more into something worth honoring."

In spite of their troubles, early April found JB on a tour of Australia with Tomi Rae performing in his revue. But during that tour, she was asked to leave, which she later said was because of her questionable marriage situation.

Tomi Rae called *Chronicle* writer Steven Uhles from Australia and told him that in spite of her problems that she still wanted to reconcile with JB.

"I was told not to talk to the press by my attorneys, but I'm tired of hiding," she was quoted as saying. "I don't want to go blow a bomb on my husband, and I don't want to put my husband down. I love my husband and I believe he deserves every honor he gets." She said the argument on January 28 had not developed over her questionable marriage status but came about from something more basic.

"That weekend, you might remember, there was no electricity [due to an ice storm]," Tomi Rae told Uhles. "We had gone for three days with no power and no heat and we were freezing to death. Mr. Brown woke up that morning disheveled and I wanted to leave. I wasn't allowed to. That's when I made the 911 call, that's when the chair was raised over my head and that's when the police came."

Tomi Rae said even then she tried to look out for JB and tried to give the deputies a comb for JB and some clean clothes so he wouldn't look as bad as the mug shot later showed. "I asked them not to take the Godfather out looking like that," she said.

And she told Uhles that she didn't think her marriage to Javed Ahmed was legal, which is why she went ahead with the wedding ceremony to JB. "That was an illegal marriage that lasted for three days and was annulled," she added. "It was done under the pretense of a man trying to stay in the country, which I didn't know. It was never consummated. . . . As far as I'm concerned, I'm not leaving my husband, and we're not leaving Augusta."

Besides the Australian tour in early April 2004, JB spent February through June performing in New York, Florida, California, Arizona, Washington state, Michigan, Illinois, and Ontario, Canada. He launched another grueling overseas tour in June (now at age seventy-one) that included: June 24, in Dublin, Ireland; June 28, Manchester, England; June 30, Glasgow, Scotland; July 2, London, England; July 3, Paris, France; July 5, Munich, Germany; July 11, The Hague, Netherlands; and July 13, Bonn, Germany.

Almost everywhere he went, JB was the toast of Europe and was showered with glowing reviews. That summer also marked fifty-five years after the summer when JB had broken into the cars on Broad Street and his life took a different direction.

"Jump back and kiss yourself two times because James Brown, The Godfather of Soul, played Vicar Street to three generations of dedicated fans last night," the Web site ShowbizIreland.com reported on his Dublin concert. "The crowd screamed as the living legend which is James Brown glided across the floor on Vicar Street. . . . One of the greatest showmen to ever grace a stage, James still has the energy and moves to keep his fans from three generations on their feet and getting down to his many hits."

Leon McDermott wrote in the Glasgow *Sunday Herald*, "In a silver and grey suit, his hair an immobile helmet that looks bound by a good liter of hair spray, he's still got the Brown smile, a wide, blinding grin that says he's here to entertain."

Yet, in late November, he told Jane Stevenson of the *Toronto Sun* by phone during a stop in Belgium, "Once I finish in Canada I will probably go into semi-retirement, I don't know." He performed in Toronto as apart of a nine-city Canadian tour that wrapped up December 8.

"I think I need to back off while I'm on top," Stevenson quoted JB as saying. He later added, "I think I should back off while I'm on top because of my health. It can take a toll if I don't rest. I have a lot of major other things that go along with it. One thing about it, I've been highly successful, and I can't find proper accountants, and it's just kind of embarrassing."

He expressed regret to Stevenson about the state of the recording industry and show business in general and said, "We need to clean up the industry, not let it continue to be a mess. . . . The business isn't fair enough anymore. I'd like to see the record companies release songs that relate more, not to try and make so much profit, but make it easier for our kids and give them a road map to a better life. Not a lot of cursing and crazy stuff. And when they get on the stage, they don't have any uniforms on, I don't like that concept. I like the old concept, from the old school, and that's what I do. When you see me on the stage, my band is immaculate and we're something to see."

In spite of his diabetes, Brown said that it had not slowed him down and boasted, "If you've seen my show, you know I don't have to work out. I put out more energy than anybody ever put out in the business. They call me The Hardest Working Man In Show Business, and I thank God that I have energy to go on that way."

Before hanging up, Brown must have been thinking about Christmas 2004 approaching, and he told Stevenson, "What I do for Christmas is my wife and myself and my staff, we get together, and we give out toys to the young people. We have a line, seven, eight, ten blocks long, and we'll just be giving out toys for young, poor people that need something. It's the way of making the kids feel good. I remember when I was coming up as a kid, I had nothing. . . . I look forward to sitting down with my kids and talking to them and being daddy for them. I got a three-year-old boy, James Brown II, and we just kind of enjoy the whole thing."

What JB didn't mention to Stevenson was that in December he would undergo treatment for prostate cancer. He finally talked about it that month in a story distributed by the Associated Press in which he said, "I have overcome a lot of things in my life. I will overcome this as well."

Following JB's procedure at Midtown Urology Surgical Center in Atlanta on Wednesday, December 15, 2004, his urologist, Dr. James Bennett, made the following statement, "Mr. Brown has successfully undergone a localized prostate cancer procedure and is resting comfortably. We expect a full recovery. With proper follow-up and care, we can also expect a full cure."

Upon his release, as he walked from the clinic to his limousine wearing sunglasses, a hat, and a big smile, JB told reporters, "I feel good."

There was no question about it. The media just loved it when JB said he felt good.

EIGHTEEN

The Final Two Years: 2005–2006

Merry Christmas. Happy New Year. May we all get together, love each other. If you bring people together, you've got something. If you don't bring them together, you've got nothing.

—James Brown
December 22, 2006
at his last public appearance, *Augusta Chronicle*

James Brown's final two years were rich and rewarding ones as he continued to tour extensively and receive new honors.

Of course there were the occasional bumps in the road such as the $106 million lawsuit brought against JB by forty-eight-year-old Jacque Hollander who claimed JB had raped her in 1988 in the back of his van while threatening her with a shotgun. Hollander said at the time of the alleged incident she was an aspiring songwriter working as a public relations assistant for Brown.

Her claim had been dismissed by a federal judge, but the decision was reversed by an appeals court in 2006.

Attorney Debra Opri, who successfully defended Brown in 2002 on the sexual assault complaint filed by Lisa Ross Agbalaya, former West Coast president of James Brown Enterprises, also defended JB in the sexual assault claim filed by Hollander.

Opri said, "This is what you call a shakedown in its most stupid form. It's too little, too late and baseless." Hollander said she was pursuing her suit—albeit several years after the alleged incident—because she had been diagnosed with the thyroid condition Graves' Disease, which she claimed was caused by her "rape and torture" by Brown.

In April 2007, four months after JB's death, the sexual harassment case filed by Hollander was rejected by the U.S. Supreme Court without comment from the justices.

While the Hollander lawsuit hovered over his head, JB performed before thirty thousand people on March 5 at the Jakarta International Java Jazz Festival in Indonesia's capital. The concert organizers said they would donate $1.60 of each ticket sold for the relief effort for the victims of the tsunami that had hit Indonesia three months earlier. The concert was the first jazz festival in seven years for Indonesia, which had been hit by terrorism, natural disasters, and financial crisis.

Brown hit another high spot when several hundred fans and local dignitaries gathered in the 800 block of Broad Street on Friday, May 6, 2005, to honor him just as they had in November of 2003.

This time, instead of gathering on the Augusta Common on the north side of Broad Street, spectators filled the parklike center of the block and stood about ten deep on the east- and westbound sides of the street for the unveiling of the $40,000 statue of JB. Sculpted by Augusta orthopedic surgeon John Savage, the statue was paid for with about $10,000 of public money; the remainder came from private donors, including the Brown-influenced, Atlanta-based rock singer Usher.

Among those present at the unveiling were U.S. representative John Barrow; Georgia state representative and gospel music TV host Henry Howard (who died five months later and was buried near Adrienne and Joe "Pop" Brown); original Famous Flame Bobby Byrd; JB's childhood friend, Leon Austin; Al Sharpton; and JB's family members, including Tomi Rae. Usher had been rumored to attend the unveiling, but instead called from Atlanta just before the ceremony started to give his best wishes.

Brown and Usher had teamed up earlier in the year for a duet at the 2005 Grammy Awards show. He was knocked out when JB called the singer, who was twenty-eight at the time, the

"Godson of Soul." Usher later said, "James Brown introduced me to soul. Because of him I was given a clear view of what a real performance is and should be. I learned showmanship from him." He also recalled that during the rehearsal for the show, JB had looked down at Usher's sneakers and told him, "You gonna fool around and break your ankles with those. You gotta have on the right shoes for your movement to be smooth."

The unveiling began with Augusta mayor Bob Young thanking the people of Augusta and the contributors who made the statue possible. Then Sharpton urged the crowd to sing "Happy Birthday" to Brown who had turned seventy-two three days earlier.

Sharpton then added, "People can now come to Augusta, Georgia, and look at a statue of a man who used to shine shoes on this street—a man who had to dance for nickels. But he believed in himself, he believed in this nation, he believed in God, and all over the world they know his name. This is not a statue for his ego. This is a statue to give young people hope all over the world."

In addition, Sharpton remarked on Brown's up and down life, and said the statue would be an inspiration for all seeing it.

Brown, wearing sunglasses, sat on the stage nearby during all the speeches and was observed once putting his head in his hands. The microphone was turned over to Danny Ray who called Brown to the microphone once again with his world-famous introduction.

Obviously deeply moved, Brown said, "It's hard to talk live when you have this much love and appreciation. I don't know how to tell you how much I love you and thank you." He then came down some steps from the stage to stand next to the statue, then he pulled off the black cloth covering and looked himself in the eye.

To conclude the program, popular Augusta performer Tony Howard, who had performed some preceremony entertainment, urged JB to the stage while Howard's band played "Get On Up (I Feel Like Being a) Sex Machine," which Brown had cowritten with Bobby Byrd.

As special as the day was for JB, it also was special for eleven-year-old Austin Hopkins of Thomasville, North Carolina, who had traveled five hours to Augusta to see JB and who got to show off his own JB-inspired dance moves.

The same month as his statue unveiling, Brown performed a free concert in historic Forsyth Park in Savannah, Georgia, sponsored by the Savannah College of Art and Design. He filled the park for the ninety-minute show beginning at 7:30 p.m. Friday, May 27. A *Savannah Morning News* reviewer called the show "explosive."

After JB's death, Ben Tucker, a retired Savannah radio station owner, said in a story published in the *Morning News*, "Anytime a man can come to Savannah and put 30,000 people in Forsyth Park, I give my hat to him. He was the last of the great rhythm-and-blues singers and dancers on the face of the earth. James Brown was a genius. . . . There aren't many who can match him; maybe Smokey Robinson or Stevie Wonder, but not many others."

In the following weeks Brown was back in Europe where his United Kingdom fans again watched the master at work in his shocking pink suit.

He was the undeniable highlight of the Live 8 free concert in Edinburgh, Scotland, on July 6, 2005, to raise awareness of poverty in Africa.

An estimated forty thousand to fifty thousand people were present from several countries. The antipoverty protest was organized by Midge Ure and Bob Geldof [known for his Live Aid concert fundraiser] on the same day that the G8 summit of world leaders began in Gleneagles.

"I know that people need help and I want to be a part of it in any way I can," Brown said at a media conference in London. "The concert will raise awareness of the problems in Africa and will make people think about humanity."

Concert organizer Geldof had come under criticism because of the few black performers slated for the show. Brown told reporters, "I'm not going to perform as a black artist. I'm going to perform as a man who makes music. . . . You don't segregate. I've fought against that years ago. I don't care if children are black, white, red, or yellow, I care that they are hungry."

Brown was asked about his December 2004 cancer surgery, and he said that illness had not slowed him down. "When I'm ripping and running, I don't have time to worry about the situation. A lot of people have the same thing and I pray for them."

According to news reports Brown stayed in the five-star Scotsman Hotel four nights while in Edinburgh for the Live 8 concert and the T in the Park music festival and ordered fish suppers almost every night. He was said to love the classic British fish and chips.

Victoria Minett reviewed his show on June 23 at the Wolerhampton, England, Civic Hall for the bbc.co.uk Web site and called it "an awesome performance by an awesome performer."

She described the evening noting, "From his starting medley, which featured 'Funky Good Time,' to a set that included the best of his back catalog, including 'Get on the Good Foot,' 'Please, Please, Please,' 'Papa's Got a Brand New Bag,' and 'I Feel Good,' it was a real roll through time that demonstrated why James Brown has attracted more cool nicknames than anyone else ever in the history of the world! Amongst the particular highlights were a fabulously moving version of 'Try Me' and the closing 'Sex Machine.' The band was achingly tight, James's vocals were spot on, and the Bittersweets kept the feeling of unrehearsed anarchy alive. As the closing strains of 'Sex Machine' passed, James Brown—who had already treated us to one burst of the famous slide and had been graced with two cloaks—made his exit." It's hard to believe this was wirtten about a performer seventy-two years old!

For Thanksgiving and Christmas 2005, JB was at Dyess Park on James Brown Boulevard in Augusta, giving away turkeys and at the Imperial Theatre on Broad Street giving away toys.

On Wednesday, December 21, hundreds of children and their parents were waiting including Denise Ray, an Augusta resident who was unemployed and on Social Security, along with her son, Dymaile, nine; daughters, Ariel, six, and Dynesha, seven; and granddaughter, Denisa, four. They had been waiting since 5 a.m. "We have a Christmas tree, but we don't have any gifts under it," Ray told Kate Lewis of the *Augusta Chronicle*. She added that she had helped Brown give away free turkeys the previous month.

Aurelia Overton, who also had been there since about 5 a.m. with her three children, remarked, "It's very nice of him to give away the toys. He knows where he came from."

Brown, who was driven up in a black limousine at about 11:30 a.m., stepped out wearing a red shirt, gray suit, and a tan overcoat and shiny black sunglasses. He smiled and waved to the crowd before heading inside. "We all see the need for a little love and a little giving," he said that day. "I wish I could do more, but I'm sure a lot of people enjoyed it and everybody's very proud of this."

Nobody was prouder of it than James Brown, Augusta's real Santa Claus.

JB's final concert date in 2005 was at the B. B. King Blues Club and Grill in New York City. He was booked for a repeat performance on New Year's Eve of 2006, but it was a show date that he would not be alive to make.

On the first week of James Brown's last year alive he was in Rama, Ontario, Canada, performing two shows on January 5, 2006, at Casino Rama in a forest green suit with silver sequins that sparkled in the reflections from four overhead disco balls.

Jane Stevenson of the *Toronto Sun*, who had covered JB on a prior Toronto visit, glowingly wrote the next day, "After a good, if not great, performance at Massey Hall in November 2004, the 72-year-old Brown was back in fighting form last night, both in terms of his vocal shrieks and trademark slippery dance moves. No song more than an extended, jam-happy version of 'This Is a Man's World,' which came towards the end of Brown's hour-and-20-minute performance, clearly demonstrated The Funky President had indeed returned to office."

At one point, JB told the crowd, "You will not be able to relax because the funk will make you move!" He was scheduled to perform return dates at Casino Rama on January 5 and 6, 2007.

Even in his final year, JB was blazing new territory and making new fans as he returned to Australia for the multicity Good Vibrations Festival with performances at the Riverstage in Brisbane on February 11;, the Sidney Myer Music Bowl in Melbourne on February 12, Sydney Centennial Park in Sydney on Februrary 18, and at Belvoir Amphitheater in Perth on February 19.

From Australia, it was on to mainland China for his debut in that country on February 22, in Shanghai at the Yun Feng Theatre, an acrobatics venue owned by the People's Liberation Army. There was even an official "Sex Machine" after-party.

"We are going to funk you up before we finish," he told the Shanghai audience, consisting mostly of European, American, and Japanese fans, and started his concert with "Make It Funky." He was dressed in a cherry red satin suit and was backed by a downsized nine-piece Soul Generals band and his backup singers.

After that Wednesday in Shanghai, he went on to perform Friday night at the Jamsil Sports Complex in Seoul, Korea; his first- ever concert in that country on February 24. That, of course, led to several times that Brown was called the real "Seoul Man."

Then it was back to the states where JB received the Reverend Martin Luther King Jr. Keepers of the Dream Award on April 6 at the Sheraton New York Hotel at an event hosted by Al Sharpton. The award honors those who best stand for the principles of the late civil rights activist.

Seven days after his seventy-third birthday, JB was rocking a packed audience at Stubbs Bar-B-Q in Austin, Texas.

On May 21 he was a celebrity guest performer for a pre–World Cup party at the Hertfordshire, England, home of Spice Girl Victoria Beckham and her soccer superstar husband, David. The exclusive event raised money for three charities—UNICEF, the Prince's Trust, and the David and Victoria Beckham Children's Foundation. JB was joined onstage by entertainers P. Diddy and Will Young. The event was filmed by the Britich ITV network for a ninety-minute program televised May 28.

From the success of the pre–World Cup party with the Beckhams, JB went to another entertainment disaster in his own hometown on May 27 with what was billed as the "James Brown Soul of America Music Festival" that was horribly organized and somewhat promoted by Charles "Champ" Walker Jr., son of jailed former Georgia state senator and minority leader Charles Walker.

Walker had boasted about who would show up for the festival and how many people would be there—fairy tales that never materialized. It ended up being a costly embarrassment to James Brown himself who was never contacted to be there.

But, not wanting to disappoint his hometown fans good-hearted JB decided to charter his own flight after a show in Portsmouth, Virginia, to reach Augusta in time to do a few songs at the festival and then head right back out to resume his schedule with a concert in Atlantic City, New Jersey.

David Cannon, Brown's business manager who would be with him for his final weekend in Atlanta, said Brown paid the expenses out of his own pocket to play in Augusta and estimated the cost of the chartered plane alone at around $20,000. "I think the man is going way overboard to be fair. I'm not against it. I'm sort of glad he has decided to do it," Cannon said.

As it turned out, Brown did just that, and enthusiastically performed four songs backed by the band of Atlanta-based Brown tribute artist Tony Wilson. "We're on the move," he said. "'Cold Sweat.' Hit me." He followed that hit with "Living In America" and "I Got You" before concluding with "Sex Machine."

"It's a beautiful picture," JB said of the music festival named after him before leading Wilson's band into "I Got You." "Me growing up here, I never knew this would happen. But this is America." During "Sex Machine," he even took time to dance with Tomi Rae, who was singing backup.

Steven Uhles, of the *Chronicle* called the three day music festival "a catastrophe from the moment it kicked off two hours late Friday until it finally wrapped Sunday with feelings of ill will between Mr. Walker and the deputies providing security." Uhles said it was "a textbook example of how things should not be done."

He told readers, "The only thing that seemed to go off on time and without a hitch was the scheduled 6 p.m. performance by James Brown. Like clockwork, the Godfather hit the stage, blasted through four of his hits and then, like the Lone Ranger after riding in to save the day, was gone. The good news is that very few people were on hand to witness the overall debacle.

"Attendance, at its peak, came nowhere close to the 7,500 that Mr. Walker had submitted to the city or the 25,000 he announced a week before the festival. Instead, it ranged from a few dozen early on to perhaps a thousand or so for Mr. Brown's performance."

Rolling Stone came out with a seven-page cover story about JB in its June 29 issue. Brown was catching a plane once again to the United Kingdom for a show on July 4 at the Tower of London and then for the annual Oxegen Festival in Punchestown, Ireland.

The Tower of London Music Festival—the first such event of its kind—took place July 28 through July 14 with a variety of artists, such as the Pet Shop Boys, Al Jarreau, Bill Wyman's Rhythm Kings, and Dionne Warwick, performing in open-air concerts near the historic British fortress.

Just before that concert at the Tower of London, Tomi Rae Hynie Brown from an Augusta jeweler bought JB a $200 pair of cuff links with the British Union Jack flag on them.

On his way from Heathrow Airport to the Tower of London show, Brown stopped off at the residence of U.S. ambassador Robert Holmes Tuttle where a Fourth of July party was under way. Brown surprised guests by getting up with the band at the party and singing "Georgia (On My Mind)." Brown performed to another sea of people at the Oxegen Festival in Ireland on Saturday, July 8. Back in the states, on September 14, JB performed his ninety-minute show—a bit late because of plane problems—to a sold-out crowd of about 650 in the VooDoo Lounge at Harrah's casino in Kansas City, Missouri.

Timothy Finn of the *Star* later wrote, "Time has diminished James Brown physically, but he can still sing. And he still puts on a dazzling live show. . . . The whole show was a blast, but the end was especially explosive: a one-two haymaker of 'I Got You (I Feel Good)' and 'Get Up (I Feel Like Being a) Sex Machine.' . . . He may have started late, but by the time he was done, James Brown had taken everyone in the room back in time."

Five days after the Kansas City show, he was performing at Indiana University in Bloomington wearing a gorgeous red shirt and red tuxedo suit—appropriate for the Hoosier audience.

On September 20, JB continued his Midwest tour with a concert at the Rialto Square Theater in Joliet, Illinois. It was his last concert in the United States.

Fannie Brown Burford, JB's fifty-one-year-old stepsister was among those in the audience as a special guest. Most people around Augusta didn't know she existed until after her stepbrother died. They had the same father [Joe Brown] but different mothers.

She told Cindy Wojdyla Cain, writer for the *Joliet Herald News*, that Brown had embraced her as a sibling when she was about ten and growing up in Chicago. She said that Brown helped raise her and helped Burford and her kids go to school.

Burford said JB had performed previously in Joliet in the early 1990s when he did a concert for the prisoners at the Joliet Correction Center. She said that she was the one who urged her stepbrother to return to Joliet. "I had been bugging him for almost two years to come," she told Cain.

On Monday, October 16, police beat reporter Adam Folk for the *Chronicle* covered a ceremony at the Augusta-Richmond County Civic Center renaming the building designed by architect I. M. Pei as the James Brown Arena. The pictures that staff photographer Rainier Ehrhardt took for the *Chronicle* that day show JB wearing black rimmed, clear eyeglasses and covering his mouth the whole time with a dark red kerchief. He cited old age and recent tooth implants.

Brown reminisced about his years growing up not far from the arena and added, "Along the way, I met some beautiful people. . . . I may look about 30 when I'm finished," he joked. And just like he had done so many times at his concerts, he urged the audience to turn to the person on their right and tell that person "I love you."

Among those present were Leon Austin; original Famous Flames Johnny Terry and Bobby Byrd, and Al Sharpton, who said the renamed civic center would stand as a place where people would know that dreams come true. Sharpton added, "Ten years ago, I wouldn't have thought this was possible, but Augusta has grown and recognized Mr. Brown's importance worldwide."

Before the ceremony ended, Brown told the crowd the same thing he had said many, many times in his interviews and at his concerts. He said, "I want to thank you. God bless America. God bless you and your family, and I hope you live 200 years, and I live 200 years minus one day so I'll never know beautiful people like you passed away. God bless."

Just days after that ceremony, Brown began his final tour of Europe with concerts at the Carling Glasgow Academy on October 25 in Glasgow, Scotland; the Roundhouse in London on October 27; the Olympia Theatre in Dublin, Ireland, on October 29 and October 30; the Larnst AutoArena in Helsinki, Finland, on November 1; the Gasometer in Vienna, Austria, on November 3; the T-Mobile Arena in Prague, Czechoslakia, on November 4;

and finally the last European tour stop at K. C. Drazen Petrovic arena in Zagreb, Croatia, on November 5.

The Roundhouse performance for the first BBC *Electric Proms* televised music festival had marked JB's third time in London in 2006 alone, and he would be back yet one more time in November. Music writer Neil Dowden saw that age was getting to Brown. His review, posted on the musicomh.com Web site, acknowledged that "few people have had more influence on popular music than him," but Dowden also pointed out the obvious.

"It has to be said that now as a Grandfather of Soul he is no longer the dynamic presence onstage which made him such a legendary performer, as recorded in his famous 1963 *Live at the Apollo* album," Dowden wrote. "These days he only attempts a few dance moves sporadically and his voice, though it remains distinctive, has lost a lot of its power. Although the showmanship is still there, the raw energy has faded with age. You have to admire his stamina for staying on stage for what turned out to be a remarkable two and a quarter hours, but a lot of that time he was sharing the limelight with various other performers."

Dowden also noted, "Although there were flashes of the old magic, you couldn't help feeling that he was coasting on the wave of affection coming from the crowd, built up over decades of outstanding musical achievement. There was too much of 'Let's have another round of applause for . . .' and 'Everybody feeling good?' rather than getting on down to the nitty gritty."

As in most cities where JB made return trips, the concert in Prague was eagerly awaited by fans. His first appearance in Prague was considered by the audience and music critics the "event of the year" for that city in 2004. And judging by the video footage that can be seen on YouTube.com, the return concert in 2006 also must have been the "event of the year" for Prague. This seventy-three-year-old guy who had suffered diabetes and prostate cancer was having one of the best concert years of his life, even though he was just weeks away from his death.

The concert in Zagreb would be the last full concert he would ever give. His emcee, Danny Ray, said, "They loved it. They came out for the show. It didn't matter how cold it was, the crowds always came out for Mr. Brown."

Lead guitarist Keith Jenkins, who performed onstage with Brown for twelve years, said the last concert in Croatia was pretty much like all previous concerts in recent years. He later told me, "I don't remember one thing about that Croatia show. I don't remember one minute about it. I remember being at the airport, and I think that I remember a little dressing room. It really wasn't anything special. I really don't have a whole lot of recall about anything revelatory. It was just another year. It was the same as any other year. It wasn't any different. We didn't do anything new that last year that I know of."

But Jenkins does remember that final year of 2006 as being particularly tough.

"Any off days we had, they [booking agents] would come up with a job. We didn't have almost any off days that last year. We just worked and worked and worked. What was supposed to have been our off days, they put in some kind of date and made us work. It was just grueling and hard. No rest. We added up the hours that we worked in some fifteen days, and it was some ridiculous amount like 150 hours of not being in a hotel."

Jenkins added that while it may have been extra money for the star, it wasn't any extra for the Soul Generals and other revue members.

"It wasn't any more money for us. If they added a show, all that did was eat up our off day, but somebody else made more money off it. We were paid per week, so they could cram as much stuff as they wanted to in a week, and so they did."

Jenkins said, while he doesn't remember the details of those final shows, he does remember Brown usually sustaining that high level of energy onstage right up to the end.

"That was incredible to see him still have so much energy and still be able to be so healthy and go out there and do such a good show at that age. I didn't record any hit records with him or do anything with him that was real spectacular," Jenkins added. "He had done what he had needed to do. He had recorded for so long and had so many good songs in such a huge catalog that anything at that point he was doing was for fun. The fact he went to work at all was for fun. That was what he did. So you could file anything that we did together under, 'Yes, he's doing this for kicks because he could have retired.'"

Although he was taking some days off before Thanksgiving and Christmas, JB fully intended to be back on the road two days after Christmas with the remaining 2006 concerts scheduled December 27 at the Palace Theater in Waterbury, Connecticut; December 28 at the Bergen Performing Arts Center in Englewood, New Jersey; and a New Year's Eve concert at the B. B. King Blues Club and Grill in New York City; as well as other dates booked for 2007.

Before he was to take time off for the Thanksgiving and Christmas holidays, Brown had one more trip to make and that was back to London for the fourth time in 2007 to be inducted into the United Kingdom Music Hall of Fame along with other American rockers Bon Jovi, Prince, and Brian Wilson (of the Beach Boys), and British rockers Led Zeppelin, Rod Stewart, and Dusty Springfield.

Also that night, British records producer George Martin would receive an honorary membership into the Hall of Fame for his legendary work in producing hit recordings by the Beatles. The honorees had been selected by a panel of sixty people who included performers, record industry executives, broadcasters, and journalists.

Dermot O'Leary presided over the impressive awards ceremony at the Alexandra Palace on the north side of London on November 14. It was broadcast live over BBC Radio 2, then later televised in its taped format on Channel 4 in the United Kingdom on November 16 and November 18, and then shown in the United States on the VH1 cable TV network on November 25.

Besides the inductees, the star-studded list of awards presenters, performers, and general attendees included Patti LaBelle, Roger Taylor of Queen, Johnny Borrell of Razorlight, Tony Iommi of Black Sabbath, David Gilmour of Pink Floyd, Swedish singer/songwriter Jose Gonzales, Corinne Baily Rae, the band Wolfmother, and Beyoncé Knowles, whose movie *Dream Girls* debuted on JB's death on Christmas Day 2006.

Brown, dressed in a pretty blue suit and bow tie, was inducted that evening by Jazzie B and, backed by the award show's band, performed a rousing rendition of his trademark song "I Got You (I Feel Good)." It was the last public performance of his life. His choice of songs later proved to be ironic when it became evident that he really didn't feel good.

One of the highlights of the night was young, British soul rock star Joss Stone singing "Son of a Preacher Man" in tribute to inductee Dusty Springfield who died in 1999. Stone had sang "It's a Man's, Man's, Man's World" when JB was honored by the Kennedy Center in 2003.

"Thank you very much," Brown said in his acceptance remarks. "I want to say thank God for this beautiful gift and a reminder that we're on the right track with good music. First thing I'd like to ask each and every one sitting in the audience today, tonight rather, would you look to the right and tell that person sitting next to you that 'I love you?'"

There were a lot of laughter and giggles and sheepish looks, but the audience did just that. Then Brown said, "Now, can you look back to the left and tell that person sitting next to you that 'I love you' too? That includes you, too, Joss [to Joss Stone]. That includes you, Joss. I have a lot of beautiful friends out there, Miss Patti LaBelle, and so many and everybody has been just great and I just love you and I thank you for everything, and my good friend here, Jazzie B, and I just thank God for doing what we do."

In his final parting words, JB quickly expressed his views about vulgarity in rap and pop music saying, "Let's change our lyrics, and clean our music up and take these kids to a better life and a better place. And I love you Tomi Rae."

And with a wave of his right hand to the crowd, Brown left the stage for the last time of his life. It had been a long, long musical journey of more than sixty years since those childhood days in Augusta, performing at Silas X. Floyd Elementary School and on the stage of the Lenox Theater.

On Tuesday, November 21, James Brown was back in Dyess Park on James Brown Boulevard for his final turkey giveaway. Scores of people lined up that cold day waiting for JB, who showed up shortly before 1 p.m. wearing a black leather jacket with a large American flag across the back, He and his helpers would give away about one thousand turkeys that day.

Augusta mayor Deke Copenhaver stood next to JB with other leaders of the community as they shook hands, hugged, and spoke words of encouragement to those coming through the line.

"We've all got to love each other," Brown was quoted in the *Chronicle* as saying that day. He was asked what Thanksgiving meant to him, and JB replied, "It means God has blessed all of us, and we need to give thanks for the things we get everyday."

Among those waiting in line that day to shake hands with the legend was eleven-year-old Joevance Green, a sixth grader a Sego Middle School, who said that waiting in the cold was worth it "because I've never met James Brown before." She added that it definitely beat buying a turkey at a store.

Also there that day was Rico Wright, who had been to previous turkey giveaways. He had been there that day in the cold and light sleet since 4 a.m. but said, "I just thank God that James Brown is giving away turkeys."

Not everybody thought JB's turkey giveaways that day or other previous Thanksgivings were a good idea, as a blogger posted on the *Chronicle*'s Web site, writing that he couldn't understand "why people stand out in the cold waiting on that man for a turkey."

That posting drew many others defending Brown's kindness, including one who wrote, "James Brown is truly a giving soul and an inspiration for the community. . . . The man still performs around the world to standing room crowds after 50 years. He could easily just sit in his big house and enjoy the fruit of his labor, but he chooses to spread some joy and good cheer."

Education reporter Greg Gelpi of the *Chronicle* was there for JB's last turkey giveaway on November 21, and he was with JB again a month later on Friday, December 22, 2006, when JB made his last public appearance.

It had been a nasty, cold, rainy morning when JB pulled up in front of the Imperial Theatre where the usual long line of children were waiting with their family members. He was driven to the theater by his chauffer of fourteen years, William Murrell, who later said, "When I took him to different cities, it was like I had the president of the United States in the car. When he got out, everybody said, 'Wow, that's James Brown!'"

Among those joining Brown that day were his daughters, Deanna and Venisha, and his personal assistant and office manager, Elif Crawford.

Three days after his Christmas toy giveaway at the Imperial Theatre, James Brown lay down on a hospital bed in Atlanta and took his last breath.

NINETEEN

The Home Goings and Name Callings

To the Brown family, to all of you that are gathered
here today, today is the end of a long journey and
the beginning of a new journey. We come to thank
God for James Brown. Because only God could
have made a James Brown possible. And only God
can give James Brown rest. . . . James Brown was
a man's man. And he stood up like a man. He lived
like a man. And on Christmas Day, he died like a
man.

—The Reverend Al Sharpton
December 30, 2006
spoken at the last of three
funerals for James Brown

The beginning of the end actually started several weeks before
the 2006 Thanksgiving turkey giveaway, when JB's business
associates, family, and close friends realized that he had a chest
cold that he couldn't seem to shake.

His tour manager and longtime friend, Charles Bobbit, later
said that Brown had been sick since returning from the trip to
London in mid-November when he was inducted into the United
Kingdom Music Hall of Fame.

But he still wanted to stand in the cold at Dyess Park to give
away turkeys and in the drafty hallway of the Imperial Theatre to
give away toys.

With Brown just days before his death were Emma Austin,
wife of his longtime friend Leon Austin, and Velma Warren
Brown Ridley, his first wife. Emma later told me:

I talked to him on Thursday, the day before the Christmas giveaway. We got to chatting, and I was saying, "You don't sound well," and he said, "I really haven't felt well since I came back from that last tour. It took a lot out of me overseas." We got on the morbid topic of dying, and he said, "Well, I want to be buried by my mother, my father, and Adrienne, because we couldn't be a family in life but we can spend eternity together."

I'm always doctoring on him and giving him advice and asking, "How's your blood pressure? Are you keeping up with your blood sugar? Are you taking your medicine?" Then I said, "What have you eaten today?" And he said, "I haven't had an appetite," and I said, "Well, you've got to eat!" So I said, "That's just an absolute must. You're taking medicine, and you can't keep your blood sugar up if you don't eat." Anyway, he loves my vegetable soup. So I made him some of that and some cornbread on the stove. We had been talking beet greens and all the healing properties they're supposed to have, so I bought some of those and prepared all that and took it to his house. He called me that night and told me he was so appreciative of the food.

Emma said her husband had wanted to go to the Christmas giveaway the next day, just as he had always been there with his friend at many past toy and turkey giveaway days and other special times.

"But it was raining so badly the day of the Christmas giveaway and [it was] cold," Emma recalled. "Leon had not been out of that hospital that long, and he had a little bug, and he called Mr. Brown because he wanted to see him so badly and wanted to be there. Mr. Brown urged him not to come. He said, 'Bro, I'm only going because they are looking forward to me being there, and I will not disappoint the children. So I have to go. But, Bro, we'll get together another time. Don't worry about it now. You stay home and stay out of this rain.'"

One of the people who also knew things were not going well for JB was "Buddy" Dallas. Later, he told me, "He called me up not long before he died, and he went on and on for twenty minutes about how much our friendship had meant to him over the years.

"I'll never forget our first conversation when he told me, 'Mr. Dallas, I want you to represent me.' I said, 'Mr. Brown, I don't know anything about the entertainment industry.' He said, 'I can teach you about the entertainment industry. I need someone I can trust.'

"Looking back, I think he knew he was going," Dallas added. "In that last long conversation, he revisited everything in my relationship with him. It was his way of saying good-bye. I told my wife, Denise, that I wish I had tape-recorded that talk."

One of the first to really know the seriousness of what was happening was his son, Daryl, who traveled with him as a musician in the Soul Generals band. Daryl later recalled at his father's Augusta funeral, "I spent a lot of time with my daddy the last two weeks, and he kept telling me, 'Son, I'm so tired.' And I said, 'Daddy, then go to sleep if you're tired. Sleep as much as you want as long as you want, because either way you look at it, I'm going to be here.' He said, 'Son, listen, you have a legacy now, and you must take this legacy and keep it going.'"

Al Sharpton also knew there was something different when Brown's personal office assistant Elif Crawford called and told him that JB had been trying to reach him. Sharpton put off returning the call a day or two later, knowing that once JB got on the line he would want to talk at least a good half hour. But this time there was more urgency in his trying to reach Sharpton.

"Mr. Bobbit called me about two hours later and said, 'You need to call him. He wants to talk to you.' It was the last conversation we had," Sharpton related during Brown's funeral service in Augusta.

He said to me, "Reverend, I've been watching you on the news. I want you to keep fighting for justice. But I want you to tell people to love one another. I want you to fight to lift the standards back." He said, "What happened to us that we are now celebrating for being down? What happened that we went from saying I'm black and I'm proud to calling each other niggers and ho's and bitches?" He said, "I sung people up, and now they're singing people down, and we need to change the music."

He said, "I want you to stay with your teacher, Reverend [Jessie] Jackson. Don't get so bigheaded you can't stay with your teacher. Y'all got to clean it up." Then he said to me, "Reverend, have you talked to Michael [Jackson]?" I said, "No, I think he's out of the country." He said, "Tell him that I love Michael. Tell him don't worry about coming home. They always scandalize those that have the talent. But tell him we need to clean up the music, and I want Michael and all of those that imitated me to come back and lift the music back to where children and their grand mommas can sit and listen to the music together.

JB spent Friday night after that day's toy giveaway at his Beech Island home, the last he would spend there alive. The next day he was driven to Atlanta for a 1:30 p.m. dental appointment with Dr. Terry Reynolds. Brown arrived several hours late, and looked "very bad, just weak and dazed," the dentist recalled. Dr. Reynolds, had been working on Brown's teeth for several months to replace twenty-five-year-old implants,. He said it sounded like JB's friends and manager had been trying without luck to get Brown into a hospital.

Road manager Charles Bobbit had arranged for a doctor to meet JB at the dentist's office to check him over for the nagging cough. Bobbit related at JB's Augusta funeral that he was disturbed by a conversation he had with Brown about a week earlier in which JB had said, "Mr. Bobbit, I've asked God to give I and you twenty more years." Bobbit replied, "Mr. Brown, I'm seventy-six years old. I don't think I can handle twenty. Maybe you can." To which, JB responded with that special wit of his, "No, man, no. They can make us young. We'll be around for a long time. We're going to do things with Michael Jackson. We're going to do things with Prince." Bobbit said he didn't argue with his friend and boss, because he knew that you didn't say no to JB.

Dr. Marvin L. Crawford, a medical doctor and pastor of Saint Paul African Methodist Episcopal Church in Lithonia, Georgia, who had been summoned to look at Brown at the dentist's office, insisted that Brown get immediate treatment at nearby Emory Crawford Long Hospital in northeast Atlanta.

The *Atlanta Journal-Consitution* reported that as JB was leaving the dentist's office to go to the hospital, Dr. Reynolds again urged Brown to take about three months off, saying, "Don't go on any dates, just relax and cool yourself out, because you're wearing yourself out." But Brown took the dentist's hand and said, "Yeah, doc, we need to talk. We need to talk man to man. As soon as I come back from the hospital, we'll talk."

Throughout that Friday and Saturday, Bobbit noticed that JB's mood was very solemn—not happy or cheerful but still never complaining. "He didn't look good," Bobbit said. "He was coughing with a lot of noise."

At the hospital, Brown went through X-rays and other tests and was told he had pneumonia and congestive heart failure. The doctor at the hospital insisted on admitting Brown. That shook up Bobbit who was thinking about the contracted dates later that week including the New Year's Eve show scheduled in New York City. The doctor said if Brown improved he might make the New Year's Eve show.

Bobbit, loyal soldier and aide and friend, stayed in the hospital with JB that Christmas Eve night getting the lemonade and water that JB requested and rubbing his feet as JB asked him to do.

"He wanted this, he wanted that," Bobbit told mourners at the Augusta funeral service, "but he didn't want to talk to anyone. He didn't want to see anyone. So that night passed through. He slept from Saturday afternoon until Christmas Day morning."

About 1:15 a.m. Brown said, "Mr. Bobbit, I'm burning up, and my chest is on fire." Bobbit put a wet cloth on his forehead. Brown was restless and would lie down and then sit up and then lie down and would then sit up.

"He said, 'Mr. Bobbit, I'm going to leave here tonight,'" Bobbit recalled. "I said, 'No, you're not.' Being the businessman, I said, 'We've got some dates to play. We've got to make some money.' And I wanted to cheer him up. And I said, 'Well, and if you're saying what I think you're saying, I can't make this trip with you.'

"So we kind of laughed. He sat on the foot of the bed. He made his peace with his God. He laid back. He laid his head back on the bed, and he exposed himself by laying back. And I took a blanket, and I covered over him. And that's how I was able to hear him breathe his last three sighs. He breathed very softly three times. He opened his eyes. He closed his eyes. And he had expired. I called the nurses and the doctors, they came, they worked on him for a long time but he was gone."

Tomi Rae Hynie was being treated in a California facility for drug addiction to legal painkillers that she claimed she was taking because of her father's recent death. She talked to Brown on the phone on Chirstmas Eve and said Brown told her, "Baby, I love you." And she said that she tried to reach him later in the evening but was told by Bobbit that JB had pneumonia and doctors were working on him but that he was going to be OK.

When Tomi Rae learned of JB's death, she caught a plane that day to head home. She said the plane trip already had been arranged for Christmas Day for her reunion with Brown, but when she arrived, she found herself locked out of the Beech Island home she had shared with JB for ten years.

Photographer Rainier Ehrhardt with the *Augusta Chronicle*

captured the dramatic moment when Hynie buried her face in her gloved hands in front of the massive, front iron gates that JB had made to resemble the ones at Buckingham Palace in London. The photo was reprinted worldwide and shown on TV stations and Web sites. *Chronicle* reporter Donnie Fetter also described the intense scene to readers saying Brown's estate trustees, attorney "Buddy" Dallas, and accountant David Cannon, were the ones who denied her access.

Dallas later explained in the *Augusta Chronicle*, "First of all, she's Mr. Brown's estranged girlfriend. She is not Mrs. Brown. She is not his widow." Dallas said JB was "offended" and "hurt" when he discovered Hynie still was legally married to another man when JB and Hynie wed at their Beech Island home. They never remarried, which meant Hynie was not JB's legal widow or wife, Dallas said.

Hynie told the media that Family Court judge Charlie Segars-Andrews in Charleston, South Carolina, had dissolved her 1997 marriage to Javed Ahmed on the grounds that they did not consummate their marriage and that Ahmed had married her fraudulently to obtain U.S. citizenship. North Augusta attorney Jim Huff, who represented JB when he sought his own annulment from Hynie in 2005 but later didn't pursue it, said he also believed Hynie was not legally married to Brown after their wedding.

But, just fourteen days before he died, JB had appeared on the Augusta cable TV local access show *Comcast Connect Live* on December 11 to promote his upcoming toy giveaway. Brown coughed frequently during the broadcast and noted that he had dental work upcoming.

During the conversation with host Austin Rhodes, Brown mentioned how much his spouse, whom he did not mention by name during the show, loved rock and roll music and said, "You know, my wife, I got her doing a big thing, but she's still a rock 'n' roll fan." Supporters of Hynie later said that JB still was referring to her as his "wife" even though they legally were not married.

Dallas, however, said it didn't matter what he called her because they still were not married. "There were other words he used from time to time, but I'm not going to repeat them," he told the *Augusta Chronicle*. "If they were not ceremonially married, and she had agreed that she would not claim to be his common-law wife, then what is she?" Dallas further contended that JB and Hynie had not lived together for at least six weeks before his death.

The afternoon of Christmas Day, Hynie showed up at the James Brown statue on Broad Street with her son in what turned out to be a memorable conversation broadcast "live" on the evening news with WRDW TV reporter Lynnsey Gardner.

"He loved Augusta and he loved his people so much," Hynie said. "He wanted to do so many things. We had so many plans for this town. We had a children's community center and the arts to get the kids off the street and not to use the drugs. We know about the drugs. We've been there. We know it ain't no way to live. We ain't just talking and not walking the walk. We've been there, you know, and we want to help the kids to put down the pipe and pick up a horn. Put down that stuff and pick up a guitar."

She told Gardner Brown loved Augusta, saying, "He was very sick when he did the turkey giveaway, and I told him, 'Honey, you don't need to go. They can do it for you.' And he said, 'No, I've got to go 'cause Augusta expects to see me. I've got to go for Augusta.' So he went. I begged him not to go, but he said he had to go for Augusta."

Even though she physically was locked out of the estate, Hynie told talk show host Larry King that she did receive money. She told him, "My husband was so smart. He told me that the day he died to go to the bank and get something that he had left for me and my son. It was left in an ITF [in trust for] under James Brown or Hynie Brown for James Joseph Brown II and to get it immediately the next day. . . . It was a check for $80,000. And then he told me I would need it to take care of him until things were over."

She also revealed that her son was receiving a Social Security check in her name, and that she was receiving a Social Security check in James Brown's name. She added, "That will help me to get by until I get a job."

Remembrances of Brown began filtering in from JB's past associates. Joe Collier, then fifty-three, had played trumpet and other horns in JB's bands for twenty-one years beginning in 1980 after JB heard him playing in a small jazz club in Augusta. Collier told Tim Cox of the *Chronicle*, "He asked if I'd like to play with them. I went to his office on a Monday morning and days later, played my first gig in Toronto. . . . He was more like a father and big brother to many of us. . . . He was truly the Bach or Beethoven of our time."

Keith Jenkins, then thirty-two, Brown's lead guitarist and one of his few white band members, said that JB had backed off from his famous fines imposed on band members in later years but still had been demanding of musical excellence. "He was hard but not impossible," Jenkins told reporter Cox. "In later years, he relaxed on fining you if you missed a note or something. We had no set lists. It was mainly improvised, so he understood that. There was no daily fear of being fined."

Tony Howard, then forty-nine, who had performed for the crowds at the unveiling of Brown's statue on Broad Street, also told Cox, "Augusta will never realize how much Mr. Brown loved this city. . . . I'll never forget the time when he called [TV music host] Dick Clark and discussed business on the speaker-phone while I was sitting in his office. That was his way of teaching me about the industry."

And JB's close friend Leon Austin told Cox, "We were like brothers. His children call me Uncle Leon. James was left-handed, and I helped him form chords with his right hand. . . . I opened up a lot of shows for him. I'll really miss my old buddy. We were very tight for many years."

Immediately following the news of JB's death fans and friends

218

started turning his statue on Broad Street into a shrine covering it with flowers, candles, photos, handwritten personal messages, and other gifts. Someone draped the statue itself with a large plastic American flag, and mourners began writing more personal messages on the white stripes. (Much of that memorabilia is on display today at the Augusta Museum of History where JB and his third wife, Adrienne, donated one of his stage outfits a few years earlier and where a large exhibit about Brown will remain on display through May 2011.

You might have known that for someone as flamboyant and famous as James Brown—remember he was a Famous Flame before he actually was famous—he would need not just one or two funerals but three to send him off to what was supposed to be eternal rest.

Charlie Reid Jr., who was manager of his Brown's Third World nightclub and who had handled the funerals of Adrienne, and Joseph "Pop" Brown, conducted all three of the star's funerals.

"I got a call about 2:30 or 3 on Christmas Day morning from his daughters, Yamma and Deanna, who told me their father had died," Reid related to me a few months after Brown's death. "Then the hospital called me, and we drove to Atlanta and picked him up and brought him back to Augusta."

Asked if JB had ever discussed any funeral arrangements with him, Reid replied, "The only thing he discussed with me was about three Christmases before he passed. He wanted to make sure that everything was done proper. I don't know why it came up. We were at his Christmas party. He just broke off and started talking to me about that. I said, 'O.K., but you're going to have to stay here as long as I do, because we need to look out for one another.'"

The family sent over three different changes of clothes for the three funerals. JB's housekeeper, cook, and friend, Ella Overton, styled his world-famous hair for the last time, just as she had done thousands of times in previous years. Reid himself changed Brown's clothing for each of the three funerals, including dressing him for the final time. "It was kind of like dealing with my father. I did that myself also. It's very touching, but you know it's something that has to be done."

The First Service

Apollo Theater
253 West 125th Street
New York, New York
Thursday, December 28, 2006

One of the most bizarre journeys in rock and roll or soul music history was hauling Brown's body more than 1,670 miles over four days.

Brown's children had gone to Reid's funeral home and picked out a twenty-four-karat gold-plated casket from a book of photos. The casket was manufactured by a company in Indiana and would be fixed up accordingly and driven in a panel van from Indiana to Reid's funeral home on Laney-Walker Boulevard in Augusta.

Since the casket was extremely heavy—about five hundred pounds plus Brown's body of about one hundred and fifty pounds—the game plan was to drive it to the Atlanta airport where it would be loaded onto a plane and flown to New York City for the first of the three funerals.

But there was a hitch in the time frame when the family decided to change the casket's interior from a red-lined one to a cream color. That slowed up delivery, and the panel van containing the casket didn't arrive from Indiana until about 7:30 p.m. on Wednesday, December 27, which was too late to drive the two and a half hours to Atlanta to catch the flight to New York at about 8 p.m.

The public viewing at the Apollo was to begin about 11 a.m., so that presented a major problem. That's when, according to

Reid, Sharpton told him, "He's got to make the Apollo. He never missed the Apollo." Reid then agreed to drive the body all night, to which Sharpton said, "Well, I'll get in the car and ride with you. You ain't going to out–James Brown me."

So Brown's body, now dressed and placed in the gold casket, was put inside Reid's own panel van with Reid, Sharpton, and William Murrell, Brown's chauffeur whom Reid hired for the trip, They drove to Interstate 20 and headed off into the night, bound for New York City. There is no telling how many hundreds of vehicles passed the panel van on those more than eight hundred miles without ever knowing what precious cargo it contained.

"We stopped at two or three fast-food places and for gas and that was it," Reid told me of the trip that took about sixteen hours. "They did recognize Sharpton at the stops, and I was hoping it wouldn't get any further. They just looked and smiled. When we got to New York, we went to Reverend Sharpton's residence, which is a gated area, and we switched Mr. Brown over to a white hearse. Then we went from his residence to the horse-drawn carriage which I think was near Sharpton's office."

The old-fashioned white, glass-walled carriage hearse was pulled by two white horses, and the driver wore a black top hat. It was driven to the Apollo where thousands of fans waited for the public viewing before the service. Reid and Sharpton walked behind the hearse along with others who had been close to Brown. Two waiting lines stretched for five blocks with many of the faithful having waited in the cold since midnight. The hearse pulled up in front of the Apollo Theater at 1 p.m.

Management at the *Augusta Chronicle* considered the event so big that it sent reporter Johnny Edwards and photographer Andrew Davis Tucker to cover it. Augusta TV stations also sent crews. Edwards had only seen JB once, more than a year earlier in May of 2005, when Brown showed up to perform four songs at the James Brown Soul of America Music Festival on the Augusta Common. Edwards had taken his five-year-old daughter, Gracie, for her to see a real legend in person. "She covered her ears, because it was so loud," Edwards said with a smile.

In his coverage of the public viewing, Edwards wrote about Brown's loyal fans,

On Thursday, some of those who heard that message back then needed canes to get up the stage stairs to see Mr. Brown's body. Their heads were gray, and some tugged grandchildren. They brought bouquets of roses, and when they approached Mr. Brown, pumped their fists or tapped their hearts. Several of them danced a few steps.

Lying in the gold coffin with white lining, Mr. Brown seemed impossibly still and impossibly silent. His face was gaunt, but still recognizable. He wore a blue-sequined suit with white gloves and silver shoes. Funk music blared from a sound system—the pounding rhythms, hard-driving horns and wailing vocals of Mr. Brown's music.

Posters of Mr. Brown belting into a microphone stood on each side of the coffin, along with a 6-by-4-foot floral arrangement with "Godfather" spelled out in red carnations.

At the Apollo service Sharpton told mourners that at his past appearances at the Apollo, JB, from backstage in his dressing room, repeatedly would ask Sharpton to check and see how long the lines were of fans waiting to get inside. Sharpton said that memory came back to him as he was walking behind the horse-drawn hearse when it pulled up in front of the historic theater. "I looked at his casket and said, 'Mr. Brown, the line's all the way up to 130th Street.'"

There was an especially dramatic moment when, at the conclusion of the service, Brown's family was called onstage. Walking up with them was Hynie. She spoke into the podium's microphone saying, "He wasn't always the nicest man, but he was always right."

Once the Apollo service was over, viewing continued until about 11 p.m., and then Brown's body in the gold casket was loaded back onto Reid's panel van for the long, long, long drive back to Augusta to get Brown back in time for his second funeral scheduled the next day at Carpentersville Baptist Church in North Augusta, South Carolina. Sharpton, Reid said, opted to fly back to Augusta.

"We put him back in the van and hit the road back to Augusta," Reid said. "That was the only way we could get him back in time for the North Augusta service. We didn't leave the Apollo until about 11:30 that night and got in the next morning. We changed his clothes, put him in my black [actually dark blue] Mercedes hearse and went on to the service at the Carpentersville church."

The Second Service

Carpentersville Baptist Church
415 Carpentersville Road
North Augusta, South Carolina
Friday, December 29, 2006

JB's second funeral took place in a small, plain, brick church building capped with a white steeple behind a former Kmart turned flea market about two miles from downtown Augusta on the South Carolina side of the Savannah River.

In his opening paragraphs covering that funeral for the *Augusta Chronicle*, reporter Justin Boron wrote, "James Brown, always spectacular in life, transformed a little-known street in a poor North Augusta neighborhood into a grand boulevard Friday.

"Behind the dark blue Mercedes hearse that carried The Godfather of Soul's body in a golden casket, a motorcade of 15 limousines and cars lined the narrow street outside Carpentersville Baptist Church on Friday, where Mr. Brown's family had planned a small, private funeral at his daughter's church in North Augusta."

The Reid funeral home hearse arrived with JB's body at 2:28 p.m., or roughly ninety minutes after the funeral was scheduled to begin. James often did like to keep the crowd waiting, building up the anticipation before his appearance.

More than three hundred people—ushered in by deacons dressed uniformly in baby blue ties and navy blue suits—packed the church, including Al Sharpton; Leon Austin, dressed in a lime green suit; Leon's wife, Emma, formerly an employee of James Brown Enterprises; Charles Bobbit; civil rights activist and comedian Dick Gregory; boxing promoter Don King; music star Stanley Burrell (aka MC Hammer); fellow Georgia Music Hall of Fame inductee Janis Lewis Phillips of the Lewis Family bluegrass gospel group; and her husband, Earl.

Another seventy-five mourners was left to stand in the church's courtyard when the seats ran out.

"When he started singing, we were sitting in the back of the bus. When he stopped singing we were flying Lear jets," Sharpton said of the transformation that JB had made in improving the rights of black citizens.

The Carpentersville ceremony was marked by caustic remarks from Sharpton directed at JB's "widow." Sharpton, apparently still tired from that long drive from Augusta to Harlem and miffed by Hynie's comments at the Apollo and in the news media, looked in her direction and warned, "If you really are all that you say you are, you don't place yourself in the story. The story puts you in your place. We don't want to hear your story or your mess. We're here because of James Brown. The reason I am here is because I walked with James Brown."

Hynie, seated in the front row of the small church with her five-year-old son, already was being excluded from the Brown family. She had arrived at the church in a Ford Taurus an hour earlier than the family who arrived in limousines.

That service concluded about 4:50 p.m. with Sharpton, carrying a Bible, dramatically leading the mourners out of the church. Brown's body was loaded back into Reid's Mercedes hearse and driven to Reid funeral home to be prepared for Brown's third and largest funeral the next day.

If Reid thought he was finally going to get a few hours of good sleep that Friday night, he was badly mistaken. For late that night a special visitor who had requested a private viewing showed up, and that visitor, as Reid would tell me, was pop superstar Michael Jackson. Reid got a call about 10:30 p.m. asking "if it would be permissible" for Jackson to have a private viewing.

"He came by our funeral home the first time about 11 p.m. with about twelve or thirteen of his Nation of Islam bodyguards and stayed about forty-five minutes to an hour, and then he left," Reid said. "Apparently, they had landed in Atlanta and had come straight here from off the road. I think they were staying at the Partridge Inn. Then we got a call that he wanted to come back. So he came back about 1:30 and stayed until about 3:30 or 4 that morning. Then we got Mr. Brown ready [dressing him for the third time] and put him in the civic center [James Brown Arena] about 5:30 that morning."

When asked about Jackson's demeanor during the two visitations, Reid said, "The first time he just stood and watched Mr. Brown for God knows how long, and the next time he came he did basically the same thing and asked a few questions about the coffin. He just talked in general basically and said that he [JB] was his idol. He was very emotional about it."

Within hours after Jackson left Reid funeral home for the final time, Brown's body was loaded back into Reid's Mercedes hearse and driven just a couple of miles to James Brown Arena where the casket was positioned for James Brown's final Augusta appearance.

The Third Service

James Brown Arena
601 Seventh Street
Augusta, Georgia
Saturday, December 30, 2006

In the black gospel vernacular, Brown's funerals were called "home-going" services, meaning JB was being given his big send-offs, bound for his heavenly home. Most people agreed that although JB had done some hellish things in his life, overall he had tried throughout his seventy-three years to do the right thing for others, he truly did love his fellow human beings, and he always gave his God the credit for his talents, wealth, and world fame.

There was no question that the final "home-going" service for James Brown in his hometown of Augusta in James Brown Arena was going to be a major, major event, even though the last time he was there in concert was a disaster with extremely poor attendance in the nine-thousand-seat building.

It was the first funeral held in the thirty-two-year-old building and had the largest attendance in one building for a funeral in Augusta. Other large funerals in Augusta had packed large churches and Bell Auditorium (2,690 seated at the funeral of Augusta's first black mayor, Edward M. McIntyre in 2004), but those attendances were nowhere near the turnout for Brown's funeral. The closest of any size was that of the Reverend Charles T. Walker, a black evangelist known nationwide who died in 1921. It was reported in the *Chronicle* that 10,000 people filed past his coffin before his funeral in the roughly 2,000 seat Tabernacle Baptist Church that he had founded.

Augusta mayor Deke Copenhaver, who had stood next to Brown about a week earlier giving out toys in the Imperial, offered the use of James Brown Arena for the funeral because he expected thousands to attend. He also ordered all

Augusta-Richmond County consolidated government flags to be flown at half-mast until Brown's service was over.

Copenhaver said he was "completely shocked" by JB's death and remarked in a press release, "Today, Augusta mourns the passing of music legend James Brown. I was honored to call him a friend and to be able to share with him just how much he has meant to our community prior to his passing. Mr. Brown was a true icon in the world of music and his influence will certainly be felt for generations to come. Augusta has lost one of its greatest advocates in a man who truly loved this city. His generosity was legendary and he kept on giving right up until the end. My thoughts and prayers go out to the family during this difficult time."

The Brown family working, with Reid and arena officials including brand new general manager Robert "Flash" Gordon, a former employee of Brown's WRDW-AM radio station, arranged for a public viewing to begin at 9 a.m. followed by the service at 1 p.m.

The gold casket was placed on the north end of the arena floor in front of a large constructed stage similar to the ones that JB had performed on for his celebrity birthday party bashes in the same building and on the very spot where JB had performed. There was an elevated press area for the media and TV cameras at the south end of the floor.

Facing the stage, the left front of the arena floor was reserved for guest celebrity mourners. Most of the right side floor area was reserved for family members, politicians, close friends, and other dignitaries. That would leave, taking away the stage and elevated media area and reserved seats, 8,100 seats available to the first-come, first-seated public.

Behind the stage a black drape covered the floor-level hockey rink boards for the Augusta Lynx, that had a scheduled game the next day at 7 p.m. George Croft, arena operations manager and a musician himself, and his crew would have to remove the floor chairs and put ice back onto the arena floor after the funeral and in time for the game.

As for me, I called the last person who spoke with JB, Charles Bobbit, and asked if I could tag along with him for the day. He told me that he wasn't sure but to meet him in the lobby of the Marriott Hotel & Suites at Reynolds and 10th streets at 9 a.m. that Saturday.

When I walked into the almost empty lobby, the first person I saw was Sharpton, who would be conducting the service. I went up and shared some words with him about our past meeting at JB's Christmas party and about his getting his public start on the "Parade of Quartets" program on WJBF in Augusta, whose studio is just outside the Marriott Hotel.

A few minutes later, I was talking with comedian and civil rights activist Dick Gregory, who ended up giving one of the funniest and most emotional speeches of the day. He was dressed in a jogging suit and about to head out for a run on the Riverwalk next to the hotel. I showed him a *Chronicle* news article I had found from 1946 about JB's boxing in Bell Auditorium.

When Bobbit came to the lobby he agreed to let me ride with him to the arena and leave my car at the Marriott. We ended up going through about three or four police checks until we got to the backstage ramp of James Brown Arena.

At the intersection of Telfair and Eighth streets, we crossed through a line of people that stretched a couple of blocks down the street even though the arena had been opened to the public about an hour earlier. Brown would have loved it.

After going through the door of the arena that celebrity performers generally use, we passed other police officers until we got to a secured area just to stage right. There Robert Howard, assistant director of the Augusta-Richmond County Recreation Department, and arena general manager Gordon helped me obtain a media badge.

For a couple of hours, before taking my seat on the seventh row, I stood a few yards from the open, cream-satin-lined, gold casket where JB lay in state dressed in a black suit with sequined lapels, red shirt, black gloves, black bow tie monogrammed with the initials JB, and rhinestone-studded boots.

The coffin itself was surrounded on both ends by floral arrangements of red, yellow, white, and peach roses along with yellow daisies and peace lilies.

Near the head of the casket was a large color painting of JB by Chouaieb Saidi, which was on loan from the Lucy Craft Laney Museum in Augusta.

As the mourners filed past in a steady stream about five feet in front of the casket, Robert Howard up onstage frequently reminded the mourners not to take photos—even though many did—and that this was a funeral service and not an entertainment event. Many would disagree with that assessment—the service would include performances by Brown's band, former backup vocalists, and guest celebrity performers including MC Hammer.

Shortly after the celebrities began filing into the arena, Bobby Byrd and his wife, Vicki, walked in. It would be the last time I got to briefly say hello to him. He would be dead within seven months. Two more of James Brown's great band members—Fred Wesley and Parliament Funkadelic leader Bootsy Collins with his trademark star glasses covered with gold dust—took seats in the row in front of me as the now-filled arena crowd applauded.

Superheavy comedian Bruce Bruce also got a large round of applause from the crowd when he took his seat, as did Carlton Ridenhour, better known to his fans as Chuck D of the rap supergroup Public Enemy. Public Enemy had sampled Brown's recordings on its albums *It Takes a Nation of Millions to Hold Us Back* and also *Fear of a Black Planet*. Chuck D told the media, "He was almost like a black king or president, an international ambassador of culture and soul. Simple as that."

While those celebs attracted generous applause, pandemonium broke out when Michael Jackson entered the building, ushered by Nation of Islam guards in bow ties and crisp starched shirts. Jackson himself wore long, straightened hair and was dressed casually in a black leather jacket, black slacks, a white shirt, a thin black tie, and dark sunglasses.

He ended up sitting six rows in front of me with the Reverends Jesse Jackson on his left side and Sharpton on his right. At one point, Jackson and Sharpton led Michael up to the casket so he could grieve, and obviously to provide some great camera shots with him. Michael leaned over and kissed JB's face.

Augusta-Richmond County Fire Department officials closed the arena doors at 12:30 p.m., thirty minutes before the service started, with hundreds of mourners shut outside. They listened to the service on outside speakers. Many others outside watched the service on a portable television set up outside Augusta Presstech printing shop, two blocks from the arena, or in nearby restaurants and businesses.

The service began about 1:30 p.m. with a twenty-minute video tribute in which Brown professed his pride in Augusta. It featured his last performance in Augusta at the James Brown Soul of America Music Festival, followed by Ali "Ollie" Woodson, former lead singer of the Temptations, delivering an emotional rendition of "Walk around Heaven (All Day)."

Derrick Monk, who had produced JB's 1998 CD *I'm Back,* performed a crowd-pleasing version of Brown's favorite gospel song, "God Has Smiled on Me" that had been released as a single with Brown as producer.

Famous Flame Bobby Byrd performed "I Got You," "Georgia (On My Mind)," and the Byrd-Brown classic "Sex Machine"—in his last-ever public performance—backed by Bootsy Collins on bass guitar; Brown's band, the Soul Generals; and his backup vocalists, the Bittersweets; while Brown's daughter Venisha danced onstage, followed by MC Hammer performing JB's signature dance.

The Soul Generals were in great shape. They had rehearsed the previous night in the arena with former Brown solo vocalist Marva Whitney, who was sitting in one of the vacant seats watching. Whitney had accompanied Brown and his trimmed-down band on the trip to Vietnam in 1968. She came to Augusta from her hometown, Kansas City, to sing for Brown one last time; appropriately she sang "(Going to) Kansas City." "He was a great mentor," she said. "There's never going to be another one like him."

Other vocalists who delivered their musical tributes were Vicki Anderson Byrd, performing an incredible version of "It's A Man's, Man's, Man's World"; Jesse Jackson's daughter, Sanita, performing "Going Home," The Greatest Love of All," and "Remember Jesus"; and the Swanee Quintet led by Percy Griffin singing "True Friend."

Possibly, the strangest performance was when the grieving widow—who had been locked out of the Brown homestead —got onstage and sang the Sam and Dave hit "Hold On, I'm Coming" backed by the Soul Generals. It was a song she had been singing in recent concerts with the Brown revue, but the choice seemed a bit tasteless for the home-going service.

At the conclusion of her song, Hynie knelt down on the edge of the stage and gazed forlornly and dramatically and silently for several moments at the open casket below on the arena floor. She then pulled a rose from a nearby floral arrangement and, with a sweep of her right arm, tossed it down on JB. Spectators in the higher arena seats said that it landed on his crotch. She then kissed the casket lid before getting up and leaving the stage.

Topping that dramatic moment was an even bigger one when JB's family gathered on the stage for Shirley Lewis, president of Paine College, to present JB with a posthumous honorary degree. Reportedly, Brown had known before he died that the honor was forthcoming.

During that presentation, many television viewers and arena spectators were able to observe an intense conversation between Tomi Rae and Sharpton who were at the rear of the stage behind the family members.

Larry King later asked Hynie about that moment, and she said that Sharpton, in assisting with the presentation, had given the collegiate graduation cloak to one of the family members, the mortar board hat with tassel to another, and the degree itself to still another.

Hynie told King that Sharpton had announced to the audience, "As I sit and watch Hynie cry behind me, I know that she would be happy knowing that Mr. Brown sees that his daughter get these doctrines." She added to King, "And he looked around and he said to me, 'See, I recognized you.' And I said, 'You still aren't going to give me the dignity of calling me his wife.'

"And he said to me, 'You see, I tried to be nice to you and look what you did. Now I ain't going to be nice to you no more. That's it.' And he turned around and I started crying tears, tears, tears. And I walked off the stage. That's when they told me that there was no more funeral, and that I was to go this way. And that's when the eulogies were held, and I wasn't able to say anything about my husband."

The family's position on Hynie was made clear when several of JB's children were to take part in a tribute to their father on Larry King's TV show on January 4 but pulled out when they were told Hynie also would be taking part. They, instead, sent James Brown's lawyer Debra Opri to set the record straight. She went on camera live immediately after Hynie had her say.

"There are many signed documents wherein Ms. Hynie can't discuss the relationship of her and Mr. Brown and she does," Opri said. "She gave him a scathing review in the BBC and in a London newspaper and it's horrendous. It's a scavenge of his reputation. She had a relationship with him as a companion. . . . The family, Deanna, Venisha, and Yamma, did not invite her [to the Augusta funeral]. Hynie was there, but Hynie embarrassed herself and embarrassed the fans and the family the way she conducted herself."

Opri also said, "James Brown loved Hynie, but the last conversation Hynie had with James Brown was that she didn't love him, she never loved him, she was just in it for the business arrangement." Opri further said she was unimpressed with Hynie's sincerity at the funeral and added, "I was totally not impressed with Hynie's performance during the funeral. I was embarrassed for the James Brown family."

When asked about Hynie's right to speak at the funeral as the mother of his child, Opri told King, "You know, you're asking . . . that's another issue. James Brown intentionally did not do any DNA testing of that child during his life. And there was a reason for it. And he uttered comments to his attorneys before he died and he said, 'When I'm gone, get it done so my family knows.' Now, I'm not making allegations. I'm not here to disparage Hynie, but what she did with the BBC and the London newspaper and here again tonight and at the funeral is inappropriate to the memory of James Brown, the Godfather of Soul, and it should stop because she is contractually obligated not to discuss the business and personal issues of James Brown."

An amazing moment was when Michael Jackson—rarely seen in America since his exoneration in June 2005 by a jury in Santa Maria, California, of child molestation, conspiracy, and alcohol charges and his subsequent move to Europe—went up the stage steps and to the microphone. The crowd was screaming, thinking and hoping he might sing something. But he respectfully didn't.

"James Brown is my greatest inspiration," Jackson said in a soft but clear voice. "Ever since I was a small child, no more than like six years old, my mother would wake me no matter what time it was . . . to watch the television to see the master work. And when I saw him move, I was mesmerized. . . . And right then and there, I knew that that was exactly what I wanted to do for the rest of my life, because of James Brown." He added, "James Brown, I shall miss you, and I love you so much, and thank you for everything."

Another emotional delivery came from Jesse Jackson, leader of the Rainbow Coalition and fellow South Carolina native, who said, "James Brown did not just happen. He did not just fall out of the sky. He came out of the womb of rhythm and brass sounds of Augusta and Savannah, Georgia.

"We sum up his life: he was born with little, inherited nothing, and left a lot. Born with little, inherited nothing, and left a lot. Many are born with a lot, inherit more, and leave nothing. Sons and daughters of inheritors, looking at life top-down, see life different than sons and daughters of work ethic and cold sweat."

Not long after Jackson spoke, Danny Ray walked to the front edge of the stage holding one of Brown's large, sparkling, red-sequined capes. And without saying a word, he unfurled the cape wide as if throwing a fishing net and draped it for one final time over his boss.

At the close of the service, Sharpton administered last rites before the coffin was closed and remarked, "Thank you, Mr. Brown. You can get your rest now. We won't forget you, and we won't let the world forget you. Sleep on."

The long weekend, with rehearsal on Friday night and the funeral all day Saturday, wasn't the end of the mourning and home-going celebration for the Soul Generals, who ended up playing two forty-five-minute sets at the Soul Bar at 984 Broad Street. Owner Coco Rubio had invited the band members to take part in an informal jam session that evening and they did just that. Rubio named his club in honor of Brown's music in 1995 and had several posters of Brown in the building.

Roughly four hundred people who had gotten word of the possible jam session packed the bar. Longtime band member Keith Jenkins later said, "We got a chance to reflect and consider our future options. We're not sure when we'll all get together again."

And that's how the third and final funeral day ended—with the Soul Generals playing JB songs in the Soul Bar as their personal tribute to the King of Soul, James Brown.

Charlie Reid Jr., still had two more trips to make with Brown's body that day. First he saw that the body was safely driven from the James Brown Arena to Brown's Beech Island home, where the media and general public were told it was going to be until moved later to an "undisclosed location."

Several hours later in secret Brown's body was driven back to Reid's funeral home There it remained in storage until the family had it moved more than two months later to an above-ground mausoleum on his daughter, Deanna's ranch about three miles from JB's estate.

Presiding over that brief noon ceremony on Saturday, March 10, 2007, was Al Sharpton, with Tomi Rae Hynie—by then being described in the media as "Brown's partner"—attending, along with Brown's children and other family members who sang, prayed, and released balloons.

Not present was Brown's attorney and estate trustee, "Buddy" Dallas, who told the Associated Press, that JB was deserving of a public burial place, adding, "Mr. Brown's not deserving of anyone's backyard."

Less than two months after JB's death, the forty-ninth annual Grammy Awards was held on February 11, 2007, in Los Angeles. One of the emotional highlights of that international TV broadcast was when pop singer Christina Aguilera performed a passionate rendition of "It's a Man's Man's Man's World" and Chris Brown performed a Brown-like dance routine.

At the conclusion of the tributes, Danny Ray came out onstage carrying what appeared to be the same sparkling, red-sequined cape he had thrown over JB's gold casket at the Augusta funeral. This time Ray approached a single microphone on an upright stand, and he wordlessly draped his cape over the microphone and backed away as the single spotlight faded out on it.

And once again the full-house crowd went wild with cheers, and applause, giving a standing ovation in tribute to the man the world would forever know as Soul Brother Number One, the Hardest- Working Man in Show Business, Mr. Dynamite, and the Godfather of Soul.

EPILOGUE

I hope you live two hundred years, and I live two
hundred years minus one day so I'll never know
beautiful people like you passed away. God bless.

—James Brown

James Brown often was prompted by reporters to utter his
famous phrase "I feel good," which actually was the hook line
for his song titled "I Got You." The truth is, there were many,
many days—like most of us have—when James Brown didn't feel
anywhere close to good.

In the forty years that I crossed his path off and on, he would
go from incredible career or personal highs one day to very low
points in his life the next.

The only difference between JB and most of us is that his
lowest days became headlines in newspapers, magazines, on radio
stations and TV shows and in recent years, on countless Internet
Web sites. I truly think it was those kinds of days that kept him
living in America and in the Augusta area when he easily could
have packed his bags and moved like several celebrities to larger
or smaller cities or even other countries.

On several occasions he threatened to move from the Augusta
area, but he never did. It was the people of this area, you see,
like his seventh grade teacher Laura Garvin at Silas X. Floyd
Elementary School, who had encouraged his talent and told him
he was special. It was those unknown judges at the Lenox Theater
on Ninth Street who had patted him on the back with his first
official recognition by voting him the winner on amateur talent
night.

It was his closest Augusta childhood friends, like Leon Austin
and the late William Glenn, who hung in there with him through all

his history-making achievements and his heart-breaking failures, through the marriages and the divorces, through the poor times and wealthy ones, and through the days when people wanted to be seen with him, and the days when the same people acted as if they didn't even know him.

There are many people around Augusta and elsewhere who will tell you it wasn't always easy being James Brown's friend. He could get mad at you for the strangest of reasons, or maybe it was one of his wives who didn't like you. But, by the same token, he was one of the greatest friends you could have—who would brag about you, sing songs to your face giving you a personal concert, hug you with the same arms he used to box others, and touch you in your heart by simply asking, "How's your dad doing?"

He stayed around the Augusta area for several reasons: It is where he grew up, where the friends lived who knew him before he was famous, where he could eat a meal, watch a movie, hear a band, or just simply have a conversation without having a million flashbulbs popping in his face as when he visited New York City, Los Angeles, London, Paris, and other international capitals.

James Brown was so visible in the Augusta area that he almost was taken for granted as the guy who would be here forever. He was totally approachable. The other day a guy at my health club remarked, "You never saw him around here with a bodyguard." And that was true.

He did have an entourage for the bigger occasions like a media conference or a toy giveaway, but most of the times he would be out driving his own car, pumping his own gas, eating at fast-food restaurants, shopping in local stores, going to church services and parties, and, in recent years, taking his young son, James Brown II, to the Exchange Club of Augusta's fall fair on the same grounds where Ty Cobb started playing professional baseball in 1904.

More people in the Augusta area, I would wager, had the opportunity to say hello to James Brown than had the chance to even visit the fairways of the Augusta National Golf Club, much less play there. No matter where Augustans travel in the world, they usually are greeted with: "Oh, the home of the Masters tournament" or "Oh, the home of James Brown."

In spite of the police chases and the nasty incidents and bitter letters that Augustans sometimes wrote about him to editors of local newspapers, James Brown was deeply loved and admired by thousands of Augusta-area citizens of all races and educational backgrounds for both his amazing talents and his uniqueness as a person. He may have been Soul Brother Number One to the world, but to those from the Augusta area waiting in long lines for turkeys and toys and just having the joy to know him—with some racist exceptions—he was Friend Number One.

In writing about his years growing up in Augusta, I was reminded of what one of his childhood friends, Allyn Lee, told me about the neighborhoods where they lived as children in the 1940s. He said each had its own gangs and the members would beat up any kid who was not supposed to be in that area and who didn't basically crawl while passing through that section.

But he said his young friend, James Brown, never was scared of anyone and always stood tall and held his head high—walking anywhere in any neighborhood about town. And it hit me that what Lee had described was exactly the pattern of JB's entire life.

He was undoubtedly often defiant, frequently arrogant, and never ever afraid to take on anyone who had done him wrong—whether it was powerful IRS agents, white record company owners and promoters who tried to cheat him, trusted friends who broke his heart, or even police who arrested him even though it may have been deserved sometimes.

That exactly is why people the world over loved James Brown—not only because of his enormous musical contributions but also because he was a person who was not about to let anyone put him down or put him "in his place." He was the one who had the guts to proclaim, "Say it loud, I'm black and I'm proud" when blacks in America were still being called that horrible "N" word. No wonder in his later years, he hated it when young black rappers used that same "N" word to refer to women and men of their own race.

I will miss his smile more than anything else and his infectious laughter that made you feel good even more than he felt good. He was a joy to be around for the most part, and I was honored and privileged to share so many good and bad times in his life. He was not only this genius whose music creations will live forever, but he was also a truly extraordinary human being, even on his most terrible days.

Almost any given day in downtown Augusta, if you go to the Augusta Common in the 800 block of Broad Street to the statue of James Brown in the middle of the street, you will find one or more visitors there taking photos, posing with the statue, reading the bronze marker, laying floral tributes or other special gifts at its base, or simply sitting on a nearby bench quietly resting in his presence.

The statue is kept lighted twenty-four hours each day, which must really please the Godfather who loved being in the spotlight. And surely the steady stream of visitors also must please JB who dearly loved his fans and friends and family with a love that transcended all of his personal troubles and all of his enormous successes.

It would be easy to feel sad every Christmas Day in the future knowing what happened on Christmas Day 2006 if you did not know what Thanksgivings and Christmases meant to JB. He would want you to give a turkey or a toy to someone who needed it, because he always remembered where he came from as well as knowing where he was going.

He could be just as comfortable dancing onstage with the female president of Finland as chatting with someone while pumping his own gas at a station in Beech Island. He had the same ease dining at the White House as driving up to the take-out window at the chicken wings place on Sand Bar Ferry Road in

Augusta. He could exude the same dignity in accepting praise at the Kennedy Center as in shaking hands with average workers at Augusta's Bush Field airport whenever he was flying off to begin world tours.

James Brown, was simply one of those people who rarely ever comes into your life, and yet was someone you remember with joy and gratefulness the rest of your life.

In wrapping up this book, I once again called his first wife, Velma, at the large brick home in Toccoa, that JB had built for her and their children after he had left to move on to other wives and other relationships.

"I look at it like this, if a man leaves and takes care of his family, then he's all right," Velma said, "because a lot of men leave and forget about their family."

She mentioned how proud JB was of the way Augusta had treated him in his final years with the naming of the street and civic center after him and with the statue on Broad Street. She said it was true that JB took friends, family, and other visitors to see the statue.

Yes, he would always talk about how they recognized him down there [in Augusta]. At first they didn't, but after they started doing it and everything, he was real proud of that.

I'm glad they recognized him, because anything he did, he did it wholeheartedly. He did it from the heart. Everything he did, he did it from the heart. He was so proud of being able to give those children toys at Christmas, and he was so glad to give the turkeys out at Thanksgiving. And he really believed in children having an education. Those three things were his pet projects. That's what he wanted. He said, "Nothing would kill ignorance but education."

There are people who want to believe the bad things about him, and they don't want to look at the good, but in my heart, I know he was a good person. That's all that matters—no matter how many books are written, because I've read a lot of stuff that I knew wasn't true about him and heard a lot of stuff that I knew wasn't true about him.

And finishing up her thoughts, Velma choked up some as she told me with a heavy tone in her voice, "The way I loved him in life is the way I love him in death, and that's just the way it is."

APPENDIX A:

An Interview with Gloria Anderson Daniel

N ear the completion of this book, I was told by James Brown's attorney, "Buddy" Dallas, about Gloria Anderson Daniel, who was in and out of James Brown's life for thirty-eight years (between 1968 and 2006). She rarely appeared in the media even though JB sometimes introduced her as his "fiancée" but JB's associates, friends, and family were well aware of her presence in JB's life whether they approved of her or not. This is the story she told me. You can decide for yourself what you want to believe.

Thursday, February 28, 2008
The phone rings; someone picks up the receiver. A toddler is heard crying; heard almost above the voice of the person answering the phone in an extremely nice, Tudor-style home near Atlanta:

Gloria: Hello.
Don: Is this Gloria?
Gloria: Who?
Don: Gloria Daniel.
Gloria: Yes.
Don: This is Don Rhodes in Augusta, Georgia.
Gloria: Uh-huh.
Don: Did Buddy Dallas tell you I'd be calling you?
Gloria: Yeah. Didn't I talk with you before?
Don: No, no. We haven't talked.
Gloria: What's your name?
Don: Don Rhodes. R-h-o-d-e-s.
Gloria: Attorney general? The attorney general? No, he didn't, but what's up? [she laughs]
Don: I'm wrapping up a book that I've got to have completed this weekend about James that is coming out in October.
Gloria: Uh-huh. . . . Hold on. [She then is heard saying sternly] Don't write on that furniture! Write on the floor on your paper! [Then she says to me] I have a two-year-old granddaughter I'm

watching. [Then she says sternly again] You write on the floor on your paper! I said, No, no! I'll take it from you! You don't write on the furniture! [Then back to me she says] I was with him those last two days before he went to Atlanta.

Don: So you were with him on Thursday and Friday [December 21 and 22, 2006, before his death on Monday, Christmas Day]?

Gloria: Uh-huh.

Don: Now, Velma Brown, his first wife, told me she was with him that week also.

Gloria: Maybe so, but I doubt it. Washington [JB's chauffeur David Washington] picked me up. So, he can verify that I was there, but I don't know if Velma came unless she came in the earlier part of the week, because he [JB] left Saturday [for Atlanta] and he also told me that he had been alone all week. But, you know, he could have had other guests. I don't know. He was in bad shape when I was there. His feet were swollen, and I had to rub him, rub him, rub him. And he had this terrible cough. When you rubbed his back, you could hear the cold all in him.

Don: But you didn't think he was going to die [that Christmas weekend] just like everyone else didn't?

Gloria: Oh, of course not. I asked him to go to the doctor. I've been with James since 1968, and we never stopped seeing each other through all of his little marriages and affairs. I lived at his house with him three times starting in 1980.

Don: The first time was where he was living on Walton Way Extension?

Gloria: No, no, no. The first time I moved in he was still where he is [at death] on Douglas Drive.

Don: In 1980, was that after he and [his second wife] Deidre split?

Gloria: Well, it was shortly after, but he had another girl named Peggy staying there, and she stayed there for about a year. He and I were still dating, and he wanted me to come there, so he and Peggy split up and I came. He was trying to get me there to live. I would always visit the house, but I never would stay.

Don: Did y'all meet in Atlanta?

Gloria: We met in New Orleans. I was from New Orleans. I went to his show—[Toddler is heard shouting] Excuse me. [To toddler] Write on the paper! [To me] She is writing on her face! [To toddler] If you write on your face again, I'm taking the pen! [To me] I'm sorry. Let me see, I went to a concert, and I knew

Larry McKinley who was a disc jockey in New Orleans, and he let me and my friends in. They went inside to watch the show, but I had my paper and pen to meet him. So I got backstage and I waited the whole show, and then Mr. Bobbit told me, 'You can't see him unless you go to the airport.' So, of course, I did, wanting to meet James Brown. I rode in a separate limousine right behind his, and when I got there, he came to the car and said, 'Get out of the car and let me see you.' He put me on his plane, and that's how it started."

Don: He put you on his plane? Where did you go?

Gloria: He took me to Dallas. That's where we went. I remember that trip on his jet distinctly because he said, 'We don't have a restroom. You have to do it in a bag or something.' But I waited until we got there. But I was only there only a couple of hours because his fiancée at the time was Dee Dee [Deidre Jenkins]. She flew in, and I had to come right back, which I was happy to do, because I went for an autograph, not an affair actually, you know. I was young then, and he frightened me, you know.

Don: Did y'all do anything on the plane going to Dallas?

Gloria: Oh, no, no, no. Just talked. He was a perfect gentleman, but when we got there I realized it was more involved. I looked around and I said, 'Oh, God, I don't want to sleep with this man.'

Don: Now, why did you say that? He was a good-looking guy.

Gloria: I know, but out of his clothes, I didn't like it. He came into the [hotel] room naked, and I was shy at the time. I'm like, 'Oh, God, cover it up.' I was naive, you know. He said, 'Be in the bed when I come back.' He was in the next room having business with his managers and stuff. So I got in the bed with my clothes on, and he came and he pulled the covers back and said, 'I said, be naked.' I'm like, 'Oh, God,' so I went in the bathroom and got in my underwear. He went back out and came back in and I still wasn't naked, so we went through that. By the time I did get butt naked in bed, a knock came on the door, and I was like relieved because I was getting ready to get myself in a situation I wasn't ready for.

Don: How old were you then?

Gloria: I was eighteen.

Don: So, who was the knock at the door?

Gloria: It was Mr. Bobbit letting him [JB] know that Dee Dee had flew in. So James said, 'I'm going to call you. Stay home,' and he gave me a lot of money, and I flew right back [to New

Orleans], so it was just like a couple of hours that I was gone. I had called my cousin . . . at that time we used to take acid and all kinds of silly drugs in the sixties, and she knew me and my friends used to get high sometimes—and I said, 'I'm with James Brown, and I'm going to Dallas,' and she said, 'Yeah, right' and hung up on me. So, when I got back from Dallas in a couple of hours after he flew me back commercial, I called her from the [New Orleans] airport and said, 'Oh, God, I've been with James Brown, and I've got all this money.' She said, 'Bitch, get off that stuff! You need to stop!' and hung up on me. We later laughed about that, how she didn't believe me until he gave me the first call to come to Philadelphia.

Don: How long after the Dallas trip was that?

Gloria: It must have been a month. I stayed in. I wouldn't go anywhere waiting on James Brown. Everybody said I was fantasizing, and that I had went to the show and made up all that stuff. Everybody thought I was really tripping until my cousin got the call, 'cause the night I went out was when he called. I had given my cousin the number of where I'd be, and she said, 'Yeah, I'll call,' not really believing me. Then she called the place where I used to hang out at this little club with five girls from my school, and she said, 'Get home quick! James Brown called, and it was really him! He sounds just like on his records!' That's how it really began with that trip to Philadelphia. . . . He would send me round-trip tickets.

Don: Then you started hooking up with him at shows and everything?

Gloria: No, no, no. He would send for me. He talked to my parents 'cause I was married and had two small kids. I left my husband when I met James. He would send money for them and my mom to keep my kids so I could see him. And so it continued that way. But anyway, let me ask you, what are you doing, an interview?

Don: Yes, for this book, because I thought you should get your credit because I have never have read in any article or any book—

Gloria: About me.

Don: About you.

Gloria: I know. You know I did an article with the *Globe* [the American tabloid magazine] last year. Did you read it?

Don: No, but I'll look it up.

Gloria: It was March 26, and it was the first time I had talked with anyone about our affair even though people knew about it in all the entourage. He always talked about Gloria, and that's me. I recently talked with a man with *GQ* [magazine], and he said, 'Why did you stay with him, and why didn't you want to marry him?' I said, 'I never wanted to marry him because he was hard to live with.' He asked me to marry him several times. He was fun, and then he was hard to be around when he was doing drugs and everything. He changed in the last four years with this Tomi Rae girl. His drug habits, it got worse.

Don: I always thought it was Adrienne who got him on PCP.

Gloria: Adrienne didn't get him on PCP. He already was on it. Oh, James was on that for years. In the first years when I met him, he was smoking weed, but shortly after that, he knew about PCP I guess when it first came out, like with Jimi Hendrix and the rest of them. He got on that and he never stopped.

Don: Did James ever do heroin?

Gloria: No, no, not to my knowledge.

Don: I heard you were at one end of the house while Tomi Rae was at the other end of the house.

Gloria: Not exactly. Tomi Rae never had a key to his door, so during the marriage we never stopped seeing each other. You know, I could come at any time he wanted me to, because he always told me he wasn't really married to her, and I wouldn't disrespect her if she had been his wife. [heavy breathing]. [To toddler] Come here! [To me] I'm sorry. I was walking up these steps, and I'm trying to get this girl to come down. [To toddler] Come here! [To me] Hold on a minute.

When James met me, my married name was Gloria Steele. I had married James Steele, my high school sweetheart at sixteen. We had two kids, and I met James at eighteen. Then in 1978, I met a guy at General Motors, James Daniel, and married him briefly and that's how I got the name Daniel. . . . Now, you write for the *Augusta Chronicle?*

Don: Yes, that's right. I write a music column for it.

Gloria: Could you find out—they got videotapes on when he and I went to the Super Bowl right after Adrienne died. It was around that time in January we went to the Super Bowl in my home of New Orleans. They did film on us. I never did get my copy. There was a lady with the Augusta TV station. That was the time they shot him up through the floor. I was with him on that, and I was wondering if you could get any footage of that. He did the whole show.

247

Don: Well, I don't have any connection with the TV station, but I can ask.

Gloria: I was with him in Cincinnati at the Rock and Roll Hall of Fame, and I went with him in Chicago where he was getting inducted into something with music. Jerry Butler, Aretha Franklin, and others were there.

Don: How did he introduce you when you were with him?

Gloria: Well, he did at shows. He would say, 'my fiancée,' and he brought me out onstage several times.

Don: He would introduce you as his fiancée?

Gloria: Yeah, oh, yeah, several times.

Don: Were y'all really ever engaged?

Gloria: Oh, noooooo. He just would always say that we lived together, you know . . . this is my fiancée, but I told him no several times about marriage. He gave me diamonds and mink coats and cars and stuff—the same things he gave everybody else.

Don: When was the first time you lived together?

Gloria: We lived together the first time in 1980, but I met him in '68, 'cause a lot of years before that [1980] he tried to get me to live down there but I didn't like Augusta. I would come and visit but I wouldn't live with him. When I first met him, he was still with Dee Dee. He would fly Dee Dee and her kids out to California and fly me and my kids out to California at the same time. We would be at different hotels. He just did it like that. He spent a lot of money flying me here and there, flying her home, flying me out.

Don: Do you think Dee Dee knew about you?

Gloria: Well, she did in 1980 I'm sure because I kept her kids at the house at Beech Island along with mine. He let my kids visit that summer and brought Deanna and Yamma out—they were little girls—and Neecie [Vanisha] from California, she came out too. My daughter—she's dead now—was about Deanna's age, so they played together.

Don: How long did y'all live together that time?

Gloria: That time, I stayed about a year and a half, and then we had a fight and I moved back to Atlanta where my mom lived. The next time was about '96 or '97 whatever year it was that Adrienne died [1996]. She died that January, and I moved in the day of her funeral in California. He was away for her funeral in California, and I was at the house. Then he came back and they had the funeral in Augusta. I didn't go to her funeral there. I was just at the house with him.

Don: Do you think he loved Adrienne the best or Velma?

Gloria: I don't know who he loved, you know. He said that he loved us all. I just know through all of his marriages and his affairs we stayed on a basis where we always saw each other. I never stopped seeing him. Anytime he called, I came.

Don: When was the third time you lived with him?

Gloria: 2001. He had met—what's her name?—Tomi Rae. He bought me a Jag that year. We went back together, but it didn't last for about two months because we had a bad, bad fight in Las Vegas. We ended up getting into it, and I flew back to Atlanta. So that was the last time we lived together, but I continued to go see him. That [fight] didn't last but about a week or two and we were all right again. But all my clothes and stuff were at his house, because that was a major move again. And then she found out she was pregnant, and we busted up for a little bit.

Don: Do you think that kid [James Joseph Brown II] is James's?

Gloria: He said it wasn't. In fact, I heard he had a vasectomy, so we'll see if she ever does the DNA.

Don: I heard this wild rumor that he won a lottery of about $100,000 just before he died. Do you think that's true?

Gloria: I don't know, but I just know—had he lived—he said something big was going to happen in January, and he was going to give people this and that. He had promised friends like Bobby Byrd other things. He didn't tell me what. I thought it was something with the record deal or something. I never heard anything about the lottery, but I knew James used to play it. He was really lucky with gambling. He would go to Vegas and overseas like in France and gamble, and they would make him stop. That's how lucky he was. They would.

Don: What do you think he's best going to be remembered for?

Gloria: His music. You know a lot of people in the music field didn't get along with him because he didn't take to listening to anybody. He was always the boss, and he had to be the one to have the last say and he didn't like being told what to do. And I always said he deserved that because he worked for it. He's the boss. He took care of a lot of people through his life. I know he took good care of me.

Don: Did you go to his Augusta funeral?

Gloria: I watched it on CNN. I was so upset. What happened that Christmas Eve was that I got up that night to go to the bathroom, and I leave the TV on all night. I saw his picture, and I turned the TV up, and when they said he was dead, I almost fainted. I screamed, and my son [Daryll] and his wife came in, and my grandson. It was Christmas morning, and I thought, 'Oh, God, I just left there.' He had given me money for Christmas and everything. I had no idea he was that sick. I knew he was sick, but I didn't think he was that bad. I knew it was bad enough for him to go to the doctor, and I kept saying, 'Baby, you need to go to the doctor.' And he said, 'No, I just got to get my feet down [from being swollen] 'cause I got to go to work for New Year's.' That's all he talked about.

Don: Did you leave that Friday afternoon after the toy giveaway or did you stay that Friday night?

Gloria: No, no, no. I left that Friday morning about 12.

Don: That was a nasty, nasty, cold, rainy day.

Gloria: It was and he looked so bad. He was very upset because Tomi Rae wouldn't come home [from California at the drug abuse clinic]. It was so sad around his house for Christmas with him being sick. The Christmas tree was up with nothing under it. The house just had a gloom over it. . . . Tell me this. I'm trying to get a connection with [director/producer] Spike Lee or whoever is doing his movie. I want to be known now about my friendship with him—my love affair—because a lot of people just didn't know that he had other people in his life—I mean regular. I put a lot of my youth with him and my old age with him. So I want to be there. So if you can, could you maybe send a copy of your book to him when you do it?

Don: I promise you I'll do that. You don't mind me quoting you, right?

Gloria: No, I don't.

Don: 'Cause I think your story needs to be told.

Gloria: Oh, yeah, I have a helluva story.

APPENDIX B:

A Brief Chronology of James Brown's Life

March 29, 1911, Joseph Brown, who would become James Brown's father, was born in Barnwell County, South Carolina, reportedly as "Joseph Gardner." He later assumed the name Brown from a woman who cared for him as a child.

August 8, 1916, JB's mother, Susie Behling, was born in Colleton County, South Carolina, where Walterboro is the county seat.

May 3, 1933, James Brown is born in rural Barnwell County, South Carolina, near Snelling.

About 1936, JB's family, including his father, Joseph, and mother, Susie, move to Augusta, Georgia, where they initially live with Joseph's aunt, Hansone "Honey" Washington.

January and February, 1946, James is boxing in the welter weight class in the city auditorium.

May 31, 1949, Richmond County Grand Jury returns a true bill against JB (meaning there was enough evidence for a trial) for "four cases of breaking and entering and larceny from an automobile."

June 13, 1949, James Brown is sentenced by Superior Court Judge Grover C. Anderson to serve two to four years in prison for each of the four breaking and entering cases or a total time of eight to sixteen years.

June 14, 1952, JB released from Georgia Boys Industrial Institute prison in Toccoa exactly three years and one day after being sentenced in Richmond County Superior Court.

June 27, 1953, marries Velma Warren in living room of the house of the pastor of Trinity CME (Colored Methodist Episcopal) at 326 West Franklin Street in Toccoa.

November 1, 1955, JB and the Famous Flames record demo session of "Please, Please, Please" at downtown Macon radio station WIBB-AM, then located in the basement of the old Professional Building at 830 Mulberry Street. Charles "Big Saul" Green, a popular WIBB disc jockey, was at the reel-to-reel tape control board which JB later donated to the Georgia Music Hall of Fame.

January 23, 1956, Ralph Bass signs Brown and the Famous Flames to the King/Federal records label.

February 4, 1956, JB and the Famous Flames record in King/Federal studios in Cincinnati, Ohio, "Please, Please, Please," "I Feel That Old Feeling Coming On," "I Don't Know," and "Why Do You Do Me?"

251

March 3, 1956, single version of "Please, Please, Please" released on the Federal label, and by April 11 was peaking at Number 6 on the nation's rhythm & blues sales charts.

October 1, 1958, Brown's first No. 1 hit, "Try Me," is released.

October 24, 1962, Brown, then 29, personally pays to rent the Apollo Theater in Harlem at 253 West 125th Street, and all other expenses to record a "live" album that his record company owner didn't want him to do. The emcee is Lucas "Fats" Gonder who also played organ in JB's orchestra. King/Federal records company owner Syd Nathan is so convinced it will be a disaster that only 5,000 copies were pressed initially.

June 30, 1963, the live album titled *The Apollo Theatre Presents In Person The James Brown Show,* becomes a benchmark in recording history, remaining on *Billboard* magazine's music charts for a then-unprecedented 66 weeks, peaking at No 2.

May 10, 1964, Brown is back in Augusta headlining a show in Bell Auditorium that also features the Famous Flames, the James Brown Orchestra, Otis Redding, Dionne Warwick, Solomon Burke, Garnet Mims, the Tams, the Orlons, and others. Tickets are $3 advance or $3.50 at the door.

October 28-29, 1964, Teenage Awards Music International show filmed in Santa Monica, California, auditorium with JB, the Supremes, the Beach Boys, the Rolling Stones, and others. The resulting film is titled *The T.A.M.I. Show* with JB and the Famous Flames stealing the show.

February 1, 1965, Brown records what will be his monster cross over charts hit "Papa's Got a Brand New Bag."

June 1968, JB with a minimum number of band members and with backup vocalist Marva Whitney performs for American soldiers in Vietnam with the author of this book seeing him at Long Binh Post.

August 1968, Brown releases what will become the anthem of black citizens worldwide: "Say It Loud, I'm Black and I'm Proud."

February 4, 1969, "James Brown Day" in Augusta, with JB riding in a parade on Broad Street being cheered by thousands and performing a fundraising concert for Paine College at Bell Auditorium.

February 18, 1969, *Look* magazine issue has JB on cover with headline asking, "Is he the most important black man in America?"

August 26, 1969, JB and Velma officially divorce. They had been separated since 1964 but will remain in each others' lives until his death.

May 12, 1970, JB flies from Flint, Michigan, to Augusta in his private jet to meet with Georgia Governor Lester Maddox at Brown's WRDW radio station to appeal for calm in Augusta and Richmond County in wake of a racial riot following the death of 16-year-old Charles Oatman in the old Richmond County jail.

October 22, 1970, JB and Deidre (Dee Dee) Jenkins are married on the front porch of a probate judge in Barnwell, South Carolina.

July 1, 1971, Brown signs with Polydor Records.

June 14, 1973, 19-year-old Teddy Lewis Brown killed with two others in a one-car accident near Elizabethtown, New York.

October 17, 1973, JB's plush Augusta nightclub, The Third World, is destroyed by fire.

January 5, 1974: Brown releases *The Payback* album which was recorded in Augusta. It will become one of the best selling albums of his career and be regarded as the real start of funk music.

September 1, 1974, Brown scores personal high by being on a show with B. B. King, Etta James, Bill Withers, and the Spinners performing for more than 120,000 people at a music festival in Zaire, Africa, which preceded the legendary "Rumble in the Jungle" boxing match between George Foreman and Muhammad Ali.

March 10, 1979, JB is a guest artist on the Grand Ole Opry in Nashville after being invited by Opry member and Dolly Parton's former duet partner, Porter Wagoner.

January 10, 1981, Brown's second marriage of 10 years to Deidre Jenkins officially ends. Their union had produced two daughters, Deanna and Yamma.

March 11, 1982, James Brown is a speaker at the memorial service in the Cathedral of Saint John Divine in New York City for actor John Belushi. JB always will credit Belushi and Dan Aykroyd for resurrecting his fading career by having him featured in their movie *The Blues Brothers.*

September 24, 1983, Brown is inducted into the Georgia Music Hall of Fame with the ceremony being in Atlanta.

September 21, 1984, Brown marries Adrienne Rodriguez.

November 21, 1984, Brown attends the world premiere of the *Rocky IV* movie. He is seen in a cameo appearance in the film singing "Living in America" before a crucial boxing match.

May 30, 1985, Brown's Beech Island, South Carolina, home on nearly 40 acres is sold at public auction, purchased by his attorney Albert "Buddy" Dallas for $9,500.

January 23, 1986, Brown becomes one of the first inductees into the Rock and Roll Hall of Fame with the ceremony being in New York City.

June 28, 1986, "James Brown Day" is held at Augusta Riverfront Marina, marking the second official time that his adopted city had honored him.

September 24, 1988, JB at his Executive Office Park office suite armed with a shotgun and a pistol confronts a group attending a seminar in another section of the building.

December 15, 1988, Brown found guilty in Aiken County General Sessions Court and sentenced to six years in jail by Circuit Court Judge Hubert E. Long.

February 27, 1991, JB granted parole after hearing before the South Carolina Parole Board in Columbia and freed after two years and two months in custody. His parole officially would not expire until October 23, 1993, after which he would be on probation for five years.

June 10, 1991, JB stages come back with live, Pay-Per-View concert broadcast from Los Angeles's Wiltern Theater with the event arranged by boxing promoter Butch Lewis.

February 25, 1992, Brown accepts a Lifetime Achievement Award at the 34th annual Grammy Awards.

July 10, 1993, Joseph "Pop" Brown, JB's father, dies at 81.

November 20, 1993, an estimated 5,000 people turn out in the cold to see part of Ninth Street (originally known as Campbell Street) between Broad and Twiggs streets renamed James Brown Boulevard including JB's mother, Susie, and wife, Adrienne.

January 6, 1996, Adrienne Brown suffers cardiac arrest at The Hidden Garden upscale after-care facility in Beverly Hills, California, after cosmetic surgery. She is taken to Century City Hospital where she is dead on arrival. She will have a memorial service in California attended by celebrities as well as her funeral in Augusta's Imperial Theatre with burial following in Walker Memorial Park in Augusta.

January 10, 1997, JB finally gets his "star" on the Hollywood Walk of Fame.

January 26, 1997, JB performs at the Super Bowl in New Orleans.

April 28, 2000, fire set by arsonist burns James Brown Enterprises office complex on West Augusta Parkway.

August 1, 2000, James Brown signs his will. It never is amended legally and, therefore, does not include his future wife, Tomi Rae Hynie, nor their son.

June 11, 2001, Tomi Rae Hynie, backup and featured vocalist in JB's touring revue, gives birth to James Joseph Brown II. Those close to Brown later will say that Brown himself told them that the child is not his.

December 14, 2001, Brown marries backup vocalist Hynie in a ceremony at his Beech Island, South Carolina, home, only to later discover Hynie was still legally married to someone else. He was 68. She was 32. Their son was six months old.

July 21, 2003, JB takes out a full page advertisement in the show business magazine *Variety* saying that due to their "heavy, demanding tour schedule," that JB and his wife had decided to go their separate ways.

December 7, 2003, JB, now reconciled with Hynie, takes her to the Kennedy Center in Washington, D.C., where he is honored with a lifetime creative achievement award.

February 26, 2004, Brown's mother, Susie Behling Brown, dies at 87. Her funeral service is held in Mt. Carmel United Methodist Church in Bamberg, South Carolina. She was buried in Walker Memorial Park cemetery in Augusta beside her former husband. At this writing, she still doesn't have a gravestone.

December 15, 2004, JB undergoes prostate cancer treatment procedure at Midtown Urology Surgical Center in Atlanta.

May 6, 2005, Brown is present in the 800 block of Broad Street in Augusta for a statue unveiled in his honor.

September 20, 2006, JB performs last concert in the U.S. at the Rialto Square Theater in Joliet, Illinois.

November 5, 2006, JB performs his last concert ever at the K.C. Drazen Petrovic arena in Zagreb, Croatia.

November 14, 2006, JB sings publicly for last time after being inducted into the United Kingdom Music Hall of Fame at the Alexandra Palace on the north side of London.

November 21, 2006, JB for the last time presides over his annual turkey giveaway at Dyess Park on James Brown Boulevard. The turkey giveaway will be continued after his death by his family and friends.

December 22, 2006, JB makes his last public appearance at his annual Christmas toy giveaway at the Imperial Theatre in Augusta. It also will be continued after his death by his family and friends.

December 25, 2006, JB dies at Emory Crawford Long Hospital, 550 Peachtree Street in northeast Atlanta, about 1:30 a.m. with his longtime friend and road manager Charles Bobbit with him.

December 28, 2006, first of three services for JB held at the Apollo Theater, 253 West 125th Street, Harlem, New York City. Thousands line up for blocks to view the body.

December 29, 2006, second of three services for JB held at the Carpentersville Baptist Church, 414 Carpentersville Road, North Augusta, South Carolina, mainly for family members and very close friends.

December 30, 2006, the third and final of his three funeral services is held in James Brown Arena in Augusta with more than 8,000 attending and being broadcast live over CNN cable news TV network.

March 10, 2007, James Brown's body is placed in a crypt at the Beech Island, South Carolina, home of his daughter, Deanna Brown Thomas, not far from JB's home. The Reverend Al Sharpton presided over the private ceremony.

September 12, 2007, Bobby Byrd, cofounder of the Famous Flames and writer and arranger of many James Brown songs, dies of cancer at his home in Loganville, Georgia, at age 73. His last public performance was singing at James Brown's funeral service in Augusta.

June 12, 2008, JB's close childhood friend Leon Rhodes Austin, who taught JB to play piano with both hands and styled his hair for twenty years before shows and other media events, dies at his home in Augusta at age 74. More than 1,000 attended the funeral service at the United House of Prayer in Augusta with the Reverend Al Sharpton delivering the main eulogy.

APPENDIX C:

Suggested Further Reading

Brown, James. *I Feel Good: A Memoir of a Life of Soul.* With an introduction by Marc Eliot. Penguin Group, New York: New American Library, 2005.

Brown, James. *James Brown, the Godfather of Soul: An Autobiography.* With Bruce Tucker. Macmillan Publishing Co., New York. 1990, reprint, Thunder's Mouth Press. First published 1986 by Macmillan.

Charles, Ray. *Brother Ray: Ray Charles' Own Story.* With David Ritz. Perseus Publishing, Cambridge, MA: Da Capo Press, 2004. First published 1978 by Dial Press.

Eng, Steve. *Satisfied Mind: The Country Music Life of Porter Wagoner.* Thomas Nelson publishers, Nashville: Rutledge Hill Press, 1992.

George, Nelson, and Alan Leeds, eds. *The James Brown Reader, 50 Years of Writing About the Godfather of Soul.* New York: Plume, 2008.

Guralnick, Peter. *Sweet Soul Music: Rhythm and Blues and the Southern Dream of Freedom.* Back Bay Books, Boston: Little, Brown, 1999.

Loewan, Nancy. *James Brown, Profiles in Music.* Vero Beach, FL: Rourke Enterprises Inc, 1989.

Miller, Zell. *They Heard Georgia Singing.* Macon, GA: Mercer University Press, 1996.

Robins, Wayne. *A Brief History of Rock, Off the Record.* Taylor & Francis Inc., New York: Routledge, 2008.

Smith, R. J. *The Great Black Way: L.A. in the 1940s and the Lost African-American Renaissance*, Public Affairs, New York, 2006.

APPENDIX D:

Selected Discography

<u>NOTABLE SINGLES</u>

- "Please Please Please" / "Why Do You Do Me?"—Federal 12258 (1956)
- "Try Me" / "Tell Me What I Did Wrong"—Federal 12337 (1958)
- "I Want You So Bad" / "There Must Be a Reason"—Federal 12348 (1959)
- "I'll Go Crazy" / "I Know It's True (I Found Someone)"—Federal 12369 (1960)
- "Think" / "You've Got the Power"—Federal 12370 (1960)
- "Bewildered" / "If You Want Me"—King 5442 (1961)
- "Lost Someone" / "Cross Firing"—King 5573 (1961/2)
- "Night Train" / "Why Does Everything Happen to Me"—King 5614 (1962)
- "Prisoner of Love" / "Choo-Choo" (Locomotion) (Instrumental)—King 5739 (1963)
- "These Foolish Things" / "(Can You) Feel It" (Part 1) (Instrumental)—King 5767 (1963)
- "Oh Baby, Don't You Weep" (Part 1) / "Oh Baby, Don't You Weep" (Part 2)—King 5842 (1964)
- "Caldonia" / "Evil" (Instrumental)—Smash 1898 (1964)
- "So Long" / "Dancing Little Thing"—King 5899 (1964)
- "Out of Sight" / "Maybe the Last Time"—Smash 1919 (1964)
- "Think" / "Try Me"—King 5952 (1964)
- "I Got You (I Feel Good)" / "Only You"—Smash 1989 (1965)
- "Papa's Got a Brand New Bag" (Part 1) / "Papa's Got a Brand New Bag" (Part 2)—King 5999 (1965)
- "Ain't That a Groove" (Part 1) / "Ain't That a Groove" (Part 2)—King 6025 (1966)
- "It's a Man's Man's World" / "Is It Yes or Is It No"—King 6035 (1966)
- "James Brown's Boo-Ga-Loo" (Instrumental) / "Lost in a Mood of Changes" (Instrumental)—Smash 2042 (1966)
- "Don't Be a Drop-Out" / "Tell Me That You Love Me"—King 6056 (1966)

- "Think" (with Vicki Anderson) / "Nobody Cares" (with Vicki Anderson)—King 6091 (1967)
- "Cold Sweat" (Part 1) / "Cold Sweat" (Part 2)—King 6110 (1967)
- "Funky Soul No. 1" (Instrumental) / "The Soul of JB" (Instrumental)—King 6133 (1967)
- "I Can't Stand Myself" / "There Was a Time"—King 6144 (1967/8)
- "I Got the Feelin'" / "If I Ruled the World"—King 6155 (1968)
- "Licking Stick" (Part 1) / "Licking Stick" (Part 2)—King 6166 (1968)
- "America Is My Home" (Part 1) / "America Is My Home" (Part 2)—King 6112 (1968)
- "Say It Loud—I'm Black and I'm Proud" (Part 1) / "Say It Loud—I'm Black and I'm Proud" (Part 2)—King 6187 (1968)
- "Santa Claus Goes Straight to the Ghetto" / "You Know It" (Instrumental)—King 6203 (1969)
- "The Popcorn" (Instrumental) / "The Chicken" (Instrumental)—King 6240 (1969)
- "Mother Popcorn" (Part 1) / "Mother Popcorn" (Part 2)—King 6245 (1969)
- "Ain't It Funky Now" (Part 1) (Instrumental) / "Ain't It Funky Now" (Part 2) (Instrumental)—King 6280 (1969/70)
- "It's a New Day" (Part 1) / "Georgia on My Mind"—King 6292 (1970)
- "Get Up, I Feel Like Being a Sex Machine" (Part 1) / "Get Up, I Feel Like Being a Sex Machine" (Part 2)—King 6318 (1970)
- "Super Bad" (Part 1) / "Super Bad" (Part 2) / "Super Bad" (Part 3)—King 6329 (1970)
- "Hot Pants" (Part 1) / "Hot Pants" (Part 2) / "Hot Pants" (Part 3)—People 2501 (1971)
- "King Heroin" / "Theme from King Heroin" (Instrumental)—Polydor 14116 (1972)
- "Get on the Good Foot" (Part 1) / "Get on the Good Foot" (Part 2)—Polydor 14139 (1972)
- "I Got Ants in My Pants" (Part 1) / "I Got Ants in My Pants" (Part 2)—Polydor 14162 (1973)
- "The Payback" (Part 1) / "The Payback" (Part 2)—Polydor 14223 (1974)
- "Papa Don't Take No Mess" (Part 1) / "Papa Don't Take Bad"—Polydor 14255 (1975)
- "Sex Machine" (Part 1) / "Sex Machine" (Part 2)—Polydor 14270 (1975)

- "Dooley's Junkyard Dogs" / "Dooley's Junkyard Dogs" (Short Version)—Polydor 14303 (1976)
- "Get Up Off That Thing" / "Release the Pressure"—Polydor 14326 (1976)
- "For Goodness Sakes Look at Those Cakes" (Part 1) / "For Goodness Sakes Look at Those Cakes" (Part 2)—Polydor 14522 (1978)
- "God Has Smiled on Me" (Part 1) (with Rev. Al Sharpton and The Gospel Energies) / "God Has Smiled on Me" (Part 2) (with Rev. Al Sharpton and The Gospel Energies)—Royal King 7-900 (1981)
- "Unity" (with Africa Bambaata) (Part 1) / "Unity" (with Africa Bambaata) (Part 2)—Tommy Boy 847 (1984)
- "Living in America" / "Farewell" (by Dicola)—Scotti Brothers 05682 (1985/6)
- "Move On" / "You Are My Everything"—Scotti Brothers 72392 75286-1 (1991)

NOTABLE ALBUMS

- *Please, Please, Please*—King 610 (1959)
- *Try Me*—King 635 (1959)
- *Think*—King 683 (1960)
- *The Always Amazing James Brown*—King 743 (1961)
- *Presents His Band/Night Train*—King 771 (1961)
- *The Apollo Theater Presents, in Person, the James Brown Show*—King 826 (1963)
- *Prisoner of Love*—King 851 (1963)
- *Pure Dynamite!*—King 883 (1964)
- *Showtime*—Smash 67054 (1964)
- *Out of Sight*—Smash 67058 (1964)
- *Papa's Got a Brand New Bag*—King 938 (1965)
- *I Got You (I Feel Good)*—King 946 (1966)
- *James Brown Plays James Brown Today and Yesterday*—Smash 67072 (1966)
- *It's a Man's Man's World, Soul Brother No. 1*—King 985 (1966)
- *Christmas Songs*—King 1010 (1966)
- *The James Brown Show*—Smash 67087 (1967)
- *James Brown Live at the Garden*—King 1018 (1967)
- *Cold Sweat*—King 1020 (1967)
- *I Can't Stand Myself When You Touch Me*—King 1030 (1968)
- *I Got the Feelin'*—King 1031 (1968)
- *Live at the Apollo* (2-LPs)—King 1022 (1968)

- *Thinking of Little Willie John and a Few Nice Things*—King 1038 (1968)
- *Say It Loud—I'm Black and I'm Proud*—King 1047 (1969)
- *The Popcorn*—King 1055 (1969)
- *Ain't It Funky*—King 1092 (1970)
- *Sex Machine* (2-LPs)—King 1115 (1970)
- *Super Bad*—King 1127 (1971)
- *Hot Pants* (Vol. 1)—Polydor 4054 (1971)
- *Get on the Good Foot* (2 LPs)—Polydor 3004 (1972)
- *Black Caesar*—Polydor 6014 (1973)
- *The Payback* (2 LPs)—Polydor 3007 (1974)
- *Reality*—Polydor 6039 (1975)
- *Take a Look at Those Cakes*—Polydor 6181 (1979)
- *The Best of James Brown*—Polydor 6340 (1981)
- *Bring It On*—Churchill/Augusta Sound 22001 (1983)
- *The Federal Years* (Part 1)—Solid Smoke 8023 (1984)
- *The Federal Years* (Part 2)—Solid Smoke 8024 (1984)
- Gravity—Scotti Brothers 40380 (1986)
- *Live at the Apollo* (Vol. 2) (Part 1)—Rhino 217 (1986)
- *Live at the Apollo* (Vol. 2) (Part 2)—Rhino 218 (1986)
- *I'm Real*—Scotti Brothers 44241 (1988)
- *Live at Chastain Park*—Bulldog 3005 (1990)
- *Star Time*—Polydor 331 (1991)
- *Love Over-Due*—Scotti Brothers 75225 (1991)
- *Universal James*—Scotti Brothers 75274-2 (1993)

INDEX

ABOUT THE AUTHOR

Don Rhodes, publications editor with Morris Communications Company, based in Augusta, Georgia, has been writing about music celebrities for more than forty years, since he was fresh out of high school, interviewing Ethel Merman and Bert Parks the summer of 1963 in Atlanta.

He has crossed paths within arm's length of the Beatles, Bob Dylan, Tom Jones, Joan Baez, Bob Hope, Barbra Streisand, Dolly Parton, Tammy Wynette, Garth Brooks, Brenda Lee, Captain Kangaroo, and scores of other political and entertainment celebrities. He is one of the rare journalists to have interviewed all of Georgia's "Big Soul Four:" Otis Redding, Little Richard, Ray Charles, and, of course, James Brown.

He first crossed paths with JB while he was a student at the University of Georgia in the mid-1960s, saw him perform in Vietnam, and cemented his friendship with the soul music legend in the early 1970s, which lasted until JB's death on Christmas Day 2006. He wrote the text for the metal plaque at JB's statue in Augusta, Georgia; he attended JB's private Christmas parties; and he was invited to JB's fourth wedding to Tomi Rae Hynie.

Don has authored music articles for national and international magazines, such as *Smithsonian Performing Notes, Bluegrass Unlimited, Performance, Country Music, Pickin', Frets, Bluegrass Now, Music City News, Success Unlimited, Muleskinner News,* and others. He is the author of the *Augusta Chronicle*'s weekly *Ramblin' Rhodes*, the longest running country music column in America, which is now in its thirty-seventh year and can be found on the Internet; has been nominated several times to the Georgia Music Hall of Fame in the nonperformer category; has written CD liner notes for Grand Ole Opry artists; has composed songs recorded by artists (one was sung on the Grand Ole Opry stage); and has reviewed more than one hundred musical and dramatic plays.

His previous books include *Down Country Roads with Ramblin' Rhodes* (Hartwell, GA: North American Publications Inc., 1982), *Entertainment in Augusta and the CSRA* (Charleston, SC: Arcadia Publishing, 2004), and, most recently, *Ty Cobb: Safe at Home* (Guilford, CT: The Lyons Press, 2008). He lives in North Augusta, South Carolina.